This book is dedicated
to Blanche

Contents

One. Freedom   1

Two. Rendezvous at Bar Harbor   12

Three. The Knickerbocker Athletic Club   26

Four. Henry Barnet   36

Five. Alienation   49

Six. West End Avenue   58

Seven. Letter Box 217   69

Eight. General Molineux   78

Nine. Death of a Friend   91

Ten. A Curious Honeymoon   105

Eleven. Death of a Stranger   119

Twelve. Retreat to Brooklyn   130

Thirteen. The Inquest   146

Fourteen. Indictment   161

Fifteen. Prelude to Prosecution   174

Sixteen. The Trial   185

Seventeen. Conviction   203

Eighteen. Sing Sing   218

Nineteen. The Last Chapter   229

Acknowledgments

This story of Roland and Blanche Molineux is the culmination of four years' research and writing; it has been a labor of love throughout.

I am indebted to several American libraries for material from which I was able to reconstruct the events that are laid out on these pages. The New York State Library at Albany, the New York Public Library, the Wilson Library at the University of Minnesota and the Minneapolis Public Library all yielded information that contributed to the fabric of this tale.

Illustrations were obtained from a variety of sources, principally the New York Public Library picture collection, the *The New York World* from 1898 through 1902, and a volume entitled *The Molineux Case*, published in 1929.

I acknowledge with appreciation the skillful editing of Barbara Field, who so ably smoothed over the rough spots, and the contributions of Barbara Seifred, who keystroked the entire manuscript.

Finally I am deeply indebted to my husband Arthur, who encouraged me to write the story "one chapter at a time" and who undergirded the entire effort with his constant support and friendly criticism.

And now, I invite the reader to step back in time to the waning days of the Victorian Age . . .

The Molineux Affair

ONE

Freedom

Justice Lambert's courtroom was normally the most dignified one in New York City's Criminal Courts Building, but on this afternoon of November 11, 1902, it was in a state of pandemonium. The judge's efforts to quell the unexpected outburst were of no avail, for Roland Burnham Molineux had just been acquitted of first degree murder. Rejoicing spectators crowded forward in the courtroom to shake his hand and also to congratulate his father, General Edward Molineux. Roland's attorneys—no less than four of New York's most eminent—tried in vain to intervene and shield their client from the press of humanity. Roland, on the other hand, was doing his best to respond to the well-wishers with a smile and a word. He seemed to treasure this opportunity to touch his fellow human beings and to share this joyous moment with them.

Finally Judge Lambert beckoned to the sheriff, and within a moment his deputies went into action. Reporters and spectators alike were summarily ushered toward the doorway at the back of the courtroom. When order was finally restored to the chamber and the doors closed, all that remained were those who had played an important part in the four-year odyssey just concluded.

1

The sordid affair had first come to light with the death of an obscure middle-aged woman, one Katherine Adams, shortly after Christmas in 1898. Mrs. Adams had died suddenly, less than a half hour after taking a teaspoonful of Bromo-Seltzer powder to cure a mild headache. It was soon discovered that the powder was not Bromo-Seltzer, but cyanide, and that the bottle containing the mixture had been received in the mail by her nephew, Harry Cornish, athletic director of the Knickerbocker Athletic Club on Madison Avenue. These circumstances prompted investigators to examine the internal political squabbles of this stylish club, where New York's amateur sportsmen gathered and competed.

The newspapers very early suggested that Roland Molineux, a former member of the club and the privileged son of a highly respected Civil War general, was a prime suspect in Mrs. Adams's death. A year earlier, it was reported, Molineux had tried unsuccessfully to have Cornish removed from his position at the club.

Less than a week after Mrs. Adams's demise, inquiries were made into a second death, also having a connection with the Knickerbocker Club. Henry Barnet, an amiable stockbroker who made the club his home, had died six weeks earlier of what had been thought to be diphtheria. However, later investigations revealed that he too had died of cyanide poisoning. According to reports in the newspapers, Henry Barnet and Roland Molineux had once been the best of friends, sharing adjacent rooms at the club, but the friendship had ended over the attentions of an exceedingly attractive young woman, Blanche Chesebrough, whom Molineux married less than a month after Barnet's death.

Following an inquest into the events surrounding the death of Katherine Adams, Roland was indicted in February 1899. Later that year he was brought to trial for first degree murder. The prosecution, orchestrated by New York's formidable Assistant District Attorney, James Osborne, drew heavily on evidence linking Blanche Molineux with Roland's erstwhile friend, Henry Barnet. The implications of this evidence were such that, throughout the trial, public sentiment generally went against Roland. It was therefore a surprise to no one, not even to Roland and his family, that he was convicted of murder and sentenced to die in the electric chair. Nor was anyone surprised when Roland's attorneys promptly mounted an appeal of the verdict.

A year and a half later, while Roland sat in his cell on Sing Sing's Death Row, the New York Court of Appeals overruled his conviction and ordered a new trial. The court also·set aside as inadmissible much of the evidence that James Osborne had used to convict Roland, including all references to the death of Henry Barnet. Justice Lambert, who had presided over this second trial with an iron hand, used his power to ensure that all of the evidence presented lay within the narrow limits defined by the Appellate Court. The result was acquittal.

Now, with the completion of his responsibilities and the removal of the undisciplined spectators from his courtroom, the judge's demeanor softened. He turned to the jurors and thanked them for fulfilling their collective obligation with so few complications. There was no doubt that the twelve men had reached their decision efficiently, for they had spent just thirteen minutes deliberating. As they filed out of the jurybox to return to their respective lives, Roland, ever the gentleman, stepped forward to shake the hand of each one.

Then James Osborne, whose prosecution was unsuccessful in this second trial, took Roland's hand and offered his personal congratulations, as if to show his sportsmanlike attitude now that the case was settled. He also extended his hand to each of Roland's attorneys, especially to George Gordon Battle and his partner Bartow Weeks, who had stood by Roland from the day he was first implicated in Katherine Adams's murder. Osborne was particularly cordial to Weeks, whom he had ridiculed unmercifully during the trials. It was not in the interest of any of the attorneys to jeopardize their relationships with each other, for they were all members of New York's elite legal community.

George Battle was the first to leave the courtroom. He walked through the corridors amidst the cheering multitude, left the building and entered his carriage alone. He was off to Thorley's florists for a dozen red roses. He had an important appointment to keep at the Murray Hill Hotel.

A few minutes later, both Molineuxs left the courtroom. Roland took his father's left arm, and Bartow Weeks walked at the general's right side. They pushed their way through the applauding crowd toward the little bridge that connected the Courts Building with the Tombs prison across the street. Word of the acquittal had already spread to the inmates there, and a cheer rose from the cellblocks as Roland entered for the last time. He responded with waves and greetings as he strode past the cells of those less fortunate than himself. In his own cell, with the help of Weeks, he packed his few belongings into a valise and then returned to his father's side.

Father and son emerged together from the Tombs to be confronted by a reporter who had recognized the waiting Molineux carriage and now pressed for a statement. The general pulled from his pocket and handed to the reporter a scrap of paper on which he had written two lines:

The strife is o'er, the battle done, and Might has lost but Right has won.

Father and son entered the carriage. Roland pulled the curtains shut and shouted to the driver: "Fort Greene Place, Bert, as fast as you can take us!"

In 1902 Fort Greene Place in Brooklyn was an avenue of stately brownstone mansions, and among the most elegant of these was number 117, the Molineux family home. On this late November afternoon the residence was surrounded by a large contingent of the Brooklyn police, who had received word that Roland had been acquitted and was on the way home with his father. Within minutes after the arrival of the police, a host of friends, neighbors and strangers also gathered at the front of the house.

Suddenly a mounted police officer galloped up to the front stoop to announce that the Molineux carriage had just crossed the bridge from Manhattan. A reporter pressed the officer: "Is Molineux's wife with him in the carriage?" The reply was negative. The whispered speculation of the reporters as to her whereabouts soon spread to the spectators; all the more reason to await the arrival of the carriage and determine whether Blanche Molineux was inside the house with Roland's mother. From time to time a drape was pulled back from the front door window and the face of the older Mrs. Molineux was clearly visible behind the window glass. However, there was no sign that her daughter-in-law was with her.

A thunderous cry arose from the crowd when the Molineux carriage finally appeared from around the corner and slowed to approach its final destination. As soon as the vehicle came to a halt, Roland stepped jauntily out without waiting for the driver to descend from his seat. As he turned to help his father from the vehicle, the front door flew open and Mrs. Molineux came running out. In the presence of the large throng, mother and son embraced and remained in each other's arms. The general, somewhat flustered by this public display of private emotions, gently separated the two, and taking each by the arm, escorted them into the house.

The Murray Hill section of New York was considered old, even at the turn of the century. It took its name from the property on which the home of a Mrs. Murray stood a century earlier. Legend has it that on one occasion during the Revolutionary War, Mrs. Murray entertained the British officers, detaining them long enough for General Washington's embattled troops to escape. Over the years the area had changed considerably, and in 1902 the spot was occupied by a quiet residential hotel, appropriately named the Murray Hill Hotel, home to a number of genteel permanent residents and also a shelter for occasional transients. In early October, about the time the second Molineux trial commenced, a handsome young woman was registered, and through a quiet understanding with the management, her identity was kept secret.

The mysterious woman was the young Mrs. Molineux, for-

merly Blanche Chesebrough, who had married Roland Molineux in November of 1898, shortly after the death of Henry
Barnet. Before her marriage, Blanche was known to have been
a very charming, talented and somewhat coquettish young
woman. She came from a good family of English descent, and
through her sister and brother, as well as the connections of her
deceased parents, she traveled in very respectable circles. She
had studied voice in both Boston and New York and showed
promise of becoming an accomplished singer. In spite of these
credentials, Blanche Molineux was virtually penniless before her
marriage, depending from time to time on the generosity of her
older sister, who had married well in Boston.

The death of Katherine Adams occurred just a month after
Blanche and Roland were married, on the day before they
moved from their honeymoon quarters in the Waldorf-Astoria
Hotel to newly decorated rooms on West End Avenue. They
were to spend but two nights in their new home, for with the
first public mention of Roland Molineux as a potential suspect
in Mrs. Adams's death, General Molineux convinced the newlyweds to move to the Molineux home in Brooklyn.

From that day on, Blanche had remained with General and
Mrs. Molineux, much of the time behind closed doors and shuttered windows on Fort Greene Place. She had acceded to every
wish of her father-in-law, more out of respect for him than out
of affection for her husband. Yet it was clear to her, perhaps to
the Molineuxs also, that this sacrifice—this loss of youth, as
Blanche viewed it—could not overcome the barrier that loomed
between her and the Molineux family. This barrier, by itself of
little consequence, was the well-publicized, though ill-defined,
relationship that had existed between Henry Barnet and
Blanche prior to Barnet's death. As a public embarrassment, it
had festered like a sore, bestowing on Blanche an unwelcome
notoriety. Privately it had been like a club, which Blanche's
mother-in-law frequently wielded against her.

The general deemed it prudent that Blanche not be present
at Roland's second trial and that she leave the Molineux home
temporarily, at least for the duration of the proceedings. For

Blanche, the news that the general had found her a room at the Murray Hill came as a blessed relief—an escape from the Molineux prison—and in this spirit she gladly moved to a spacious corner room in the old hotel.

Blanche sat alone in her room the afternoon of November 11. She had followed the second trial by reading the daily newspapers, a privilege she had been denied during the first trial. Yet in that earlier trial she had not been spared the gossip, the innuendos, and the attacks on her own virtue that James Osborne had thrown so carelessly about, for she had sat in the courtroom daily and heard it all with her own ears. How different were the reports that emerged from the proceedings this time around. Much of the testimony centered on Roland's whereabouts during their honeymoon days at the Waldorf-Astoria. Roland had alibis and corroborating witnesses for each and every hour. Blanche pondered this fresh knowledge about her husband, remembering that she had spent most of her honeymoon days alone. But none of this mattered to her any longer. Besides, like those who awaited the verdict in the corridors of the Criminal Courts Building, Blanche was confident there would be an acquittal.

The afternoon light was fading when a knock on the door aroused Blanche from her musings. Opening the door fully expecting to greet one of the Molineux attorneys, she instead found herself face to face with a reporter from the *World*, who thrust a fresh newspaper at her, then promptly retreated. Blanche returned to her window seat to read the account of the day's proceedings and in that way learned of her husband's acquittal. Later she realized that the newspaper had been delivered not more than a few minutes after the verdict was announced, as if it had all been a *fait accompli*.

George Battle arrived a quarter hour later. He stepped into the room, breathless but smiling, for he thought himself to be the bearer of good news. Taking Blanche's hand in both of his, he addressed her with an unexpected intimacy.

"My dear Blanche—Roland is free and awaits you at home!" Blanche said nothing lest she betray her innermost feelings, but Battle misinterpreted her silence and thought to allay her fears.

"The others have driven directly to Fort Greene Place—in fact, they are probably already there waiting for you . . . Blanche, I know what you are thinking. You have been through more than any of us can ever imagine, but you should understand that it is best to come with me, to appear at this time with Roland and his parents. Please do what I say and come with me. My carriage is waiting on the street."

When there was still no response, he chose another tack.

"As distressed as you no doubt feel, you nevertheless look lovely—your outfit is most becoming."

At this point, his eyes brightened mischievously.

"There will be a flock of reporters at Fort Greene Place; let's see what they write about it tomorrow. I venture it will begin, 'Mrs. Molineux arrived in an exceedingly tasteful costume, on the arm of the dashing . . . ' "

Battle interrupted himself, for it was obvious that his attempts to cheer her were having no effect.

Blanche's eyes glistened and her voice trembled.

"No George, you do not understand. They do not want me. They only wanted their son back, and they held onto me just as long as I could be useful to them. They have no need of me now."

But Battle would not give in.

"It is imperative, Blanche, that you go with me immediately to the Molineuxs', before the reporters leave to file their afternoon stories. You may do with your life what you will after that, but you and I together must dispel any gossip as to the affairs between Roland and you and between you and his mother. No one must be allowed to say that you have not rejoined the family," he insisted. "If you revere the general at all, you will come with me."

With that he pressed her hand once more and stepped to the doorway. Under any other circumstances, Blanche would have dissolved in tears, for this had increasingly been her habit over the past three years. But the persistent manner of this kind

8

counselor dissuaded her from any such inclination. Rather, she donned her hat, turned to the mirror for a last look, gathered up a fur piece, and took his arm.

As the pair descended the stairway into the lobby, it became apparent that Blanche's identity was not the secret that she and her father-in-law had intended. Residents of the hotel, as if forewarned, stood at attention smiling warmly as she swept by. Blanche put the irony of this from her mind; her thoughts were focused on the dreaded family reunion that lay ahead.

George Battle's carriage stood before the hotel entrance, and as Blanche climbed in, she noticed a large bouquet of American Beauty roses on the seat. Battle was quick to inform her that he had procured the flowers not for her, but rather for her to present to her husband as a token of their long-awaited reunion. Blanche replied with a stony silence, reminded once again that George Battle, like all the others, was beholden to the Molineuxs and therefore was not to be trusted.

As the carriage drove through the streets of Manhattan and across to Brooklyn, Battle ventured to break the silence, suggesting sympathetically that Blanche would now need a good rest. Blanche stared straight ahead, ignoring Battle's feeble attempts at consolation. Instead she pondered the future and her decision to leave Roland, though she knew no one would understand. For no one could understand how completely and irrevocably the events of the past years had destroyed any feelings she may have once had for Roland. Nor could anyone know how tenuous the threads of their relationship had been, even at the start.

Life—not rest—was what she needed now. Had she not earned her right to a release from this suffocating existence? Blanche had long since convinced herself that this was so and she had already made the necessary arrangements. There was just this one last hurdle to overcome—the imminent reunion at Fort Greene Place.

A crowd was still milling about as Battle's carriage drove up before the Molineux home, and reporters flanked the front steps. George Battle opened the carriage door for Blanche. She descended elegantly, and as they walked up the steps together, he did his best to shield her from the onlookers. Blanche was quite aware of the reporters on both sides, writing in their little books and no doubt looking to see whether she would smile or weep at this dramatic moment.

Every friend and acquaintance of the Molineux family had beaten a path to their door that afternoon, and George Battle wisely concluded that he was not needed. He therefore escorted Blanche just to the front entrance, then returned immediately to his carriage. But as the vehicle pulled away, he discovered the bouquet of roses on the seat. Not knowing whether Blanche had left them accidentally or with purpose, he ordered the driver to turn around and delivered the bouquet to the door himself. The *New York Times*, ever vigilant, reported this fact the following day.

General Molineux received Blanche at the door, with Mrs. Molineux close behind, but Roland chose to remain in the sitting room beyond, occupying himself with the floral tributes and messages of congratulation that continued to arrive. As the general turned to lead his daughter-in-law to her husband, Blanche, without a word, left his side and walked straight through the panelled hall to the stairway. To the astonishment of all, she ascended the stairs and went to her room — the room into which she had moved almost four years earlier and the only space in the world she could call home. She removed her wraps and sat down at the window, amazed at the courage and independence she had exhibited. Darkness slowly descended and the lights gradually appeared all over the city. Still Blanche did not leave the room, and throughout the evening no one bothered her. Only the maid knocked later and left a tray of tea and cakes, which Blanche barely touched. All night she sat at the window, and intermittently she wept, as if these last hours under the Molineux roof were more than she could bear.

When dawn broke, Blanche dried her tears. Opening her portfolio on the desk, she began to write a letter to General Molineux. In another hour she would be going away; it was her decision and she would not change it. She would board the *Century* and be on her way to her ultimate destination — a little town in South Dakota called Sioux Falls. (At the turn of the century, Sioux Falls provided the means for a simple, quick divorce, much as Reno did in later decades.)

She wrote of the slow death that had overcome her. She wished only happiness to him and to his family, and she hoped that God would bless them all. Then she concluded by reiterating her love and respect for her father-in-law. Blanche placed the letter in an envelope and sealed it with wax by the flame of the candle on the desk. Into the wax she pressed the signature of the *Mizpah* ring that Roland had given her a lifetime ago. Blanche left no message for her husband. She simply removed the ring from her finger and laid it beside the letter on the desk.

She hastily packed her writing portfolio and the contents of her wardrobe into two leather bags. She would have to abandon her wedding gifts and the few household items she had accumulated, for they were all in storage. On her dressing table stood a lovely antique silver bowl of early Flemish design, a gift from the general before her marriage. This alone she chose to call her own, and she carefully wrapped it within her folded gowns.

At the appointed time a carriage stopped in front of the house. Blanche picked up the two bags, quietly descended the stairs, and left the Molineux home, this time forever. Despite the early hour, a reporter stood outside to record her departure.

Once inside the carriage, Blanche drew the curtains and ordered the driver to the Murray Hill Hotel, where her arrival and subsequent departure with all of her belongings were also duly noted. From there she rode to the railroad station, boarded the *Century*, and left New York for the West.

Twenty-four hours later the *New York Times* reported:

Mrs. Roland B. Molineux left the family home yesterday morning and drove over to the Murray Hill Hotel, where she staid [sic] several weeks past. She gave up her room there, and returned to the Fort Greene Place house, where she will remain with her husband. All disagreements between young Mrs. Molineux and her mother-in-law, it is said, have been settled.

For the first time in her life, Blanche had outwitted them all.

TWO

Rendezvous at Bar Harbor

It is difficult to place blame or to give credit unilaterally when pondering the acquittal of Roland Molineux and the subsequent departure of his wife Blanche. One would be hard-pressed to view as worthwhile the events that occurred in the five years preceding the day on which Roland gained his freedom. A determination as to whether the entire affair was tragic or wicked, or just foolish and unfortunate, falls into the realm of the subjective. However, it makes for an interesting exercise to reconstruct the events and perhaps to ruminate on them.

At this late date, much remains to aid us in this reconstruction. There are voluminous newspaper accounts, a plethora of court records, and even some biased reminiscences of the attorneys. These records have of course always been available. Now, however, it turns out than an additional record remains—one never before published—namely Blanche's own recollections, written during the last decade of her life. Together these diverse sources tell a complex story, in which ambition, jealousy, revenge and regret all have a part.

Our account of the Molineux affair begins with the day on

which Roland Molineux was introduced to Blanche Chesebrough. It was in August of 1897 at Portland, Maine. The
Portland harbor had been a mass of yachts and other watercraft
since the opening of the season in May. Every yacht club along
the east coast seemed to have planned a cruise to Bar Harbor
with a stop at Portland, perhaps to emulate *the* great race of the
season, that in which competitors vied for the prestigous
Vanderbilt cup.

On this particular day in August, the Vanderbilt race was
over. In response to the ensuing August doldrums, the New
York Yacht Club had organized a week-long cruise, in which
the well-to-do bachelor Albert J. Morgan was participating. His
steam yacht, the *Viator*, while hardly a competitor to the great
yachts of the day, nevertheless attracted considerable attention
as it lay at berth in the harbor. It was a lovely morning, with
sunshine to warm the decks and a brisk wind to tease the flag
of the New York Yacht Club, which fluttered gaily at the stern.

Morgan and his two friends, Roland Molineux and Walter
Baldwin, also New York bachelors, made themselves comfortable under the striped awnings that protected the deck chairs
from the sun. Shortly before noon a sailing yacht slid gracefully
into the neighboring berth. It carried the name *Mohegan* on its
stern and proudly displayed the flag of the Larchmont Yacht
Club. Judging from the craft and the flags, any knowledgeable
observer would have known that the owners of the two yachts
either knew one another already or were surely potential acquaintances. It was clear that they traveled in the same circles.

As a matter of fact the owners did not know each other, but
it took very little time for them to become acquainted. The
owner and skipper of the *Mohegan* was Clark Miller. With him
were two male friends and two female friends. The names of the
male friends have been lost, but that is of little importance to
the story. It is the female friends of Clark Miller who are important. Both were dressed in muslin skirts, their heads covered
lightly with chiffon scarves. The older woman, who appeared to
be in her forties, was rather short and a little stout. She had an
aristocratic face, though, and one could see even from across the

decks that she was someone to be reckoned with. Her name was Isia Stearns, and she was married to Waldo Stearns of a prominent Boston lumbering family. The Stearnses wintered in Longwood, just outside of Boston, and summered at *Craigsmere*, their property on Conanicut Island near Jamestown, Rhode Island. Waldo Stearns was not on board. With Isia was her younger sister, Blanche Chesebrough of New York City, unmarried and twenty-four years of age. Blanche was tall and slim, a handsome young woman of elegant bearing with auburn hair and deep brown eyes.

During the first hour that the *Mohegan* was berthed, the two women were in and out of the cabin at least a dozen times. Their comings and goings intrigued young Morgan, and he called to his steward inside the cabin: "Hold luncheon for an hour; I have an errand." Releasing the dinghy strapped to the *Viator's* deck and letting it drop into the water below, he climbed down the hull into the craft, pulled out the little oars and rowed through the choppy waters over to the *Mohegan*.

"Ahoy up there! Al Morgan of the New York Yacht Club here."

Miller leaned over the side of the deck and extended his hand toward Morgan.

"Greetings! Clark Miller of the Larchmont crowd; pleased to meet you, Al."

In those days, that identification—rather confirmation—was all that was required. Without further ado, Morgan extended an invitation to Miller and his friends to join the *Viator* group for luncheon in an hour. Then he rowed back to the *Viator* and crawled up the hull to the deck, leaving the little dinghy bobbing in the water below.

"Walt, Moli! I've met the chap whose yacht is next over there. Miller is his name—from Larchmont. He's our sort, I believe, so I've invited him and his friends to luncheon in an hour." Pointing in the direction of the *Mohegan*, he continued, "Those two women with him look interesting. I'd like to know the younger one better."

With that, all three men retreated to the cabin to give a hand to the steward and then to change. Together they'd see to it that the affair was executed in good style.

On the *Mohegan*, Isia and Blanche also quickly withdrew to their cabin. Neither was really prepared for a social occasion, as their participation in the cruise had been hastily organized.

Blanche was spending the month of August at *Craigsmere* with Isia and Waldo, having given up her modest New York quarters over the summer for financial reasons. Waldo was in Boston on business much of the time, leaving the two sisters to amuse themselves alone on the island. As there was little to interest the women in that semiwilderness area, Isia had organized this little adventure during Waldo's latest absence. She had packed a few summer garments for herself, and for Blanche she had gathered some of her older frocks, from a time when she was much slimmer. The two sisters had taken the ferry over to Jamestown and there had met Clark Miller, an old friend of Isia's. Miller had insisted that the women join him and his friends on their tour to Portland. Isia offered weak protest, but they soon found themselves aboard the *Mohegan* and on their way in a spirit of adventure.

Blanche was aware of her good fortune in having a sister such as Isia. The Chesebrough parents had died two years earlier, within six months of each other. The father had been an itinerant inventor, and Blanche had grown up moving from one part of the country to another, presumably to elude her father's creditors. Hers was a childhood filled with economic uncertainties. Although she had a lovely voice and exceptional musical abilities, there had been barely the wherewithall to keep the family together, let alone provide for a musical education. Isia, who had been raised at a time when their father's fortunes fared much better, had obtained a respectable education and succeeded in marrying well. Thus, when Blanche was sixteen years old, Isia had taken her into her home and provided a year of training and education in voice, diction and piano, supplementing what the public schools had to offer. That year marked the end of Blanche's formal education.

At her father's insistence and over Isia's protestations, Blanche had gone with her parents to New York. There they lived together in genteel poverty, moving from flat to flat as their financial resources dwindled. Fortunately Blanche had obtained positions in two choirs, one at a large Manhattan church and the other at a synagogue, also on Manhattan. With her modest earnings, she had been able to afford voice lessons and still make some small contribution to her family's subsistence. In turn, her mother devoted all of her energies to Blanche's advancement. She designed and sewed so creatively and tastefully that Blanche began to be noticed in the New York musical circles where she performed and at the theatrical and musical events she attended. As her confidence in her innate assets as well as in her wardrobe increased, she gradually began to exhibit the air of an aspiring singer who perhaps someday would even become a theatrical or operatic star. At least those who came in contact with Blanche during those years expected as much.

On the other hand, Blanche had been carefully protected by her mother. Her only associations with peers of either sex had been purely professional. She had auditioned successfully for the Rubenstein Society, a choral group of some renown, whose participants often went on to successful musical careers, in many cases the Metropolitan Opera. At evening rehearsals and performances of this group, Blanche was never present without her mother, which precluded her sharing in any of the related social activities. At the time, Blanche accepted this with grace, believing that her interests lay in her musical studies and career alone. Only later did she draw a connection between the protective cocoon in which she had dwelled up to her twenty-second year and the disasters that evolved from her entanglement with two men soon thereafter.

The deaths of the Chesebrough parents had drawn the two sisters closer to one another. In fact, Isia began to see herself as a pseudo-mother, hastening to make up for the deficiencies of her sister's haphazard childhood. In New York, Blanche had been forced to give up the last family flat; in the two years since her parents' deaths she had lived in a series of modest boarding houses, continuing to press forward with her musical efforts, but with an increased sense of urgency. Isia and Waldo, always occasional visitors to New York, now came more frequently and included Blanche in their social activities. Often, with a hint from Isia to the hostess, Blanche was invited to sing, accompanying herself charmingly on the piano. The younger woman thus was becoming a welcome and remembered guest wherever she went. Blanche could thank her mother and father for passing on to her the tastes and manners that they presumed represented their superior Anglo-Saxon heritage. She could also be grateful to Isia for providing her entrée into circles where she expected eventually to find her place.

The anticipated luncheon on board the *Viator* was but another example of the opportunities that seemed to present themselves whenever Isia was around. As the two sisters sorted through their belongings, each constructing a suitable costume for the occasion, Isia tried to recall the familiarity in the name Al Morgan from New York. Suddenly it came to her.

"A. J. Morgan, why those are the manufacturing Morgans! They make Sapolio—that's who they are. Oh, Blanche darling, aren't we fortunate this afternoon? I have a feeling that Al Morgan has eyes for you!"

At the agreed upon hour, the little dinghy was dispatched to carry the *Mohegan* guests across the water, two and three at a time. In this case it was "ladies last," so there was an impressive group of men—five in all—to welcome the Chesebrough sisters as they climbed up into the steam yacht with Miller close behind. Both were dressed in chiffon waists and skirts, like two pastel flowers blooming in the sunshine. Miller presented Morgan to the ladies, and Morgan in turn presented his two guests—Walter Baldwin and Roland Molineux. Blanche noticed that Morgan was carefully observing her, even as he was introducing the others, just as Isia had predicted. But Blanche found Morgan's guest Roland more interesting. He was a bit aloof, suave, and very good looking in his white flannels. She would have liked to address him beyond the formal greeting, but for the moment she found nothing to say. After a brief awkward silence, Morgan invited everyone to be seated on the deck chairs

17

under the awnings, where Isia deftly took charge of the conversation by recalling the recent Vanderbilt cup race. Everyone present had some knowledge of the event, and each seemed to know someone who had taken part. The fact that no one on board had actually been a participant gave each a comfortable feeling of being in the same slice of that carefully constructed institution known as *society*. Sensing that everything was under control, Morgan excused himself and went below. Isia was holding her own among five men, in fact leading the conversation as it meandered from one topic to another. Even Blanche joined in. How easy it was to speak with strangers when Isia was in charge.

Presently Morgan emerged, carrying a huge silver tray laden with paté sandwiches and toasted squares piled with Russian caviar. Alongside were thin-stemmed champagne glasses. The guests gasped with pleasure at being served this sumptuous combination of food and drink in the middle of a busy harbor. Morgan himself served the champagne, leaving the other duties to his steward. The refreshments induced a higher level of conviviality and gaiety, but as the afternoon wore on and the heat of the sun finally penetrated the awnings, the guests began to seek cooler, more intimate spots, either in the salon below or in the shade of the cabin.

Blanche retreated to such a spot on the afterdeck, and as she settled on a bench, Morgan appeared from around the opposite corner. He sat down next to her and laid his arm along the railing behind her, and the two began exchanging pleasantries. Blanche wished so that she had Isia's ability to move beyond the customary trivia, to take advantage of this encounter with her host. The opportunity vanished, however, as Morgan peered around the corner. There sat Roland Molineux in a deck chair, his feet on the lower railing, reading a book. Blanche found it odd that he had appeared so suddenly, for he had not been there when she passed by a quarter of an hour earlier.

"Moli," called Morgan, "Where in heaven's name did you come from?" Then, as though Roland's mere presence compelled him to defer to the other man, he stepped aside gracefully. "Take care of this lovely lady while I check on affairs below. My steward has probably finished off the champagne by now. If so, there will be no dealing with him."

Blanche giggled. Roland closed the book, dropped his feet from the rail, tossed his cigarette overboard, and came toward Blanche. So simple and uneventful was Blanche's first meeting with her future husband.

Roland was not very tall, hardly taller than Blanche. But he had a slender, muscular and well-proportioned body. He carried himself in a very erect manner and had an unusual air of self-confidence. All this Blanche had observed previously. Now she noticed his quiet, infectious smile. Blanche began to speak and the words tumbled forth like a waterfall. At the same time, Roland's aloofness vanished, and they found themselves conversing freely. For the rest of the afternoon they remained seated there by themselves, laughing and chatting as if they had known each other for years. To this new friend Blanche related her modest musical sucesses and confessed her grand musical ambitions, including the dream of one day singing with the Metropolitan Opera. She assured him that such ambitions were not unrealistic in view of the great obstacles she had already overcome in her young life.

Roland expressed his great admiration for Blanche's determination and his support for her aspirations. He eagerly confessed his own great interest in opera, an interest that was matched by his extensive knowledge of both composers and performers. He told Blanche of the Opera Club to which he belonged, of their social gatherings after the performances, and of certain members who themselves were aspiring opera singers. Blanche acknowledged that she knew of the Opera Club, by reputation only, not wishing to reveal how isolated she was from the most important musical circles. In an attempt to bolster this privileged young man's opinion of her social stature, Blanche described to him the details of her recent audition with the great Madam Nellie Melba.

The audition had been arranged by Jean DeReszke of the Metropolitan, for whom she had earlier sung. Blanche was invited to Madam's private residence, and there she sang for the great diva. Melba was so approving that she immediately insisted it was time for Blanche to go to Paris and continue her studies. For an American singer at that time, Paris was the only route to a successful career in America. In truth, Melba was so insistent, she sat down at her desk and wrote Blanche a letter of introduction, in French. Blanche confided to Roland that this audition before the great Melba had been the high point of her life so far. What she did not tell him was that the realization of the impossibility of ever reaching Paris, even with the diva's letter, had filled her with despair ever since.

Before the afternoon was over, Roland had invited Blanche to join him for the entire New York winter opera season, a luxury far beyond Blanche's financial circumstances. That evening when she returned to the *Mohegan* with the others, Blanche was already spinning fantasies about her musical career. She had the feeling that its success had been sealed that afternoon, that she might in her life actually find a way to study in Paris, from which all good things would emanate. In the privacy of their cabin the sisters embraced. "Oh Isi, this the happiest day of my life!"

Both the *Mohegan* and the *Viator* were scheduled to leave Portland the following morning. Earlier Miller had promised Isia that the *Mohegan* would return promptly to Jamestown. The *Viator* and its crew were of course on their way to Bar Harbor. That night Miller consulted with Isia about changing the itinerary and heading north. With such congenial guests aboard, why not delay their return and instead rendezvous at Bar Harbor with the *Viator?* Isia was faced with a dilemma. On the one hand, a delayed return created the possibility that her husband Waldo would return to *Craigsmere* from Boston and find her absent. On the other hand, an opportunity for Blanche had finally presented itself, an introduction of immense benefit. Isia chose to place Blanche's interests before her own and concurred in the changed itinerary.

As the *Mohegan* sailed up the coast, Blanche rejoiced in Isia's decision and looked forward to the expected reunion with

Roland. She was now twenty-four years old. She had had several male friends in her adult life, but she had never been even close to intimate with a man. Certainly both the lack of opportunity and her protective upbringing influenced her behavior in these early adult years. However Blanche had changed perceptibly since the death of her parents. Now, for the first time she had met a man to whom she was definitely drawn, a man she would like to hold onto. It was clear to Blanche that the situation called for a new technique, so to speak. The unfettered environment of the cruise had already bent a number of the Victorian rules that normally applied in social intercourse. As Blanche stared out to sea, she contemplated the current situation carefully and decided that it was the time and place for her first seduction. Roland possessed the attributes she valued at the moment, and she smiled at the thought that with his strong, yet poised, stance, he would play the part of the seducer very well.

For Blanche, the arrival at Bar Harbor was akin to the first step on a social ladder that had eluded her so far. She thrilled at the rugged beauty of the landscape and even more at the knowledge that she was sailing into a harbor that had been the mecca and playgound of America's well-to-do for several decades. The *Mohegan* glided gracefully into the harbor and slid into the berth adjacent to the *Viator*, just as at Portland. For two nights the schooner and the steam yacht lay side by side while, several times each day, the little dinghy carried passengers to and fro between the craft.

At Bar Harbor, Isia applied all of the charms she could muster. Her goal was to provide enough diversion on the *Mohegan* to amuse both Walter Baldwin and Al Morgan for hours at a time, leaving Blanche and Roland alone on the *Viator*. In this she succeeded well. Blanche had given much thought and care to preparing for the hours alone with Roland, expecting that he would eventually draw her below into the cabin. She was ready for this moment, in fact longed for it. But Roland did not, even when he realized that his caresses were arousing passions in Blanche and making her eagerly responsive to him. Blanche had been educated to believe that young men did not behave so shyly under such circumstances, and she was left somewhat baffled each time. She rationalized that Roland was indeed a gentleman beyond her wildest expectations, a real jewel in his respect and admiration for her. She chided herself that her disappointment during these tender moments was only a sign of her own weakness. What Blanche learned of Roland in their hours together more than compensated for this discontent. Each intimate detail reaffirmed her conscious decision that she would make him the man in her future.

It was quite evident that Roland Molineux was the son of an eminently successful man, though Blanche did not learn until later how very distinguished and respected General Molineux really was, both in the community and in the nation. Roland preferred to tell her of his own successes, particularly those he had achieved without any assistance from his father.

Born in 1866, Roland had grown up near Fort Greene Park in Brooklyn in one of those massive brownstone homes where a respectable well-to-do family would be expected to reside. He had two brothers — Cecil and Leslie — who, like his father, were in business in New York. His parents still lived in the family home, but Roland made his residence at the recently organized Knickerbocker Athletic Club on Madison Avenue, in the center of Manhattan life. Roland had always exhibited a keen interest in gymnastics, not only through his support of an athletic club in which gymnastics played a major role, but also as a performer. Roland himself had excelled in gymnastics since he was fifteen years old. At seventeen he was enrolled at the Sedgwick Institute in Massachussetts, where his gymnastic abilities were further developed. Returning to Brooklyn the following year, he became one of the star performers in the gymnasium of the Brooklyn Young Men's Christian Association, and in 1885, at eighteen, he won the first national championship on the horizontal bars in the United States.

Blanche of course communicated to Roland her fascination with his physical prowess, and Roland was quick to assure her that he viewed his athletic interests as those of a gentleman. By this he meant that he traveled in a company of athletes who

22

were proud to remain amateurs, pursuing other professions appropriate to gentlemen. He noted regretfully that even in the finest athletic clubs one would find a few members who considered themselves professional athletes. Among such men were the rougher elements, which he and others like him did their best to avoid.

Roland was no less accomplished in his professional life. He explained to Blanche that at a very early age he had shown a bent toward science, particularly chemistry. He had studied at the Brooklyn Polytechnic Institute and later for two years at Cooper Union. Upon completing his education, Roland had worked as a chemist with the firm in which his father was a partner — C. T. Raynolds paint manufacturers. But he had sought an opportunity to establish his reputation independently from his father and had seized on one that presented itself in 1892. Leaving the Raynolds firm, and taking a number of the employees with him, he joined Morris Herrmann and Company, a new partnership also in the business of manufacturing paints. Neither of the firm's partners — Mr. Herrmann and Mr. Levi — was acquainted with the processes of color manufacturing. Roland possessed this expertise and was given the position of factory superintendent. He also had administrative duties, which meant that his time was divided between the firm's offices in New York City and the factory in Newark, New Jersey. Roland hinted there was a strong likelihood that he would soon be invited to join the partnership. He was not sure he would accept such an invitation since the partners were Jews. Nevertheless, for the time being, Roland was most content with the association.

Almost shyly, Roland confessed to Blanche his real ambitions, which had to do with opera and theater. He hoped someday to be financially able to pursue these interests, perhaps to publish a book or a play and also to study music. He had often been told that his baritone voice was exceptional. It seemed to Blanche that Roland was too good to be true.

Just as Blanche held back from Roland some details of her past life, so Roland did not share everything with Blanche. For instance he did not tell her that he had been named co-respondent in a divorce case when he was but sixteen years old, and that his father had sent him to the Sedgwick Academy to remain until the scandal blew over. Nor did Roland tell Blanche about Mary Melando, a young woman not quite Blanche's age with whom he had maintained a lengthy alliance.

He had met Mamie, as she was called more often, when she came to work in the Raynolds factory at the age of thirteen. Mamie's disarming innocence, combined with her ample physical attributes, immediately sparked Roland's interest, and she in turn responded to his attentions. Roland had been involved with Mamie for ten years. In fact, she was one of the employees he took with him to the Morris Herrmann firm. In recent months, however, he had been attempting to disassociate himself from Mamie altogether. First of all, he was aware that he no longer commanded Mamie's exclusive attentions. There were rumors, and confirmations, that she was consorting with the baser elements of society. More worrisome to Roland was the fear that he might have contracted some debilitating disease through Mamie. Off and on he had experienced uncomfortable physical symptoms, including loss of virility, that could be connected with venereal disease, and it was not shyness, but rather dismay over his impotency, that had restrained Roland during the intimate hours he shared with Blanche aboard the *Viator*. All of this he kept to himself.

On the last day at Bar Harbor, Roland and Blanche made tentative plans for the fall season in New York. Roland promised to deliver to Blanche certain books, which he had himself enjoyed the previous winter. Of course they would attend the Metropolitan together during the winter season, and Roland was already soliciting Blanche's preferences as to concert selections. He laughingly theorized that, with such a schedule, Blanche would certainly have no time for any other suitor in her life. Blanche teasingly begged to differ, but of course there were no other suitors in her uncertain life. It embarrassed her that she could not even tell Roland where he could reach her in New York, for she had no permanent address.

Before parting that last evening, Blanche and Roland spoke tender words to each other and indulged one another with tender caresses. Yet when the *Mohegan* pulled anchor the next morning, Blanche was in full possession of her virginity. She and Isia stood at the deck railing, throwing kisses and calling farewells across the water to those aboard the *Viator*. For now, it was home to Jamestown and *Craigsmere*; and if Waldo had already returned from Boston, there would be some explaining to do.

THREE

The Knickerbocker Athletic Club

Waldo's return to *Craigsmere* brought to an abrupt end the carefree meanderings of the Chesebrough sisters. Indeed he had a number of questions regarding their whereabouts during his absence, and Isia was less than candid with her answers. A rift formed between the two, causing an unfriendly pall to descend on the island for the remaining days of August.

At summer's end, Isia decided it would be best for her to make a visit to New York rather than to return home with her husband. Presumably a separation would help clear the air between them. Also, Isia rationalized, her presence in New York would relieve Blanche's financial problems resulting from her absence over the long summer. Isia selected the Mystic Flats as a temporary residence and of course invited her sister to stay with her until Blanche could pick up the pieces of her career.

In early September, a day after her arrival in New York, Blanche sent a note to Roland at the Knickerbocker Club, informing him of her new address. Roland responded with all of the enthusiasm of a young man in love. Baskets of hothouse fruits, flowers and sweets arrived almost daily for Blanche. Then came the invitations—to join Roland for dinner, at the theater, or the concert. Never had Blanche experienced such enjoyment as the attentions that Roland showered upon her. Her life became one feverish round of activities, from which she took the greatest pleasure. Isia, on the other hand, did not share Blanche's enthusiasm. Not that Isia did not like Roland. On the contrary, she saw in him and his family an excellent connection for Blanche, a sort of extension of her own efforts on Blanche's behalf. But true to her role as the older sister, Isia observed that Blanche was not picking up her musical career. She had made little effort to reinstate the musical contacts from which her income derived, or to continue her voice lessons. In Isia's view, procrastination was one of the deadly sins, and she in no way wished to encourage it in her younger sister.

Without warning, Isia announced one morning that she would be giving up the rooms at the Mystic Flats and moving to the home of her friend, Alice Bellinger, on West End Avenue. Blanche would have to manage on her own from now on. Blanche pouted a little at the news, but eventually came to see the wisdom of Isia's forcing her to come to terms with her situation.

With Roland's help, Blanche found her own rooms at the establishment of one Mrs. Bell at 251 West Seventy-fifth Street. Always anticipating Blanche's every need, he arranged for a maid from the Knickerbocker to spend a day at the Mystic Flats, helping her prepare for the move. And not unexpectedly, there was a huge bouquet of roses to welcome Blanche to her new home. Roland had a way of remembering every detail.

Later Blanche was to remember this month of October 1897 as the high point of her life with Roland. He presented her with an extraordinary gift—a jeweled ring from Tiffany's. It had been designed especially for Blanche to Roland's exacting specifications. The ring was a circlet of diamonds, the jewels forming the word *Mizpah*, on which was engraved "GEN.XXXI.49." The citation referred to the Biblical phrase, "The Lord watch between me and thee when we are absent from one another." In the *Mizpah* tradition, such a ring signified a deep and abiding friendship between the giver and the receiver. In Blanche's case, the elegance of the diamond circlet may have obscured this deeper significance of the ring. Roland made it known to Blanche that he placed great importance on her acceptance of this visible witness to their friendship. Though as yet he had not proposed marriage, all of his conversation presumed a future together, one that included an extended stay in Paris. Blanche was ever mindful of this. She was also increasingly aware that their relationship was mainly on an intellectual basis. Roland did show affection to her, but even in their most intimate moments, he appeared to have every bit of his mind and body in tight restraint. For Blanche, it became a challenge and a game to penetrate this controlled exterior, either by teasing or through an especially seductive move on her part. But Roland was impenetrable.

Increasingly, Roland came to orchestrate less intimate gatherings at which he proudly introduced his intended to both fellow club members and musical acquaintances. Blanche's introduction to the Knickerbocker Club was arranged by Roland in such a way that she would also meet his closest friend, Bartow Weeks. The three of them had dinner together one evening in the Knickerbocker dining room. The other club members and staff were witnesses to the event, which of course was Roland's intention.

Bartow Weeks was already a successful attorney in New York, partner in the law firm of Battle and Weeks. In addition he had served two terms as president of the New York Athletic Club, a much older and somewhat more exclusive club than the Knickerbocker, and was currently captain of the club athletic team. In spite of the prestige surrounding the New York Athletic Club, teams from the Knickerbocker had surpassed those of the older club in the previous season. This fact caused a great deal of good-natured ribbing between Roland and Bartow at dinner. To some extent the conversation amused Blanche, but she soon tired of the continued references to athletics which dominated the conversation and seemed to pervade the entire club. Her relationship with Roland had been built on their common interest in music. This other side of Roland—the club, the athletic events and the gossip—rarely surfaced when the two were alone. In the company of Bartow Weeks it predominated, and indeed it bored Blanche.

Blanche could excuse Roland and his athletic club crowd, for the opera season had opened and provided sufficient glamour to satisfy her fondest desires. With every performance she could count on dinner beforehand, or supper afterward, usually with other members of the Opera Club. True to her upbringing, Blanche made do quite well with what she had in the manner of clothes. A ribbon here, a pin there, or a new scarf smartly tied transformed a stale gown into a creation with real style. Roland greatly admired this talent of Blanche's and was proud to present her to his fellow opera buffs and to escort her to their after-theater haunts—Delmonico's, the Waldorf, Martin's or the old Brevoort.

Certainly Blanche enjoyed the operas and concerts to the fullest, but most of all she treasured this circle of acquaintances into which her friendship with Roland had brought her. Years later she acknowledged that her real interest had not been so much the music as the social contacts to which the music led—the people of talent and cleverness who shared Roland's enthusiasm for opera. Surely this was a difficult admission for one who had previously thought she would devote her entire life to a musical career.

Unfortunately, things were not quite as they seemed to Blanche that happy autumn of 1897. Roland's constant attentions to her were masking two very serious crises which he faced. The first had to do with Mamie Melando, who formerly had played an important role in his life. Younger than Blanche, she too had been pretty at one time, but in Roland's eyes she now was faded and soiled, an object of contempt.

Mamie had been born and raised in Bayonne, New Jersey. The prototype of an American industrial city in the late nineteenth century, Bayonne was not a pretty place. Short on greenery and long on fumes, it was a center for chemical factories and oil refineries as well as a busy harbor. The dreary residential areas of Bayonne housed the laborers who were required to keep the heavy industrial plants in operation. This was a time when there were no child labor laws of any consequence and it was not uncommon for children to work along with their elders in the factories. The Bayonne paint factory belonging to the Raynolds Company was no exception. Thus in 1887 Mamie Melando, just thirteen years of age, left school and entered the factory workforce as a full-time employee. At that time Roland was newly employed there as a chemist, and this winsome young girl, eight years his junior, quickly attracted his attention. No doubt the attraction was mutual, for an intimate relationship developed that was to last almost ten years.

When Roland moved to the Morris Herrmann Company, Mamie went with him. She advanced rapidly from a simple factory worker to forewoman in the green dye department, a position she would never have reached without Roland's intervention. The Herrmann factory was located in Newark, some distance from Mamie's home in Bayonne as well as from Roland's in Brooklyn. It was therefore convenient for Roland to maintain private rooms above the factory, rooms to which Mamie had easy access. In time Mamie took over responsibility for the housekeeping of the little apartment. As long as Roland used the rooms for his principal residence, Mamie could play house there, a situation in which she was quite contented.

However, when the Knickerbocker Club opened in 1896, Roland took a room at the clubhouse on Manhattan. Though he still frequented his apartment when he found it necessary to be in the Newark factory, he no longer slept nor spent his leisure hours there. Mamie continued to care for the rooms, and Roland often left a box of sweets or a bowl of fresh fruit on his dresser, perhaps to repay her. Mamie found it convenient to treat herself accordingly, and on occasion would also "borrow" a pen, or perhaps a few sheets of writing paper and other items of little value.

By early 1897 the relationship between the two had become very tenuous, and Mamie seemed to sense that a final disengagement was approaching. Roland had become very embarrassed about the whole affair. In the first place it did not fit into the life he was actively pursuing in New York, and secondly, he no longer cared for Mamie to spend time in his rooms during periods when he was seldom there. In addition to clothing and other personal items, Roland kept a number of chemical compounds in the apartment, one area of which he used for experiments with new color combinations.

The fact that Mamie was from a background quite dissimilar to Roland's and was totally uneducated by his standards had previously mattered very little in their association — that is, until Mamie's lack of discretion impinged on Roland's own reputation.

With Roland no longer dominating her every move, Mamie began to look for other diversions. Unfortunately, either through force of circumstances or lack of good judgment, she began to frequent an establishment in Newark that was viewed by the authorities as a disorderly house. One night the police raided the house, and Mamie was arrested. Compelled to spend the night in jail, she succeeded the next morning in sending a message to Roland at the Knickerbocker Club. Roland was in the gymnasium at the time, and the message was relayed to him through the club's athletic director, Harry Cornish. To Roland's credit, he acted immediately to extricate Mamie from her predicament, traveling to Newark so that he could intercede directly with the police. Mamie was released forthwith; clearly the influence of the Molineux name was not limited to the State of New York!

When Roland returned to New York after the summer, he vowed that he would get rid of Mamie once and for all. For reasons of health, he did not wish ever to have contact with her again. Besides, any connection with Mamie could only be a liability in his courtship of Blanche. In view of all this, and the proximity of Mamie's place of employment to his private rooms above the factory, Roland was compelled to terminate her employment. To soften the blow, he offered her a new dress, provided that she promise never to return to the Herrmann factory premises. Mamie left the Herrmann factory for good and accepted the dress. It was the only evidence of her years of service to the Morris Herrmann firm, not to mention Roland Molineux.

Gossip regarding Roland's relations with Mamie Melando, in particular as these related to Mamie's arrest in early 1897, had taken firm root at the Knickerbocker. Ths gossip precipitated the second crisis with which Roland was forced to deal during his courtship of Blanche.

The impressive clubhouse in which the Knickerbocker was housed stood at Forty-fourth and Madison. The building itself was not new, having formerly housed the now defunct Manhattan Club. It had been renovated extensively, however, thanks to the substantial financial investment of Herbert Ballantine, a prominent New York brewer. To enhance the athletic reputation of the fledgling club, Ballantine had personally arranged for the hiring of Harry Cornish as athletic director. Cornish had made his name at the Chicago Athletic Club and had also co-authored with Spalding two books on athletics for which he had gained national notice.

The Knickerbocker Club boasted a first-rate gymnasium that attracted not only Roland Molineux, but many other young men about town. By the time the club was two years old, its membership numbered 1300. Roland's athletic reputation, albeit as an amateur, was instrumental in his becoming secretary of the important house committee.

In this capacity, he found it necessary to deal extensively with Cornish, a man who seemed to possess not one attribute normally associated with a gentleman. At least this was Roland's opinion. Roland's responsibilities on the house committee included updating and maintaining the gymnasium equipment, but very early it became clear to him that Cornish viewed the gymnasium as his kingdom. He appropriated a room off the gymnasium as his office and soon transformed it into his sleeping quarters as well. Roland also noted that Cornish used the club stationery for his personal correspondence. He concluded that Cornish was a man to be watched and that the responsibility for this had fallen on him.

Roland felt it was his mission to maintain the reputation of the Knickerbocker as a gentlemen's athletic club. The athletic performers and teams should never lose sight of their amateur status, even as they strived for quality and competitiveness. He viewed himself as a patrician and expected as much from his club.

Cornish on the other hand was well-acquainted with the professional sports figures in New York City. He frequented their haunts and he spoke as they did — bluntly and coarsely. He even had ideas of incorporating some of the professional aspects of athletics into the Knickerbocker environment and boasted that he could count on Herbert Ballantine to stand behind him. An early clash between Cornish and Roland was inevitable.

Soon after the swimming pool opened in late 1896, Roland noticed that Cornish was allowing outsiders to bathe with the club members. Roland regarded these strangers as uncouth and given to using foul language. Their presence was not in keeping with his vision of the club, and he felt compelled to report the situation to the Board of Directors. The result was a more restrictive club policy on visitors to the pool area and the beginning of Cornish's overt hostility toward Roland. The opportunity to retaliate came shortly thereafter when Cornish found himself in the position of delivering to Roland Mamie Melando's message from the Newark jail. Cornish extrapolated on this knowledge to suggest that Roland owned the house of ill-repute in which Mamie had been arrested. Roland, in a rare outburst of anger, threatened to sue Cornish, but nothing came of the threat.

Then in the spring of 1897, the Knickerbocker Club members organized an Amateur Circus, which was to become an annual event. Roland had prepared extensively for his own act on the horizontal bars and, as secretary of the house committee, instructed Cornish to order a new set of bars for the performance. Unknown to Roland, Cornish had substituted for Roland's preferred manufacturer of bars the name of a firm in which he had an interest. Roland did not discover the substitution until the actual performance; due either to his surprise on discovery or the lesser quality of the bars, Roland fell and came close to being seriously injured. In his fury over this insubordination, he went directly to Ballantine, outlining his grievances. Ballantine must have had some sympathy for Roland's point of view, for Cornish's privileges were somewhat diminished—his private room was eliminated and his desk was moved out onto the floor of the gymnasium. To Roland this was visible indication that he had been vindicated, and in this respect, at least, his mind was at ease when he left for his summer holiday.

When Roland returned to the Knickerbocker in September, his mind was filled with thoughts other than those related to Harry Cornish. Events, however, soon changed this.

Cornish had learned of Roland's little dinner party at the Knickerbocker, during which he had entertained both Bartow Weeks and Blanche Chesebrough. Well aware that Roland and Weeks were good friends, Cornish took it upon himself to write a letter to a major figure in New York amateur athletic circles belittling the New York Athletic Club and in particular its team captain, Bartow Weeks. The letter, written on Knickerbocker stationery and signed by "Harry Cornish, Athletic Director," found its way to Weeks himself, who showed it to Roland. It is surprising that Roland was able to give Blanche the attention that he did during October, for this matter of Cornish and the letter almost got the better of him. He appeared before the Board of Directors of the Knickerbocker and presented them with an ultimatum: either Cornish must go or he would go; the Knickerbocker Club was too small for both. Roland outlined to the directors Cornish's transgressions as he had observed them for almost a year. He called upon them to vindicate the slander that had been cast against his friend Bartow Weeks in the name of the Knickerbocker Club.

Roland pleaded and threatened, but when the matter was finally given over to the Board for a vote, Cornish was not removed, but rather reprimanded, particularly as to his use of the club stationery and name. Since Bartow Weeks was also a man to be dealt with, as a lawyer of some reputation in addition to his position at the New York Athletic Club, the Board voted to give a dinner in his honor. Subsequently the dinner took place at the Union League Club.

Bartow Weeks and Roland Molineux attended the dinner together. The club directors apologized to Weeks and expressed their admiration for the New York Athletic Club and its leadership. The gesture satisfied Weeks, and he carried back to his own club directors the greetings and compliments expressed by the Knickerbocker governors.

By all appearances the petty animosities within the Knickerbocker Club had also been laid to rest.

FOUR

Henry Barnet

The room adjacent to Roland's at the Knickerbocker was occupied by Henry Barnet, an amiable and rotund stock and commodity broker. Barnet was thirty-two years old, just a year older than Roland. The two bachelors had joined the club at about the same time and soon established an easy friendship. Actually their personalities seemed to complement each other—Roland somewhat reserved, and Barnet outgoing and jovial in any company. Where Roland's club interests centered on the athletic activities, Barnet was more amenable to the club's sociability and dining pleasures. The two young men occasionally shared a meal in the dining room and more often a smoke in the lounge. Though Barnet found Roland an agreeable friend, he carefully avoided taking sides on the Cornish question. Rather he strived to treat each member and employee with equal good humor; even Roland could not quarrel with that.

During the autumn of 1897 there was by necessity a curtailment of this congenial friendship. The courtship of Blanche, the Mamie affair, and the Cornish unpleasantness all vied for Roland's attention. Except for a friendly "Hello" in the bathroom or hall, the two men went their separate ways.

In early November Roland and Blanche attended the Metropolitan Opera performance of Gounod's *Faust*, in which Jean de Reszke sang the leading role. The performance held high anticipation for Blanche since she had auditioned before de Reszke several years earlier. That audition had led to the one with Madam Melba, which would always ensure de Reszke a place in Blanche's heart. During the first act Blanche's thoughts were already on the late supper at Delmonico's, to which she and Roland were invited and at which de Reszke was likely to be present. However, during the intermission an event took place which made the Delmonico supper party pale in comparison. As was the custom, Roland and Blanche promenaded in the foyer, along with a crowd representing the musical and the famous as well as the not-so-musical and the not-so-famous. Suddenly Roland raised his arm and called across the crowd, "Hello, Barney!" Henry Barnet, in the company of a rather plain woman, came through the throng and returned the greeting with a hearty "Hello, Moli" and a vigorous handshake. Greetings and introductions were made all around—Miss Chesebrough, Mr. Barnet of the Knickerbocker, Miss so-and-so (there is no longer a record of her name), and Mr. Molineux, also of the Knickerbocker. The foursome exchanged pleasantries, but all that remained with Blanche was the intensity with which Barnet's eyes had followed her. Barnet later confessed to Blanche that his only remembrance of the *Faust* performance was the animation in her voice and the piercing look from her eyes during those few minutes when they stood together in the foyer.

The following evening Blanche was Roland's dinner guest at the Knickerbocker. Several of the club members greeted them cordially as they entered the dining room; Blanche had dined there a number of times that autumn and her presence always enhanced the rather staid atmosphere of the male sanctuary. Immediately Blanche was aware that Henry Barnet was dining alone across the room, but she looked away and attempted to rivet her attention on Roland. Toward the end of the meal, Roland himself noticed his friend. He called Blanche's attention to Barney, then excused himself. Roland crossed the room and in a moment returned with his friend. The two men stood by Blanche, chatting with each other and with her. Etiquette dictated that the lady invite the visiting gentleman to sit down; Blanche had learned her lessons well and asked Barney to join her and Roland for coffee and liqueur.

A delightful camaraderie developed over the coffee and Benedictine. Barney brought up the subject of the Club Carnival, which was to take place the following week. Did Blanche know about it? Did she know that Roland would be performing? Was she aware of his excellence on the horizontal bars? Then he turned to Roland and lightly scolded him for not yet having invited Blanche to the event. Roland noted that he would be in a difficult position to escort Blanche, as he would be involved during the evening's entertainment, not only in his own performance but behind the scenes. How about Barney escorting Blanche to the entertainment? Roland would join them both after the show, as soon as he could change. A splendid idea, they all agreed.

The Club Carnival was a magnificent occasion. Roland clearly outshone all of the other club performers, and Blanche, one of the few ladies present, was breathless in her enthusiasm over his achievements. At the same time, she was thrilled at the chance to be with Barney alone, ignoring of course the presence of the hundred or so other members and friends who crowded the Knickerbocker gymnasium. Afterward Blanche trailed up to Roland's room with Barney and others, where they all drank a toast to their amateur champion "Moli," the hero of the evening. Whatever attraction Barney held for Blanche that night, she also relished her role as the champion's lady.

Henry Barnet was actually better liked among the club members than Roland. He flirted outrageously with every woman he met, whether it be the housemaid or the wife of the club manager, but his exceedingly good nature caused most everyone, the women as well as the men, to overlook whatever foibles he might possess.

Roland was highly respected by members and employees

alike. He was often called upon for advice out of regard for his well-established athletic reputation, and of course the Molineux name demanded respect in most New York circles. However the very attributes which had so attracted the aspiring Blanche seemed to put off some of his club associates. Roland was debonair and suave, smiled constantly, and often waved his hand in a condescending manner. Later it was recalled that he would often appear out of nowhere in the midst of a conversation, apologize for his intrusion, bow, and slip away, leaving the participants feeling uncomfortable and exposed. It was clear that Roland considered himself a gentleman with an excellent pedigree. He aspired to be on the Board of Directors at the Knickerbocker, but so far had attained only the house committee. Nevertheless Roland had clout and he had connections, including Herbert Ballantine himself; he was a man with whom every member wished to maintain good relations.

Blanche's presence in the Knickerbocker dining room became even more frequent with the advent of Henry Barnet. Blanche had all she could do to keep her conversation and attention directed toward Roland when Barney was present. Admittedly Barney's presence tended to take from the seriousness of the conversations—music and books were not his principal interests—but he liked people and had a seemingly unlimited supply of amusing anecdotes with which to entertain her. In Barnet's company, Roland was more reserved and often seemed somewhat bored and even a little petulant.

Not that Blanche did not see Roland alone. They continued to attend the opera and theater together, and in the weeks following the Club Carnival, Blanche had the feeling that Roland was attempting to fill every hour of her existence. Barney had obviously introduced a certain urgency in their relationship, and one evening, out of the blue, Roland formally proposed marriage. When Blanche put him off by indicating that she didn't think he was serious, Roland insisted that he was indeed dead serious, which forced her to admit, in a lighthearted way, that she did not yet care for him enough to marry him. She chose her words carefully so as not to rule out a future change of heart, for Roland still had much to offer.

The first visible sign of a break in the friendship between Barnet and Roland occurred in the presence of Blanche. One afternoon when the three sat together, Barney lamented, in mock seriousness, his state as a lonely bachelor, while Roland could look forward to the prospect of marriage to Blanche. Patting Roland on the arm he exclaimed, "Congratulations, old man." Blanche quickly explained that this was not the case—that she and Roland had no plans to be married. She was immediately conscious of an inexplicable change in Roland's manner. He seemed visibly irritated and replied cooly, "Oh yes we do." Blanche protested that they were not even engaged, then tried to cover her own irritation with a little laugh. Roland concluded the conversation by acknowledging the truth in Blanche's statement, but adding that they would soon be. Roland was smiling at Blanche, but she could sense the seriousness of his manner; then, still smiling, he turned to Barney and looked him in the eye for several moments. Roland intended to leave no doubt in either mind about his intentions. He was not ignorant of the growing infatuation between Blanche and Barnet, and he wanted them both to know it.

What was it in Barnet that so attracted and fascinated Blanche? By her own admission, she had sensed a hidden strength and brute force in the man, even at their first meeting in the Opera House foyer. Then and there she had mentally capitulated to this strain in him. In her own peculiar interpretation of the event, she noted that the temptation to yield is irresistible when a woman senses mastery in a man. Blanche believed that with some men brutality in lovemaking is the other side of tenderness. She believed further that Barney was such a man, and as events would prove, she was correct.

As winter settled in on New York and its inhabitants, Blanche found it necessary to leave her quarters on West

Seventy-fifth Street. Mrs. Bell had been a satisfactory landlady; Blanche had no complaint about her, but she had found the situation with the colored servants in the house totally unacceptable.

At the turn of the century, New York had a very highly structured society that included a very large, and largely poor, class of immigrants who performed the many service tasks required to keep such a metropolis alive. Interestingly, this immigrant class was racially integrated; black immigrants from the South and white immigrants from central and southern Europe endured a common degradation. As a result, servants in hotels or boarding houses or the better homes might be either black or white, though generally not both at a single establishment.

As a child, Blanche had been taught that there was an unbridgeable chasm between those of the Negro race and those who were of Anglo-Saxon origin, like the Chesebrough family. She carried this precept with her throughout life. At Isia's homes in Boston and on Conanicut Island, the household servants usually had been Irish immigrants. With servants such as these, Blanche had found it pleasant to engage in ordinary conversation. Even at the Mystic Flats, there had been an easy familiarity between the guests and the immigrant maids who took care of their quarters.

With the move to Mrs. Bell's rooms, however, Blanche for the first time came in contact with servants who were colored. She was astounded and annoyed to learn that they presumed to maintain the same kind of familiarity she was accustomed to only with others of her race. Moreover, Mrs. Bell's cleaning maid and janitor were both ignorant as well as colored, and Rachel, the maid, was much too curious about Blanche's affairs as well as excessively independent with regard to her cleaning responsibilities. The situation rapidly became intolerable, and after several weeks Blanche proceeded to look for other quarters.

Isia Stearns was not unsympathetic to Blanche's predicament. Since leaving the Mystic Flats, she had lingered at the home of her friend Alice Bellinger on West End Avenue; however, with the Christmas season approaching, Isia decided it was time for her to return to her family in Boston. Presumably Waldo had mellowed in the months since August.

Throughout the autumn, Isia had kept an eye on her younger sister, frequently sending notes, which usually contained a modest gift of cash, and occasionally calling on Blanche for an afternoon chat as her friendship with Roland Molineux progressed.

So far, Isia approved. But of late, Blanche had exhibited a bit of flightiness, and Isia sought peace of mind against her departure at such a critical time in her sister's life. Isia therefore suggested to Alice Bellinger that Blanche take her place, with Isia subsidizing her room and board, and Alice concurred. Blanche was ecstatic on hearing of the arrangement, marvelling once again at how fortunately everything turned out when Isia had a hand in it.

It is doubtful whether Blanche could have found a more suitable home anywhere in New York. Alice Bellinger, an exceedingly handsome and well-bred woman fifteen years older than Blanche, had been divorced from a prominent New York banker some years earlier. She was now making her way quite well in the world, having established a hairdressing and manicure salon not far from her spacious, well-maintained home. Alice lived quite comfortably and was even able to afford an Irish housemaid, who also did the cooking. Nevertheless, she found it convenient and pleasant to have a paying guest.

The move to Alice's provided Blanche with a temporary respite from financial pressures and also led to the sort of friendship that had so far been lacking in her life. Blanche admired Alice's elegance and sophistication, and most of all her moxie — a quality that Alice possessed in abundance. In New York society, a divorced woman carried a stigma that was not easily lived down. For such a woman to establish her own business and maintain a respectable clientele was next to impossible. But Alice had succeeded, and very well indeed. She treated her staff of eight employees fairly and had gained their respect and admiration. She was also respected and admired by her customers and was reaping ample material rewards.

However, even with all of her success, Alice was a lonely woman. Blanche's presence — her vibrance and enthusiasm — added a zest to Alice's somewhat isolated existence, and Blanche's current entrée into New York social circles provided Alice with a glimpse of the life that she would perhaps never know again.

Isia made all of the arrangements for the move to West End Avenue, including a helping hand in the packing and unpacking of Blanche's belongings. Alice provided her with a room which, though small, featured a tiny fireplace around which Blanche created a cozy, intimate atmosphere. In addition, she had access to Alice's parlor and the dining room on the main floor, where she and Alice shared their meals.

On the rare evenings when Blanche was not out with Roland, or more often of late with Roland and Barney, the two women could be found sitting in front of the little fireplace in Blanche's room, away from the noise of the kitchen. Blanche was eager to share with Alice the glittering details of her latest evening out, and Alice often would contribute some very astute observations on humanity, gleaned from her various business dealings with men and women alike.

One evening after supper, Alice brought up coffee and sat chatting with Blanche, who was preparing to attend the opera and an after-theater party with Roland as her escort. Blanche was particularly animated, not only because Barney too would be there, but also because she had been invited to sing for the guests. It would be the first time Blanche had sung for Barney, and she told Alice she wanted to look particularly nice for him.

As Alice sipped her coffee, Blanche took from a box a beautiful black tulle gown her sister had given her, a sort of going-away present in reverse when Isia had returned to Boston. Blanche had worn the gown before, but for this occasion she had purchased a new addition that she knew would set her apart from all of the other women at the party — black satin slippers, the high heels of which were studded with brilliants. And pinned to her breast would be the beautiful diamond butterfly pin from Tiffany's Roland had recently given her. With Alice's help, she donned her costume, then pirouetted slowly for Alice's approval. Alice declared that the gown literally breathed of Paris and that Blanche looked like a million. Blanche replied with feigned haughtiness that she ought to look that way—the jewels were from her future husband, that is, her husband in some dim and distant future.

Alice could stand no more of Blanche's vacillations between her two suitors, but as she opened her mouth to speak, there was a knock at the door, and the maid announced that Roland waited below. As Blanche scurried to finish dressing, Alice suddenly seized her by the arm and with a stern look, spoke quietly but distinctly: "I warn you as your friend, stop your flirtation with Barnet or you will find yourself in a great deal of trouble. One can see in Roland's eyes that he will not stand for it." With that, she turned and left.

A short while later, Blanche was gliding down the staircase, Alice's chinchillas draped over her shoulder and long white gloves covering her hands and arms. Roland was in a light-hearted mood and looking quite elegant in his evening clothes. As they settled into a waiting cab and headed toward the Metropolitan Opera House, Blanche forced Alice's admonition from her mind. All was certainly right in her rose-colored world on this wonderful evening, and nothing would keep her from enjoying it.

At midnight they joined Roland's friends from the Opera Club at a studio apartment on Washington Square. The rooms were crowded with guests, but the minute she and Roland arrived, Barney's eyes caught Blanche's. It soon became apparent to Blanche that there would be little opportunity for her to sing in such a lively, raucous atmosphere and at such a late hour. While Roland was detained with their host, she slipped into a nearby room with Barney. Blanche had noticed that he was not alone that evening, but when she inquired as to the whereabouts of his woman companion, Barney jested that she was off flirting with some other man. Then he made a proposition that at first seemed preposterous to her. Blanche should pick up her furpiece and gloves from the vestibule, and the two of them would escape the party for a half hour or so. In the mob, no one would miss them, least of all Roland, who was thoroughly in his element this evening. Barney had the key to a friend's apartment in the neighboring street, while the friend was in Europe.

Blanche hesitated, but her heart was pounding with anticipation at this rare opportunity—to be alone with Barney for the first time. Hadn't she been waiting for this moment all along? With no thought of the consequences, she capitulated with a nod, then quickly fetched her furs and gloves.

Once outside the building, Barney hailed a passing cab—they would save a minute or so by riding the short distance. Less than five minues later, he turned the key to the apartment door and stood aside for Blanche to enter. Blanche marvelled at the room in which she found herself—luxurious and smart, obviously a man's domicile, a man whose tastes were most cultivated. It was obvious also that Barney had prepared for her joining him here. The apartment was already dimly lighted when they entered, and a chaise lounge had been drawn up before the open fireplace, in which logs were resting on massive andirons. Barney reached for a taper and ignited the tinder, and shortly a bright, crackling fire was blazing. The firelight played on the nearest objects and threw shadows on the opposite walls. It was a scene of which Blanche would dream many times in her life.

Barney turned toward Blanche and removed her furs, exposing her bare shoulders and arms. He motioned to the cushioned chaise, then disappeared into another room. He returned with a small silver tray on which were arranged carbonated water, ice, and a flask of scotch whiskey. Barney had indeed planned every detail.

Blanche observed him carefully as he deposited the tray on a small table—so good looking and slightly thinner; had he been working out in the gymnasium? How well he looked in his well-cut, loosely fitted clothes. Barney prepared the highballs in two crystal glasses, handed one to Blanche, then lifted his own to her. "To you," was all that he said. For a few minutes they sat separately, Blanche coquettishly asking why Barney had arranged this meeting, since he had obviously set the scene ahead of time. He replied simply that he wished to have her alone, if even for a short time. Blanche continued in a playful manner, reaching over to lay her fingers on his lips as if to silence such serious talk. Barney caught her hand between his own and pressed his face into the palm of it. For a moment he held it thus.

Blanche, uncomfortable at the length of his intimate gesture, felt the urge to say something, but she soon regretted her words.

"This is terribly risque, Barney, our being here — you know that. What if Roland . . . ?"

Barney dropped her hand, stood up abruptly, and for the first time spoke to Blanche in anger.

"Molineux! Then he *does* have some claim on you!"

Reaching for his cigarette case, he snapped open the silver lid, took out a cigarette and lighted it. He drew on it and then sat down as Blanche tried to recover from her *faux pas*. She declared that Roland surely would resent their being alone, even if he did not resent the friendship itself. Barney assured her that he could survive Roland's resentment. Besides, the mere fact that he had met Blanche through Roland should in no way inhibit his own interest in her.

Blanche agreed, but they continued sparring verbally with one another. Was Blanche in love with Molineux? No. Did she intend to marry him? Perhaps some day. How could she marry a man she did not love? Well, there were many reasons for marriage — and besides he had promised to give her the opportunity to study music in Paris.

Then Blanche began to philosophize. It seemed to her that love and marriage did not really mix — that marriage often meant the end to love. She told him she didn't feel ready for that kind of commitment, that she was enjoying her life the way it was, and that she wished it to continue. Barney was quick to respond that he felt the same way, and at last the two found themselves on common ground.

Blanche then sat upright in the chaise and leaned closer to Barney, wondering if he could hear her heart beating. She had never been in such intimate circumstances before, but she knew instinctively that she wanted Barney to be conscious of the faint, indefinable perfume in her hair and on her flesh. She followed his eyes as they fell on the little hollow between her breasts, easily visible beneath the tulle bodice of her gown. Just below rested the jeweled butterfly, and as Barney's gaze fixed upon its sparkling, outspread wings, he compared the delicate creature to her on whom it perched — colorful, brilliant and fragile. Blanche denied the last, insisting that beneath her frivolity was a very sensible woman. Actually, she was paying little attention to the conversation, fascinated as she was by everything about Barney, even the way in which he inhaled his cigarette. Watching the spirals of thin blue smoke as they wavered upward from the lighted end, she felt an overwhelming desire to touch him.

Time was running out, and Blanche desperately wanted to put Barney to the test — the test that Roland had failed so miserably on the yachting trip. Barney drew back and put out his cigarette. Suddenly he rose from his chair, thrust his hands into his pockets and walked the length of the room. Then, as if overcome by desire, he turned and walked back, seized Blanche in his arms, lifting her from the chaise, and sank back into it with Blanche on top of him, her lips buried in his. In Blanche's memory it was like a storm — the kisses, the impatient undoing of closures, the pounding of two hearts and two bodies, and at last the ecstacy. After a moment, Barney's arms slipped from Blanche. She raised herself up and viewed the damage — on her flesh were several bruises just beginning to throb, her dress was rumpled but salvageable, and her hair was in disarray. But Barney looked worse. Across the back of his hand was a long, red, ugly gash from the jeweled butterfly wing. Barney did not seem to notice it any more than Blanche felt the ugly swelling on her mouth. He filled a liqueur glass with brandy and put it to her lips. There was nothing to say, for no words could do justice to that which the two had experienced together.

Their return to the party could not have gone entirely unnoticed, as the group had substantially thinned out in the meantime. Roland seemed nonchalant about Blanche's absence, but she wondered if he had noticed anything disheveled in her appearance. Surely she could not hide completely what she felt inside, and this in itself gave her an unsettled feeling. But Roland said nothing.

Over the next few days, Blanche could think of nothing but her tryst with Barney, recreating over and over again in her thoughts what had transpired in the apartment on Washington Square. But she soon gave way to feelings of doubt, for he was conspicuous by his absence. Nor were there any calls or messages from Roland. Blanche guessed that Roland had been peeved, but she was confident that after a few days all would be back to normal.

Alone one evening with Alice, Blanche confided to her friend what had happened between her and Barney. Alice was shocked and again warned Blanche that she was courting disaster. Pointing to the ring on Blanche's finger—the *Mizpah* ring which she had been wearing now for three months—she asked why Blanche was wearing it at all if she was so attracted to Barnet.

Petulantly, Blanche assured Alice that it was just a friendship ring, not an engagement ring. Then she completely reversed herself, confessing that she still hoped to marry Roland and to go to Paris with him. She had recently conferred with her voice coach about continuing her studies, and he had told her that she was wasting too much time and ought to be making preparations to study abroad. He had even offered to help her find backing, if she would only sacrifice and work a little harder.

Alice had developed a real affection for Blanche, but this was too much for her. Exasperated, she turned to leave the room, but then looked back toward Blanche. "Why don't you marry Molineux, or forget him and go back to your musical work," she demanded. "Why don't you make a decision?"

FIVE

Alienation

January is rarely a pretty month in New York, and January of 1898 was no exception. It was dark and damp and cold, and Blanche was restless and unhappy, spending day after day before the little fireplace in her room. Though she thought much about Barney, she really did not expect him to call. It was Roland's silence that weighed upon her. She could not imagine that he would break off completely with her after all of the time and resources he had invested in their friendship, and in any event she did not want this to happen. She would somehow have to take the initiative in a manner which would indicate that nothing untoward had taken place.

A plan began to emerge—she would arrange a meeting with Barney. The outcome of such a meeting could be advantageous in two ways. First of all she would have the opportunity to see him again, which was reward enough for any initiative that she might take; but in addition she could gain knowledge from Barney as to Roland's mood without revealing that she had not seen nor heard from him since the party.

Blanche "rang up" Barney at the Knickerbocker. In those days, it was not easy to have an intimate conversation on the telephone, and at the Knickerbocker Club it was nearly impossible. The telephone was located at the desk in the main lobby, and residents were called from their rooms by a bell signal.

Alice Bellinger had a telephone in her home on a party line with the one in her shop. The home phone was located on the wall in the downstairs hall, within hearing distance of every room in the house. Therefore Blanche's call to Barney had to be discreet in content. He seemed a little uneasy on the telephone, but nevertheless agreed to meet Blanche the following afternoon at an obscure uptown cafe.

Blanche had sensed a certain reticence on Barney's part to see her, and she therefore took pains to dress in a manner that would please him most. She arrived at the rendezvous stylishly late and found him already sipping a cup of Mocha coffee. As he rose to greet her, Blanche could discern both eagerness and reluctance in his eyes. They had barely exchanged pleasantries and were not yet seated when Blanche began to question Barney with mock indignation. Where had be been since their last meeting at Washington Square? Why had he avoided her so? Was it because she had capitulated to his advances that he had cast her off so shamelessly, or was it simply because of the friendship between her and Roland? Blanche demanded an explanation.

Seemingly undisturbed by this torrent of words, Barney helped Blanche remove her cloak and arrange herself on the chair, then sat down himself and ordered Blanche's coffee from the waiter. Looking at Barney across the table, Blanche felt more at ease and reached across to touch his arm in a gesture of reconciliation. But Barney intercepted her hand by grasping it in his own, an act of aggression more than of tenderness. He pointed to the *Mizpah* ring which encircled the third finger and then told Blanche of the confrontation that had taken place between him and Roland immediately after the party. Roland had referred to Blanche as his intended and had made specific reference to the ring she wore. Further he had made accusations against Barney—accusations that Barney in all honesty could not deny. He looked Blanche in the eye and spoke in a voice filled with urgency: "Roland has told me he is going to marry you and he has also told me to keep out of this. What do you say to that?"

Blanche felt as if she had been backed into a wall. She could only repeat to Barney what she had said earlier to Alice. She was not in love with Roland and at the moment she did not intend to marry him. There were many things, however, that Roland could offer her, not the least of which was the interest he shared in music and particularly in opera.

Wishing to be done with Barney's interrogation, as that had not been in her plan for this afternoon, Blanche skillfully moved from her own defense to the subject of Roland, which was still uppermost in her mind. She began with a tentative apology over not being able to join the two men for dinner at the Knickerbocker, as had been her custom in earlier weeks. There were conflicts in her schedule, as she was again singing in a choir for which evening rehearsals were required. What kind of club gossip had passed between them that she had to miss? In other words, what was new at the Knickerbocker in this midwinter season?

Barney appeared somewhat dumbfounded at Blanche's questions. Did she not know that Roland had left the club in December? There was gossip that it had been due to a feud between Roland and the athletic director. Blanche wanted to know more, but Barney was careful. He implied that he really did not know the details and did not like to pass on idle gossip. Blanche should inquire of Roland himself as to the details, if she was indeed that interested. Blanche had not prepared herself for this bit of news and quickly concluded that the less said of Roland the better.

Continuing a somewhat belabored exchange of words, the two dawdled over coffee and then brandy. One by one the street lights outside the cafe windows were turned on as evening descended, and Barney offered to accompany Blanche back to her home. He took care of the waiter, helped Blanche with her cloak, and ushering her outside, hailed a cab. In the darkness of the carriage Blanche nestled up next to Barney, putting the serious conversation of the late afternoon out of mind. The clip-clop of the horse's hooves sounded from ahead as the cab turned the corner on West End to the doorstep of the handsome brownstone that Blanche now called home. Alice was out, and the only light came from a shaded lamp burning in the inner vestibule. Blanche paid careful attention as to whether Barney would ask the driver to wait while he accompanied her to the door. He did not. Instead Barney paid the driver, and Blanche's heart skipped a beat. She knew what she might expect this night, and she was more than ready for it.

Blanche's heart may have leapt for Barney that evening, but by the next morning she had a gnawing feeling of uncertainty regarding Roland. Somehow she must get a message to him so that they could meet and straighten out any misunderstanding; at tne same time Roland must not know that she had learned of his Knickerbocker resignation from Barney. Thus she penned a message to Roland at the club, knowing full well that it would be forwarded to him wherever he might be residing. And so it was. Two days later, Roland stood at the door of Alice's home and rang the bell, expecting the Irish maid to answer it.

Blanche had realized too late that the girl had left Alice's employment and there was no one but herself at home to answer the bell. Though she expected Roland's visit, she nevertheless had procrastinated in her preparations, and a second ring was required to bring her to the door. She opened it to a sober but unruffled Roland, whom she admitted only as far as Alice's front parlor.

This parlor was the most formal room in the entire house. A loveseat and two chairs formed a semicircle at the window end of the rectangular room. Opposite the double doors that led in from the vestibule was the ubiquitous fireplace, and in the center stood a Sheraton table, beautiful to look at but of little use since no chairs were in its vicinity. Like two antagonists, Roland and Blanche positioned themselves at opposite sides of the table, and without invitation Roland laid his hat upon it. When Blanche failed to speak, he took the offensive in his own cool, calm way, asking if she had anything to say for herself as to her relationship with Barnet. When Blanche remained silent, Roland continued: "If you have nothing to say, then I wish to end our affair."

Suddenly Blanche was filled with anger; her eyes flashed and she drew the *Mizpah* ring from her finger, casting it across the table with a gesture of contempt. The ring rolled along the polished wood in a lopsided motion, then fell to the floor and rolled further until it collided with a leg under the loveseat. Without embarrassment, Roland dropped to his knees and retrieved the jeweled piece. Picking up his hat, he gave a short laugh, which Blanche would always remember for its bitterness, and turned toward her: "Tell Barnet the coast is clear—he wins!" Roland left the house with no further word.

Blanche retreated to her room in a stunned condition. She had not meant to end the affair with Roland; she had meant to mollify him at this meeting! Why had it ended this way? She sat down on her bed, laid her head in her arms, and within a few seconds was crying piteously, though there was no one but herself to hear the sobs. When the sobbing had run it course, Blanche began to inquire of herself as to the reason for her grief. Certainly it was not Roland's departure, for Roland was right; the coast was clear for Barney. The reason lay rather in her inability to control her own life. Her independent spirit notwithstanding, she seemed destined always to depend on others—whether it be Isia, or Roland, or Alice, or as she now hoped, Barney. Oh to be free like Isia—financially free—or even better, like Alice, whose only responsibilities were to those who served her, either in her home or in her shop. It was an enviable position.

From below came the sound of the front door opening; Alice had returned, and presently she mounted the stairs to Blanche's room. She knocked and Blanche invited her in by mumbling from her bed. Such a miserable, red-eyed woman she was. Alice took Blanche in her arms and solicitously inquired as to what calamity had befallen her. The conversation was punctuated by Blanche's sobs.

"I've quarrelled with Roland. I believe I hate him. It is ended between us."

"Had it something to do with Barnet?"

"Yes."

"I told you it would happen. But I tell you now that it will blow over. You will see Roland again."

"I don't want to see him again, and I doubt that it will blow over!"

"It will. He isn't going to let you out of his life, and this will only make him the more determined. Men are like that, you know! They want what they find hard to get. Roland may lay this quarrel up against Barnet, but then, a man's jealousy is always a form of flattery!"

Alice stood up to leave, gave Blanche a kiss on the cheek and laughed. "You will see that I am right. Now come downstairs in a few minutes as I am about to prepare a cup of tea for us both."

Alice disappeared and Blanche rearranged her hair and dress. How good it was to have such a friend as Alice; if only she could be more like her. Then suddenly she had an idea. There was no reason for her to be victimized by anyone. She ran from her room, leaned over the banister and called to Alice, "I don't want any tea, I'm going to call Barney! I'll tell him to meet me at Del's!"

The words rang out like a battle cry. Blanche would be seen with Henry Barnet at Delmonico's, the eating and drinking establishment of the Opera Club and the Knickerbocker set—Roland's world. Her friendship with Barney finally would come out of the closet!

Had Blanche known of Roland's present condition, had she known the circumstances of his departure from the Knickerbocker—or even had she known earlier of the departure—she might have behaved differently that winter. In a way it was ironical that Roland's loyal friend Bartow Weeks, not even a member of the club, was the catalyst in this final Knickerbocker denouement. Yet Weeks was powerless to influence the course of events.

The Knickerbocker Club organization was peculiar in that

Herbert Ballantine owned the club facilities. Though the club was governed by an elected Board of Directors, which in turn elected club officers, in the final analysis important decisions could not go against the wishes of Ballantine. The day-to-day activities of the club were overseen by John Adams, the club secretary, who also acted as private secretary to Ballantine.

Adams and Ballantine had attended Cornell University together and had established a firm friendship there, but after college they had gone their separate ways. Ballantine entered the brewery business, and Adams enrolled in a theological seminary with the intention of becoming a minister. Somewhere during these studies he realized that this was not his calling, and so for some years he worked with the Young Men's Christian Association. When Ballantine decided to organize the new Knickerbocker Athletic Club, he sought out his old friend John Adams and prevailed upon him to join in the enterprise — Adams would provide the administrative expertise, and Ballantine the business acumen. Their friendship prospered in the affairs of the Knickerbocker Club as it had years earlier at Cornell. In fact, Adams functioned as the eyes and ears of Ballantine at the club.

Roland's distress over Cornish's entrenchment at the Knickerbocker had not been alleviated by the Union League Club dinner for Weeks. Roland still viewed the removal of Cornish as a requirement for maintaining the club's integrity and respectability. Yet his efforts to effect this removal were not succeeding through the normal chain of command. Thus, following the dinner for Weeks, he called upon John Adams in his office and once more laid out the history of Cornish's transgressions and excesses. Adams was an agreeable sort of man, well-suited to his function at the Knickerbocker. He listened to Roland's story and nodded in tacit agreement. When it was all over, he reminded Roland that as Herbert Ballantine's secretary he really had no power. It was Ballantine's intention that the Knickerbocker should be a democratic organization in which the elected board made the decisions. Adams professed to be sympathetic to Roland's point of view, but helpless to do anything about it.

Roland should approach the directors once more at their December meeting. Adams was the consummate diplomat.

On the evening of December 20, Roland appeared at the directors' meeting. He restated briefly the various aspects of Cornish's conduct which he felt were detrimental to this gentlemen's club. He concluded his remarks with the statement that, to maintain his own integrity, he would have to resign from the Knickerbocker if Cornish were allowed to remain. The directors listened politely. Roland was excused for a half hour while they discussed the matter among themselves and took a vote.

Roland was invited back into the meeting room to hear the decision of the Board: Harry Cornish would not be discharged, and the directors would be pleased if Roland would reconsider any thought he had of resigning. He was considered by all to be one of the Knickerbocker's most valued members. Roland listened intently, looking around the room from face to face as if to ascertain just who his enemies were. Then he spoke: "Gentlemen, I have as of this moment resigned from the Knickerbocker Athletic Club." He then bade good evening to the assemblage, bowed slightly, and left the room.

No one will ever know whom Roland judged to be his enemies among the directors. In reality, not one wished to be his enemy. In one way or another, each director had some sympathy for Roland, but there was general agreement that Roland's feelings against Harry Cornish were out of proportion to Cornish's misdeeds and to his importance within the club structure. Cornish had offended many members, but he had certainly built good teams for several of the sports in which the Knickerbocker participated. In fact during the 1897 season, the Knickerbocker had for the first time outshone its archrival, the New York Athletic Club. Cornish was a good man to have on the staff, and there was no need to associate with him otherwise. Besides, Herbert Ballantine himself had hired Cornish. Such was the consensus of the directors. No one was angry with Roland Molineux; the more perceptive among them just wondered that a man so outwardly self-possessed as Roland Molineux could be so agitated within.

Back in this own room, Roland composed a short note to John Adams, knowing that for certain it would reach the eyes of Herbert Ballantine:

My Dear Adams,
Although I have resigned from the K.A.C., do not for one moment suppose that I wish it other than success. I entertain the highest personal regard for its officers, but I have been a disturbing element in its counsels because, and with the very best intentions, I have opposed what I am confident is a wrong policy, that of allowing an employee to use the club for personal advertisement and to get even with gentlemen who displease him. This I am not in sympathy with. Believe me, it is best that I resign, which I do regretfully. I hope you will show this to Mr. Ballantine, that he may know how I stand in this matter. Wishing you all the compliments of this happy season, I am,
      Yours most cordially,
      Roland Molineux

Late that night Roland descended the stairs and dropped the note through the door to Adams's office. The lobby was deserted, but as he walked back up to his room, he had the encounter that he perhaps wished most to avoid, meeting face-to-face with Harry Cornish on the stairs. Cornish stretched his arms across the stairway as if to prevent Roland's ascent and addressed him in an unforgivable manner: "You son of a bitch, you thought you would get me out and I got you out instead."

It appeared that Cornish was baiting Roland for a physical encounter. If that was indeed the case, then he was disappointed. Roland responded with a smile and a wave of his hand. "You win," he retorted and retreated down the stairs. By the next morning Roland and all of his belongings had disappeared from the Knickerbocker Club.

SIX

West End Avenue

Tracing the story of Roland Molineux after his departure from the Knickerbocker Club is not an easy task, for during the nine months following his resignation he retreated into a kind of voluntary exile. Knowledge of his whereabouts lay beyond the reach of the sources on which this chronicle rests. With one exception, which will be noted in due course, Blanche heard nothing from Roland between February and September of 1898. Roland did not come near the Knickerbocker Club, so those who were willing to talk about him later could shed no light on this period. No doubt he was in touch with his employer and colleagues at the Morris Herrmann Company and with his parents, but these sources did not share their knowledge with the newspapers, or with the courts, or with Blanche. Thus whatever knowledge they possessed presumably died with them.

It should be noted that the newspapers later printed a quantity of rumors, mostly of spurious origin, to explain Roland's absence from circles in which he had previously moved. There were reports that a man answering Roland's description had been seen in this restaurant or that saloon in the company of this man or that woman. Particularly damaging to him were unproven published accounts that he had been seen in China-

West End Avenue

town, in an opium den, in a house frequented by homosexuals, or in the company of known criminals.

There was little evidence to sustain any of these allegations, but there were other clues, some of which surfaced during the trials, from which one can construct a plausible account of Roland's conduct during those critical months in his life. It is prudent to begin with his departure from the Knickerbocker Club.

Roland's sudden exit occurred just four days before Christmas. It would have been reasonable for him to return to his family home in Brooklyn, at least for the holiday, but Roland did not always do what to others might seem reasonable. Instead he moved immediately back to his rooms above the Herrmann factory in Newark. The large barnlike building, with its tiny windows facing the dreary canal, did little to lift his spirits after the humiliation he had just endured. It had been well over a year since Roland last slept above the factory, and at that time Mamie Melando was still a frequent visitor. Mamie was now long gone, and without her it was indeed a lonely place. Nevertheless Roland's pride prevented him from returning to his parents' home.

Between mother and son there had always been a close relationship and fond indulgence; but the general was stern and exacting with his sons. As a youth, Roland had been the rebel among them and had even brought a touch of scandal to the Molineux name. He did not wish to take this latest humiliation to his father; he would overcome it in his own way.

It was unfortunate for Roland that the Cornish affair had climaxed precisely at a time when his relationship with Blanche was in jeopardy. The move to Newark placed constraints on Roland's mobility that could not help but affect this relationship. From Newark, any evening engagement with Blanche meant a late night ferry ride across the Hudson. It also meant meeting a 2:00 A.M. deadline at the wharf for the last ferry back. In fact, it was partly due to this inconvenience that the party on Washington Square gave rise to such serious consequences.

The party did not begin until after the opera performance, close to midnight. No sooner had Roland and Blanche arrived than Blanche disappeared in the crowd. At first this had caused Roland little concern, for he was in a group where he had many easy associations. But as the crowd began to thin out, eventually leaving him and the lady friend of Barnet looking inquiringly at each other, the seriousness of the situation revealed itself. Blanche's sudden reappearance, coinciding with Barnet's casual arrival a short time later, confirmed Roland's worst suspicions.

It was almost 2:00 A.M. when Roland unceremoniously delivered Blanche at home — too late to reach the wharf in time for the last ferry. In any case Roland had other things on his mind. He took a cab directly to the Knickerbocker and waited outside, expecting that Barnet's arrival was at hand. Roland was correct, for no sooner had his cab pulled away than another drove up, from which Barnet alighted. Roland's verbal assault was not a pleasant experience for Barnet, as he later reported to Blanche. Fortunately he was able to escape into the clubhouse while Roland remained on the street, with nowhere to go for the night.

The prospect of freezing to death before morning overcame Roland's natural pride and prompted him to hail a cab to return uptown, this time to raise his friend Bartow Weeks from bed. Under these embarrassing circumstances, Roland told Weeks of his resignation from the Knickerbocker, the late night Opera Club party, and the ferry curfew. Weeks provided a sympathetic ear and of course shelter for what remained of the night. Roland believed that this was what friendships were for, and events proved that Weeks believed this also. Within two weeks Roland was invited to join the New York Athletic Club, and he accepted. A few months later, he was elected to its Board of Directors, a stature he had never achieved at the Knickerbocker. But Roland chose not to take a room at his new club.

Blanche's note, received some days after the Opera Club party, raised Roland's spirits and prompted him to call on her. However, the encounter in Alice's parlor, which left him in possession of the *Mizpah* ring, plunged him into a period of despondency that was to last many months. By his own choice, Roland spent considerable time alone in his rooms above the factory, with ample opportunity to dwell on his misfortune. For all his efforts, the prospect of marriage to Blanche still eluded him. He chided himself for ever having introduced Blanche to Henry Barnet. But is was too late for regrets in this matter; he had acted in good faith and trust of his friend. That Henry Barnet had betrayed this friendship was clearly revealed the night of the party on Washington Square. That Blanche had succumbed to the superficial charms of such a bounder not only lay in her own foolishness, but perhaps also reflected certain of Roland's own inadequacies, which he had every expectation of overcoming. Roland might look back on the foolishness of his own youth with some regret; but he was a Molineux through and through. He had absolute confidence that Blanche would eventually come to her senses. At age thirty-one, he could pride himself on an exceptional physical build and extraordinary athletic achievements. His performance at the Knickerbocker Club Carnival had been talked of for weeks afterward, a source of continuing satisfaction. On the other hand, Barnet, just one year older, exhibited at least thirty pounds of excess weight and a noticeable lack of interest in athletic pursuits. In this respect, he was an embarrassment to the athletic reputation of the Knickerbocker. Roland wondered why this had not occurred to him while he was still a member of that club; he could have arranged to have such a member expelled. Barnet might be known for his successes with women, but he had nothing to offer Blanche in the long run, neither money nor connections. He, Roland, could offer her everything, and besides he loved her. Blanche was surely not unmindful of these facts.

Whatever the facts were, Blanche now found it convenient to set Roland out of her mind, at least for the time being. If she gave any thought to the dramatic parting that had taken place in Alice's parlor, it was to label it the turning of a page in her life. The meeting with Barney at Delmonico's, which was precipitated by this parting, had turned into a rather festive celebration at which both became a little giddy. Subsequently

Barney made a formal call on Blanche at her West End home, and before long he was a regular fixture there. His level of culture was certainly not on a par with Roland's, but he was much less complicated, and Blanche was experiencing a passion unlike anything she had known in her courtship with Roland.

If one could call Roland a man's man, then Barney was a lady's man. Alice Bellinger, shrewd as she was in judging both men and women, was captivated by him. She responded wholeheartedly to his flattery and teasing, though his pronouncements often bordered on the scandalous.

Any announcement of his arrival caused multiple stirrings in the old house. Alice had recently hired a new maid, a colored girl by the name of Minnie Betts, as a replacement for the Irish maid. Blanche did not favor such a replacement, but she did find Minnie to be much less offensive than Rachel, the colored girl she had been required to instruct at Mrs. Bell's. Minnie was unassuming and tractable, fulfilling her responsibilities quietly and without complaint. One could hardly ask for more in a servant. Only when Barney was expected did Minnie show another side. She would race Alice to the door at his ring, then stand shyly aside while Alice threw it open. If both Alice and Blanche were present, Barney would threaten to pinch Minnie or even to kidnap her, causing the girl to giggle and run to the kitchen, screaming in mock terror. Both Alice and Blanche might gasp in shock and disapproval over Barney's behavior, but they could not help but join in the merriment. Barney never meant harm to anyone.

For the rest of that winter and into spring, Blanche spent most of her evenings at home. Barney's interest in opera and theater was minimal, and he avoided entirely the cafe society into which Roland had introduced her. Blanche relished Barney's bold advances and delighted in the intimacies that they shared.

Invariably, Alice stood by when Barney came to call. The three of them might sit together in the parlor for the first half hour of the evening, and either Minnie or Alice herself would serve tea. At these times, Alice would inquire of Barney as to the state of the market and perhaps volunteer her own opinions on the state of the world. Spring of 1898 was a heady time for the Republic. There was a revolution under way in Cuba, and after much agitation and maneuvering with the Spanish government, war was declared in April. On May 1, Admiral Dewey and his fleet sailed victoriously into Manila Bay, and a few days later the Philippines fell to the United States. Business on Wall Street responded very favorably to these events, and Barney could not help but share his enthusiasm with Alice.

Even when Alice played the devil's advocate with accusations like "imperialism" and "jingoism," Barney would not be cross. The two sparred with the political questions of the day in a way that seemed to stimulate them both. Blanche was almost a little envious. She had so little interest in the newspapers that she did not even acquire sufficient knowledge to participate, and the understanding of music and literature which she had strived so to master counted for little in this company.

Alice certainly did not intend to steal any attention from her young friend. She never remained more than a half hour, then excused herself and disappeared for the rest of the evening. Unobserved, Blanche and Barney would quietly retreat to Blanche's little room at the top of the stairs for the rest of the evening. Blanche remembered in detail Barney's insatiable desires, her own passionate responses, and all that transpired on those at-home evenings long after she forgot the discussions in the parlor. Such was the memory of Barney.

Nevertheless there was an event that spring, of little consequence at the time, which Blanche would not be permitted to forget. It was the Knickerbocker Club Amateur Circus, to which Barney invited her. Like the Club Carnival in the fall, it was an occasion when the ladies were welcomed to the members' rooms as part of the festivities. After Roland left the Knickerbocker, Barney had taken over his room, turning his quarters into a two-room suite. Blanche had not set foot in the club since early December, when she was last Roland's guest. It was a peculiar experience to enter what had once been Roland's room, but now belonged to Barney; however, any reticence she might have had as far as enjoying herself was quickly overcome by the company that was present and the champagne which they all drank together.

This innocent gathering was later to be blown out of all proportion and used as a weapon against Roland Molineux in his trial for murder. Whether it had any effect on his conviction is a moot point; the publicity, however, was to cast a long shadow over Blanche's good name.

The arrival of May had a particular significance for Blanche, for she always was forced to reckon the year, at least as it related to her finances, from September through May. Thus far in her life she had been successful in finding friends and relatives with whom to spend the summer months. This was possible only because most of her relatives, and others with whom she associated, owned summer homes along the coast. Their hospitality was a blessing to her pocketbook, as lack of money had always been her lot.

No doubt this condition was somewhat responsible for her early attraction to Roland. In fact, if Blanche had looked back to the autumn, when Roland was indulging her every whim, she could easily have quantified his attentions in terms of a substantial number of dollars. With Barney, the situation was otherwise. He was very careful with his expenditures, at least as they related to Blanche's entertainment, and he had yet to give her a gift other than a bouquet or corsage of flowers. The slim earnings that Blanche received from her two choir positions— Sundays at the Episcopal Church and Saturdays at the Jewish Synagogue—hardly covered the modest sum she paid to Alice for room and board. Blanche still received funds from Isia and an occasional small payment as her share of proceeds from property her father had owned at the time of his death, but she could not expect these payments to continue much longer.

Blanche sat alone in her room one May morning, pondering the deterioration of her material situation. This was not something she wished to share with Alice, although Isia may already have done so since Alice demanded so little from Blanche for the privilege of sharing her home. Blanche saw it as her present task to write a few letters—to Isia, to her brother, and to an acquaintance in whose home she had sung a number of times in earlier years. She began with the letter to Isia, describing quite honestly her romantic predicament and her financial problems. Isia had always participated vicariously in Blanche's escapades, and Blanche derived some pleasure from describing in detail to her sister the romantic triangle of which she was the apex. It would be fair to say that Isia was even a little envious of her sister, who possessed unusually good looks and great charm, attributes Isia lacked. That Blanche should be envied by Isia who had money and status and security—precisely the elements that were missing in her own life—did much to undergird her sagging ego. What Blanche did not know was that Isia's marriage was disintegrating. The yachting adventure of the previous summer had exacerbated existing marital difficulties, and Isia's extended stay in New York had solved nothing.

The other letters Blanche wrote that morning were in a different vein. In her most charming style and penmanship, she dwelled on the unseasonably warm May in New York and the coming season, during which she would be pleased to spend time with each recipient. Naturally she alluded to the positive aspects of her singing career and offered to perform at any gatherings that might be arranged. Having completed this task, Blanche felt some relief; she could expect her summer months to be provided for once again.

A greater problem than her financial well-being, not to mention her musical career, loomed before her as certain as September follows August. With great reluctance, Blanche began to think through her feelings for Barney. She asked herself whether she really wanted to spend the rest of her life sitting in front of Alice's fireplace or cavorting on her own bed, no matter how much pleasure she found in Barney's lovemaking. She even began to wonder where Barney was spending those evenings he did not spend with her. He never went near the Knickerbocker gymnasium; his ample waist attested to that. Were there other women in his life, as Roland had earlier suggested? Could it be that Barney was making love to others as he did to her? Blanche believed not and turned her attention to more practical considerations. Her single social event that spring had been the Knickerbocker Circus. She calculated that the only cost to Barney had been the champagne, and for that she had spent precious money on a new spring hat and shoes! Where was the luster of previous months? It was not a happy conclusion to which these thoughts led Blanche. Roland had indeed provided all of the brightness in her existence through his expensive gifts, his associations and his cultural interests. By following the inclinations of her heart, she was giving up an opportunity for a life of affluence and leisure. Overwhelmed by her helpless situation, Blanche lay her head in her hands and began to weep.

There was in Blanche a very practical streak that would serve her now and in other desperate situations during her life. Her tears were always followed by a fresh resolve and often a sharp change in course of action. This time Blanche's resolve involved Barney. She did not wish to give him up, nor did she wish to continue in the status quo. She therefore would have to take some initiative in the matter. Blanche prided herself at having overcome many of the strictures of society. The yachting cruise had been a benchmark in her quest for freedom from the ridiculous constraints of the time. She smiled inwardly at the modernity of her relationship with Barney and the way in which Alice could wink at it all. She would therefore phone Barney, as she had once before, and shame him into a dinner out; never mind the protocol. They would dine in Riverside Park, she determined, on the veranda of the Claremont Inn.

The Claremont was located just above Grant's Tomb and commanded a spectacular view of the Hudson River. Just a year earlier, the Tomb had been dedicated, and she had participated by singing in a massed choir of one thousand voices. She remembered trying to find her way into the Claremont that day, but it seemed all of New York had crowded into the hostelry to view its distinguished guest, President McKinley. There would be no crowds this time, but Blanche expected the glamour to remain. There would be candlelight and violins, and it would cost a great deal. Barney would see her as the woman she wished to be.

Thursday, the twenty-sixth of May, gave every indication of being a superb day in Blanche's life. She had succeeded in prevailing upon Barney to dine at the Claremont, and since the weather was summerlike, he had agreed to arrive at West End Avenue around five o'clock. This would give them time to promenade on Riverside Drive in the sunlight before dinner. Barney was used to waiting for Blanche, so he stood casually in Alice's vestibule, a boxed gardenia under his arm, entertaining Minnie and Alice in the interim. Presently, Blanche appeared, breathless and apologetic at her tardiness, and clasped Barney's right hand between hers. She was dressed in a flowing chiffon skirt, a broad-brimmed spring hat tied with a matching chiffon scarf, and long white kid gloves. Her neckline was cut in a deep V, and where the points of the collar met, she had fastened her brilliant jeweled butterfly.

From behind his back Barney drew out his left hand and handed over a florist's box. She opened it, and thanking him profusely for the fragrant flower, begged to have him pin it on her frock. Barney found himself in a predicament. Normally he would have pinned the gardenia at the base of the V; however, since the butterfly already reposed there, he found himself desperately searching for a sufficient amount of chiffon on which to anchor it. In mock consternation, he finally settled the gardenia below Blanche's left shoulder and pointedly wiped his brow, much to the amusement of Minnie and the two ladies.

As Barney stepped aside, Blanche swept through the door and onto the front stoop. There below stood Roland, sporting a good-sized moustache and dressed somewhat casually. A cab waited in the street, and it was clear that he was just about to ascend the steps. The unexpected encounter seemed to disturb Roland's cool demeanor. His eyes looked sharply into Blanche's, then lowered to the butterfly, then raised to Blanche's eyes again; his gaze finally rested on Barney, who stood as inconspicuously as he could in the doorway. Blanche was visibly shaken, but recovered sufficiently to smile tentatively and speak. "Why Roland, what a surprise—what a delightful surprise! Barney and I were just going up to the Claremont for dinner. Won't you join us? Right, Barney?" Whether it was right with Barney or not could not have made much difference, as he stood directly behind Blanche now, out of sight. Even Blanche's friendly smile did not seem to alter Roland's visible distress. It was obvious that he had intended to pay her an unannounced visit, but the circumstances now precluded this. He beckoned to the cab driver to wait and then firmly, but politely, made his excuses—he was just passing through the area on his way to Brooklyn, where he had an engagement within the hour. Before Barney could hail his own cab, Roland was gone.

The evening did not live up to Blanche's expectations, in spite of the unseasonable weather and the extraordinary view. Barney showed evidence of being troubled by the sudden appearance of his rival and began to question Blanche again as to her relationship with Roland. Had she been seeing him? Was she or was she not free? Blanche hated such questions and chose to be evasive, even though she had nothing to hide. Barney chose to return her to Alice's door without coming in.

Later that night, Blanche pondered the consequences of the evening with Barney. Why was it that in her life she was always buffeted about by others? Every effort on her part to influence the forces that controlled her life seemed to end in failure. Now Barney was more out of reach than ever, and with the summer holidays at hand, there would be no chance for retrenchment. The future held too much uncertainty.

SEVEN

Letter Box 217

If Roland had any intention of visiting Brooklyn that evening, the idea quickly vanished when he drove off. As Blanche herself would realize many months later, he had received a mighty blow there in front of Alice's door. His only thought now was to get home — to his own little kingdom under the factory roof, where he could pull himself together. In fact, riding on the elevated to the ferry landing, Roland was feverish and trembling, though the warm spring sun had not yet set.

The day had begun in an ordinary way. It being Thursday, Roland had made the weekly call on the Herrmann office in New York to pick up the payroll. As was his custom, he stopped off at the New York Athletic Club for lunch and even took time to work out at the gymnasium. After bathing and dressing, he walked over to the Cunard Steamship office to complete arrangements for his Atlantic voyage, which was to commence the middle of June.

Roland anticipated the trip with mixed emotions. On one side he knew that a change was needed in his life. The beatings he had taken from both Harry Cornish and Henry Barnet distracted him no end, and he wanted desperately to be rid of it all. On the other hand, Roland still hoped for a reconciliation with Blanche before leaving New York. His sailing date was less than three weeks away, and this piece of unfinished business still remained.

The European sojourn was to last two months. It meant taking an extended leave from the Herrmann Company, but that had been arranged with no difficulty. The voyage was to be a gift from Roland's mother and father, who for a number of months had been aware that all was not well with their son. They knew almost nothing of the Cornish affair, though they were cognizant of Roland's resignation from the Knickerbocker Club. They were vaguely aware that their son had met an exceptional young lady, whom he would introduce to them when he thought the time appropriate. Roland's father often inquired about the lady and spoke encouraging words on the value of an engagement and eventual marriage. The old general had been only too aware of Roland's stormy youth, and he believed that marriage would have a stabilizing influence on him. Roland's mother tended to be less enthusiastic about the prospect of Roland marrying, and in fact it was she who first promoted the European interlude. Whatever was troubling her son, either of a physical or emotional nature, he would certainly benefit from the ocean voyage and the European experience.

In his adult life, Roland had come to appreciate the caring feelings of both his parents, and he genuinely regretted not being totally candid with them about the various circumstances in his life. He felt it would make them extremely happy if he could but introduce Blanche as his fiancee before embarking on his long journey. This was the source of the impulse that had brought Roland to Alice Bellinger's front stoop on that late May afternoon.

The long trip back to Newark seemed endless, as Roland sought to keep himself upright — first on the seat of the elevated, then on the ferry bench, and finally on board the primitive jitney he was able to command at the Jersey shore. By the time Roland reached No. 6 Jersey Street in Newark, twilight was turning to darkness. He unlocked the factory door, walked through the dim space to a dusty stairway inside, and felt his way upstairs to his rooms. A second key unlocked his door, and he stepped into darkness. He ignited the lamp near the entry, and the welcome light revealed his little kingdom, a small sleeping room with a larger sitting room beyond, each with a window. .

The furnishings were rather grand. A substantial mahogony bed with matching bureau stood in the smaller room and a leather upholstered settee and chair in the other. The unfinished wooden floors were even covered with two valuable oriental rugs. A visitor to the rooms would have been surprised that such dignified surroundings could be reached by climbing such a dusty stairway. The view from the sitting room was not bad; at least there was water below, though from close up the canal was both grimy and smelly. But Roland chose to keep his heavily lined drapes closed against the outside world.

At one end of the sitting room stood a handsome medicine cabinet, not unlike what one would find in the office of a physician of the time. Roland's chemist's apron hung conspicuously nearby, white against the dreary walls of the sitting room. In fact, augmented by the leather furnishings, the room gave the air of a physician's visiting room. Behind the locked glass cabinet doors were the chemicals with which Roland worked, usually in the evenings. Though his factory responsibilities were administrative, he still had the heart of a scientist and enjoyed experimenting with creative concoctions that might lead to new colors. Fortunately he could supplement his own accumulation of compounds with the vast inventory available in the factory below.

Roland's thoughts this evening were solely on his immediate discomfort. He therefore removed his hat and suitcoat, unfolded the quilt that lay across the foot of his bed and lay down beneath it. The shaking in his body subsided, and he was able to relax for the first time since leaving West End Avenue. Periodically he was prone to such attacks—feverish periods during which any stress resulted in uncontrollable shaking such as that which had seized him late that afternoon. Perhaps if he had studied medicine rather than chemistry, he would have understood these seizures and the skin eruptions that seemed to accompany them. Fortunately, the periods when he was so susceptible occurred infrequently and usually lasted no more than a few days. Roland had every reason to expect this would be the case again.

After some minutes of relaxation, Roland's attention turned to a scrap of paper on which he had earlier jotted the name of a physician, one Dr. James Burns, whose advertisement he had seen. Dr. Burns had described Roland's ailment almost exactly and had prescribed a Marvelous Giant Indian Salve, which contained secret herbs from the ancient Mohawk Tribe. Roland stood up from his bed and drew out of his pocket the piece of paper. Sitting down at his bureau he opened the top drawer to remove one sheet of writing paper and one envelope. He was a little puzzled that his ample supply of writing paper had dwindled so, as he had used few of the sheets since purchasing it the summer before; but no matter. He lit the candle on the bureau, picked up his pen, and dipping it into the ink, began to write:

Dear Sir, Please find enclosed 25 cents, for which send remedy, and oblige. Very truly, Roland Molineux, No. 6 Jersey Street, Newark, New Jersey

He reached for his money purse and selected a twenty-five cent piece, around which he carefully folded the note. He addressed the envelope to "Dr. James Burns, Burns Remedy Company . . . ," and placed the folded note inside. The sealing wax lay conveniently nearby; Roland touched it to the candle flame and then to the edges of the envelope. He would mail it in the morning.

Too fatigued to stand up, he gazed into the flame and found himself recalling the summer before, just after his return from the Maine cruise. At that time he was behaving like a schoolboy in love. He had gone down to Tiffany's on Union Square, ostensibly to buy his mother a birthday gift, but soon found himself spending the afternoon examining the magnificent offerings in the jewelry department. That was the day Roland first viewed the diamond butterfly. It would be another two months before he actually purchased it, but he carried in his mind the image of the fragile ornament resting on Blanche's bosom long before the gift became a reality. It was on that same day that Roland walked over to Tiffany's stationery department to purchase writing paper suitable for the notes to Blanche that he was already composing in his head. He had chosen the paper that lay before him now—envelopes and sheets of robin's-egg blue, each with a trio of silver crescents intertwined in the upper center. It was elegant and dignified, the sort of paper with which a gentleman could court a lady of quality. Suddenly the image of Blanche on the front stoop of the old house, that lovely butterfly sharing her bosom with Barnet's gardenia, overwhelmed poor Roland, and he dragged himself back to his bed.

Roland slept fitfully that night and continued to be out of sorts in the morning. He reported to his office downstairs well after the start of the workday, but this attracted little notice, for his unpredictable moods were well known in the factory. He seemed totally distracted the entire day as he went about giving orders and taking care of his various responsibilities. By the middle of the afternoon, he found sufficient excuse to leave the floor and undertake the tasks that he had been planning in the preceding hours. These tasks were of a peculiar nature, but Roland believed that only by their completion could he attain the peace of mind, and body, that he craved.

The first task meant a trip across to New York that very afternoon. There he would engage a private letter box, from which he could undertake the second task. And for this second task he would also need writing paper (though not his own personal paper) and postage. He made a point to pick up some of both in the factory before he left on his errand. The writing itself could be completed over at Wakeley's after nightfall.

It was just about six o'clock when Roland arrived at 257 West Forty-second Street, the modest establishment of one Nicholas Heckmann located just across the street from Jim Wakeley's saloon, a favorite watering place of the local athletic crowd. Heckmann leased private letter boxes, a kind of business not uncommon in the 1890's, before the United States Post Office leased such boxes.

Roland pushed open the door, which activated a little bell and roused Nicholas Heckmann himself. In his most patrician manner, Roland greeted the man and inquired about leasing one of the letter boxes that lined the wall behind the counter. Heckmann viewed his new customer carefully, in keeping with his practice, and decided that he was a respectable sort. He quoted his prices and opened a large book on the counter, preparing to write.

"Name?"

"H. C. Barnet," replied Roland without hesitation.

"How long a lease?"

"I cannot say exactly—probably to the end of the summer," was the response. Heckmann left the entry incomplete: May 27–

Roland gave him sufficient money to cover three months; Heckmann in turn wrote "Box 217" on a printed ticket, then handed it over to his new customer. Roland thanked him and walked out the door. The first task had been completed.

Roland crossed the street to Wakeley's. He was almost cordial in his greetings to the other patrons and walked to the bar to order a whiskey. Glass in hand, he made his way to a table at which he could count on some privacy, picking up a sporting monthly along the way. He removed his hat and sat down to undertake the second task. He arranged the sheets of paper, the envelopes and the postage stamps on the table before him, drew out a pencil, and slowly turned the pages of the magazine. For the next few hours, late into that Friday evening, Roland continued his task at the table—turning the pages, stopping occasionally to address an envelope, write on the paper, place the paper in the envelope with one or more coins, seal it with a bit of wax, and affix a postage stamp. He repeated the cycle again and again, and at one point, actually tore part of a page from the periodical. It was an order form for a marriage manual with space for personal information. Roland filled in the blanks:

What is your name?   H. C. Barnet
What is your age?   31 years
What are your measurements?   Chest - 37 inches
                              Waist - 32 inches
Do you contemplate marriage?   Yes·
From what do you suffer most?   Regret of my condition

For the next two weeks Roland had all he could do to keep up with the deliveries at Letter Box 217. Almost every day he called at the Heckmann shop to take delivery of various packages and envelopes. For instance, from the Von Mohl Company of Detroit came the "five-day Cathos treatment for impotence and other maladies." This consisted of a small cardboard box containing fifteen pink capsules, the sort that one could take apart and reassemble. Roland took care in opening the box so as not to damage the packing materials. Presumably they might be useful at a later time.

There were also other packages of medicines—for impotence, for digestive problems, and for various other delicate conditions—as well as a marriage manual and a marriage guide. The physicians and manufacturers from whence they came included a Dr. Fowler and a Dr. Rudolphe of Moodus, Connecticut, G. B. Wright of Marshall, Michigan, the Sterling Remedy Company, and the Marston Remedy Company, to name but a few. Altogether there were more than ten deliveries to H. C. Barnet at Box 217, 257 West Forty-second Street, New York, within that short span of time.

Over at Wakeley's, where Roland invariably stopped after picking up his packages, the regulars duly noted that Roland Molineux must have overcome his queer streak. As the days went by, he spoke and laughed with them increasingly. A new purposefulness had entered his life, no doubt about it. When Roland sailed for Europe on June 15, he had shaved off his moustache and looked happier and healthier than he had in months. The activities surrounding Letter Box 217 ceased as suddenly as they had begun.

Both Blanche and Henry Barnet had left the city a week earlier, Blanche to Narragansett and Conanicut Island on the Rhode Island Coast, then on to Lake George, and Barnet to the Atlantic Yacht Club in Brooklyn, a more modest destination in keeping with his pocketbook. The clubhouse, a relatively modern structure built in 1891, was situated at the foot of Fifty-fifth Street and was reputed to have the best view of the New York harbor in all of Brooklyn. The convenient location meant that Barnet could commute regularly to his office in the Produce Building, a requirement of his profession. There was a dining room overlooking the harbor, a ladies' lounge (for guests), a trophy lounge (for members only), and upstairs several large comfortable bedrooms, one of which Barnet occupied. He quickly established new friendships in the carefree social life that developed around the yachts and their owners. That Barney was not a "yachtsman" himself mattered little. He was welcome in any circle, by male and female alike.

When the month of August arrived, those who had left the city began to return one by one. Barnet came back early in the month, since an entire summer at the Atlantic Yacht Club was more than he could afford. Roland returned from Europe the middle of August; however, he found it convenient to extend his holiday by taking a room out at Traverse Island, where the New York Athletic Club owned a summer clubhouse. Blanche, who had been the first to leave in June, was able to stretch her holiday through to the very last weekend of the month.

The Knickerbocker Athletic Club was still in the summer doldrums when Barnet returned from his six-week outing. It was a Sunday afternoon, and the clerk was off for the weekend. Thus Barnet was greeted by John Adams, who seemed to be holding down the fort alone, except for his young friend Paul. Both men came out from Adams's office to welcome the returning prodigal. Adams reached for the backlog of mail that had accumulated for Barnet in his absence and set it on the counter. A few notes had been delivered while he was gone, but none of any great consequence. His brother Edmond and his close associates had known that he could be reached at the Produce Building during the week throughout the summer. Several

Knickerbocker circulars had also been collected for him, and there was one small package—from the Von Mohl Company. Barnet stood at the counter as he sorted through the papers. When he came upon the unexpected package, he promptly untied the paper, uncovering a little cardboard box. Within he discovered a "five-day Cathos treatment for impotence," in the form of five pink capsules. Young Paul peered inquisitively across the counter to see for himself just what was in the tiny box. Suddenly Barnet stood back and burst out laughing. Holding up his little treasure, he announced for the benefit of the onlookers: "Gentlemen, there is a report abroad in the land that Henry Barnet at three and thirty has already passed his prime!" The two behind the counter looked at Barnet, then at each other, and finally joined in the hearty laughter.

As it turned out, Barnet did not swallow any of the capsules. He laid them in his bureau drawer, thought little of them beyond the jesting that they had brought about, and eventually threw them away.

EIGHT

General Molineux

Blanche eagerly anticipated her return to New York City and Alice Bellinger's home, as there had been many uncertainties connected with her summer holiday. The stay with Isia and Waldo at *Craigsmere* had to be cut short because of the domestic problems that plagued Isia's marriage. In fact the Stearnses had closed *Craigsmere* and returned to Boston shortly after Blanche arrived there in June. Thus she was compelled to arrange impromptu visits with other relatives and acquaintances, not always to the convenience of her hosts and hostesses. The frequent moves meant living precariously from week to week, more or less out of a suitcase.

In addition, Blanche had gradually been coming to grips with her own fate. She was now twenty-four years old, without means to complete her musical education and with barely enough to sustain a minimum of life's necessities. Her temporary reliance on the generosity of Isia was turning into a chronic dependency, which would worsen as soon as the annuity from her father's estate ceased. For a young woman of culture, but without independent means, life could be very cruel if one did not find a suitable marriage. Such thoughts depressed Blanche greatly when she wrestled with them in lonely hours.

The summer in New York had been miserably hot, and unlike Blanche, Alice had not the freedom to flee to the seaside. Since many of her hair salon customers did disappear over the summer months, she was forced to reduce her staff and take over some of the responsibilities there herself. Thus she looked forward to Blanche's homecoming, as it would mean pleasant company once again, with the expectation of more leisure time and cooler weather in which to enjoy it.

Blanche came back to the city directly from Lake George, arriving at West End Avenue late one evening rather exhausted from the strenuous trip. She had sent word of her return by mail, and as her cab drove up in front, her heart gladdened to see that the parlor light was burning and that Alice and the faithful Minnie Betts were on hand to welcome her. Alice had thrown open the door, and Minnie had skipped down into the street to help with her bags before she could dismiss the driver. The two friends greeted each other at the steps with an affectionate hug and kisses and then went inside, both talking at once in their mutual joy at being reunited. Despite her weariness, Blanche felt the need to talk and didn't object when Alice ushered her into the parlor. Minnie served them ice-cold lemonade from a pitcher Alice had prepared earlier and then went off to see to Blanche's luggage. For an hour or more, they chatted, Alice interrogating and Blanche responding, until at last Alice had the entire picture, not only of Blanche's summer experiences, but also of the internal uncertainties with which she was struggling. Only after Blanche had completely emptied herself of an entire summer of thoughts did the two women say good night and retire for the evening.

Back in her room, Blanche found that Minnie had opened her bags, hung up her gowns, and turned back the bedcovers invitingly. She had only to undress and lie down to sleep, but she noticed a small accumulation of mail on her desk and paused to leaf through the pieces—an announcement of the Rubenstein Society's fall schedule, mailings from both choirs in which she sang, and a letter from Roland Molineux. The distinctive handwriting and the light blue color of the stationery proclaimed the sender even before she had unsealed the envelope. Surprised and somewhat hesitant, she sat down on the bed to read.

Roland's writing style was formal but friendly—a few words about his weeks abroad, good wishes relative to Blanche's summer holiday, and a request that she meet him for luncheon at the Waldorf-Astoria on the first convenient Thursday. Given the situation in which she found herself at present and the conclusions she had come to regarding her future, Blanche decided that this was an invitation she did not wish to refuse. Before retiring that night, she had written her acceptance—for the first Thursday hence.

The new Waldorf-Astoria Hotel stood in all its elegance on Fifth Avenue between Thirty-third and Thirty-fourth Streets. Roland had always had a keen sense of that which was important to Blanche, and in selecting this as the rendezvous for their reconciliation meeting he was right on target. The Waldorf-Astoria was actually two hotels, each of which occupied the site of one of the great Astor family mansions. Prior to 1893, Mrs. William Astor lived at the Thirty-fourth Street corner and her nephew, William Waldorf Astor, lived across the garden on Thirty-third Street. In 1893 William had built on the site of his home a thirteen-story hotel, which he named the Waldorf. For three years Mrs. William Astor lived in the shadow of this large building, then finally in 1897 allowed her house to be demolished and a seventeen-story hotel, the Astoria, to be erected on its site. The two adjacent hotels were connected, creating the Waldorf-Astoria, which became the social mecca of New York as soon as it opened. Blanche had visited the Waldorf when it stood alone, but she had never set foot in the stylish Waldorf-Astoria until that September day when she and Roland met in the lobby and walked arm in arm into the Palm Room for luncheon. Blanche could not help but compare the occasion to a similar meeting she had had with Barney so many months ago. Relative to class, the meeting with Barney at the little second-rate cafe paled in comparison to this Palm Room reunion with Roland.

Roland had succeeded in arranging for a window table, providing Blanche with a privileged view of the Fifth Avenue afternoon strollers. The couple dined on filet of sole and drank white wine together. Once the thrill of the occasion subsided, the two concentrated on each other and the bridging of their estrangement. Blanche observed an apparent nervousness in Roland, reminiscent of their unfortunate meeting at Alice's in May, but for the most part his old *savoir faire* prevailed. They talked of the musical season they had enjoyed together in the previous autumn, and before Blanche realized it, she had committed herself to a season with Roland again. No mention was made either of Barney or of the Knickerbocker Club. Before they parted that afternoon, Roland had slipped the *Mizpah* ring on Blanche's finger again, and Blanche had given Roland a pledge.

That evening Blanche knocked on Alice's bedroom door. Alice sat at her desk, weary from the day in her shop yet compelled to complete the entries in her business ledger. Thus she welcomed the interruption. Blanche seemed more relaxed than she had in months, and she spoke quietly. "Roland and I are virtually engaged. You see, Alice darling, I am wearing his ring again. I believe we will be married before this year is out." Alice stood up and embraced her friend. "My dear Blanche, I am sure you have made the right decision, for I am certain that Roland will take care of you."

Throughout her entire life Blanche would have difficulty in resolving her inner tensions between head and heart. And so it was even after she consented to marry Roland. Perhaps without reason she still anticipated at least a phone call from Barney. Hearing nothing, she took it upon herself to phone the Knickerbocker to ascertain whether he was indeed back in town. Blanche was surprised, and a little chagrined, to learn that he had been back at the Knickerbocker since early August. She might better have left the matter alone, but an inner compulsion prevailed one evening as she sat alone in her room. She penned a letter to Barney, imploring him to phone her. The veiled message in the letter was that Barney had no business abandoning a woman he had wronged. Blanche postulated quite correctly that this was a message Barney would not ignore. He phoned her immediately upon receipt of the note to learn for himself what the situation was. Blanche noted a distinct coldness in his voice and choice of words. He had been informed of her engagement and therefore wished to have an end to any relationship that might previously have existed between them. The result of the brief conversation was not what Barney might have expected. Rather than being put off by his distant manner, Blanche was overwhelmed with a desire to see him and in fact made arrangements to see him that very afternoon.

It was highly unusual for any woman, other than an employee, to enter the Knickerbocker Club alone, except on those rare occasions such as the Amateur Circus. Nevertheless, on the hunch that Barney would remain there at the dinner hour, she dressed herself to please him and ordered a cab to take her to the club.

It had been some months since Blanche had last entered the almost exclusively masculine world of the Knickerbocker, and on this particular evening, she wished to remain anonymous. Her eyes darted quickly among the faces in the lobby, and she was relieved to find none that looked familiar. But as she approached the counter, where a slender youth was fulfilling the duties of clerk, a man's voice called to her, "Good evening, Miss Chesebrough."

Blanche's heart sank as John Adams, Mr. Ballantine's secretary and the de facto manager of the club, came out of his office and around the counter to greet her. "What a complete and enjoyable surprise! You look as charming as ever, and we have all missed you since you have avoided the Knickerbocker for so long. Welcome back, and may I be of service?"

Blanche began hesitantly, not wanting to reveal her mission but knowing that inevitably she would have to. "Mr. Adams, good evening to you. I have a message for Henry Barnet . . . you know, he is Roland Molineux's good friend, and therefore my friend also. I should like to speak with him for just a minute, if it is no imposition."

John Adams took Blanche's arm to lead her to a sofa, and as they walked across the room, he became more serious. "There will be no problem in finding Mr. Barnet for you, Miss Chesebrough, for he is taking his dinner in the dining room at this very hour. However, before I send for him, there is something that has been bothering me for some time. How is Roland?"

Blanche, distressed at being on the subject of Roland and inwardly chiding herself because she had been the one to raise it, could think of no quick answer.

Adams continued, "You know he was a very respected member of our club until he resigned over a severe misunderstanding with our athletic director. It is a year now since he first spoke to me about the situation, and I have always felt that perhaps I did not pay sufficient attention to the problem. I see my role here as Mr. Ballantine's representative, but also as a sort of secular pastor to my flock, the members of the club. They often come to me with their personal problems, and I always try to be helpful. But I am afraid I failed in the case of Roland. What is his situation these days?"

Blanche was not about to tell this rather casual acquaintance about her engagement, and certainly not about the estrangement of the previous winter. What she wanted was to extricate herself quickly from the conversation; in fact, had she known how to proceed, she might have left the club without bothering to see Barney at all.

"Mr. Adams, I see Roland frequently and he is in fine spirits," she replied, then carefully added, "He is serving on the Board of Directors of the New York Athletic Club and is also an executive now with the Morris Herrmann Company. I shall be happy to convey your greetings if you wish, and shall encourage him to drop by some evening and call on you personally. Tonight, however, I have a message from Roland for Mr. Barnet, and I would appreciate your calling him."

Adams took the hint well, and after seeing to it that she was comfortably seated, returned to the counter and sent the young clerk to the dining room to summon Barnet. Within a minute, Barney was in view, coming almost at a run, his face uncharacteristically pale. Blanche stood up as he approached her, ready to extend her hand for his usual gentlemanly kiss. To her surprise, he seized her firmly by the arm, and instead of escorting her back to the dining room, as Blanche expected, he led her into the empty library beyond and closed the door behind them.

"Blanche, what are you doing here? What do you want of me? It is you who have erected barriers between us, and you cannot expect me to climb over them."

Blanche responded, almost in a lighthearted manner, "You are silly, Barney dear. There need not be barriers between us. If I had thought it would hurt our friendship, I would never have promised to marry Roland. Barney, don't change toward me . . . please, can't we stay friends?"

There was a beseeching quality in her last plea, and she stepped closer to him so that he was compelled to take hold of both arms. "It is impossible, can't you see? I don't want to see you again, ever!"

Barney's own words somehow reverberated back to him. His face flushed, and impulsively he pulled Blanche to his body until his lips met hers. She yielded effortlessly to this last flood of passion and showed resistance only to the sudden release of his grip. Then, as if his courage were too fragile to depend upon, Barney spoke his final words to Blanche.

"Good God! The breach is there with Molineux! You must know that. This widens it and therefore means goodbye. I know that Molineux hates me, and you ought to know that too!"

Then, with one hand still on Blanche's arm, he propelled her toward the library door, opened it, and escorted her through to the front entrance of the club, where a cab happened to be standing in the street below. He led her down the steps, delivered her unceremoniously into the vehicle, and with neither a backward glance nor a farewell gesture, made a hasty retreat back into the club. The finality of the encounter dealt a mighty blow to Blanche, and great tears welled in her eyes as she rode silently home through the darkened streets of New York. It was several days before her disappointment lifted and she was able to console herself with thoughts of her coming marriage.

Blanche and Roland were to be wed on the twenty-ninth of November in a relatively private ceremony. Blanche might have wished it otherwise, but this was Roland's decision. There were preparations to be made and arrangements to be decided upon, most important of which would be her first meeting with General and Mrs. Molineux.

For over a year, General Edward Molineux had been on the edge of Blanche's existence, and each time she heard his name her curiosity was heightened. Here was a man whose deeds both during and after the Great Rebellion were still talked about more than thirty years later, yet his own son barely made reference to him. Here too was a man who stood staunchly among New York's Republican leaders—a force of decency and honesty—seeking to overcome the corruption and power of Tammany. All New York revered him, yet Blanche, who would soon carry his name, had never met the man. As she pondered this odd situation, she was inclined toward memories of her life shortly after the death of her parents. At the time, she was living in the vicinity of Grammercy Park, and would often walk along the adjacent street, taking her pleasure from the park by peering in through the lovely wrought iron gates. Since her family did not possess a key to such paradise, she occasionally perceived this to be her lot in life—to be forever looking in from the outside. For a time she feared this would be the case even in her relationship to the Molineux family, until one day she learned it need not be so.

Roland announced in early October that he and Blanche had been invited to his family home for an entire weekend. Thus late on a Friday evening, he fetched Blanche in a cab and took her across the Brooklyn Bridge up to Fort Greene Place, which was in the area known as Columbia Heights. As Blanche might have guessed, General Molineux was master of a handsome brownstone home that stood among others just as handsome, no doubt inhabited by families just as substantial as the Molineuxs. The general himself stood at the door awaiting the arrival of his son and the young woman who would soon join their family. Blanche was immediately struck by the aristocratic bearing of this white-haired gentleman with the distinguished aquiline nose. She extended her hand to him and was greeted not only with a firm clasp, but also with a warm smile and a look that seemed to convey tenderness and understanding. This surprised her the most since Roland had painted his father as a stern and exacting man. Just behind the general stood Roland's mother, who was rather plain looking but nevertheless bore a remarkable resemblance to Roland. Blanche bowed slightly to the woman who would soon be her mother-in-law, while Roland embraced her with genuine affection. Soon mother and son were leading the way through the long hallway to the family sitting rooms, all the while engaged in a witty and diverting conversation. Blanche was left to be escorted by the general, a situation that she did not mind one bit.

As Blanche viewed the surroundings with which she would soon be associated, she regretted only that her father and mother were not present to share this moment. What joy they would have experienced in knowing that this daughter of theirs had found her way into a family of such social standing.

Whatever attributes Roland had to recommend him (and Blanche acknowledged there were many), they could not compare with those of his father. Overwhelmed with his charm and dignity, she made it her task that weekend to learn all she could about him. For this the family album provided a guide and a point of departure. For several hours at a time, Blanche sat with her future father-in-law in the library, poring over the family portraits and mementos and learning the old general's story from the man himself.

Edward Molineux was descended from an old English family. When he was hardly more than a lad, his adventuresome spirit had caused him to leave home and seek his fortune in the new world. By the time the Great Rebellion commenced, he had already established himself as a businessman in New York; but

loyalty to his adopted country and belief in the cause of the
Government prompted him to volunteer at the very start of the
conflict.

Early in the war he obtained the rank of Lieutenant Colonel
of the Twenty-third Regiment of New York Volunteers. Later
he commanded the Seventh Regiment and was brevetted Major
General in the field. Thus it was that Edward Molineux became
"General Molineux," as he was to be known throughout the re-
mainder of his life. After being wounded at Irish Bend, the general returned to his home state, where he figured conspicuously
in efforts to suppress the draft riots in 1864. When the Great
War ended in 1865, he returned to the South as occupation
commandant for the State of Georgia. It was perhaps in this capacity that his humanity and integrity were most visible. When
the occupation ended and the general returned home, he
brought with him many letters written by the citizens of Georgia in appreciation for the fairness and compassion he had
shown while undertaking his onerous responsibilities there.

General Molineux took great pride in these letters, which
were now carefully preserved in the family album. As he turned
the pages for Blanche, he stopped frequently to read aloud one
or another of the messages, which he had in fact committed to
memory. There was a tinge of sadness in his voice as he recalled
the heroic undertakings of wartime, for which there had been
no counterpart in the prosperous decades that followed.

Those same qualities of leadership which had served so well
on the battlefield brought General Molineux into every area of
respectable peacetime politics. He had been one of the founders
of the Republican Party in New York State; he was a leader
among the veterans of the Grand Army of the Republic; he involved himself in the civic life of Brooklyn and the politics of
New York City; and he had still found time to build a splendid
fortune. The paint manufacturing concern where Roland had
begun his own professional career was only one of the general's
several enterprises. Blanche saw in him a man to be greatly admired and also a man who in turn would take an interest in
those talents she had to offer. She sensed that she had estab-

lished an immediate rapport with this fine man, not unlike that which existed between her and Alice Bellinger.

Blanche also sensed that this was not true with Mrs. Molineux. She was not slow in perceiving that between mother and son there existed a relationship which the pending marriage would alter and that the anticipation of this event had a disturbing effect on the mother. She thought this might possibly be the reason Roland preferred a private wedding. This introductory weekend therefore produced a dichotomy in the household—Blanche quietly perusing the Molineux papers in the library, often with General Molineux at her side, and Roland in the family sitting room in animated conversation with his mother.

However, Sunday afternoon tea brought the four together in the music room, so named because of the large upright piano that stood against one wall. The occasion gave Blanche the opportunity to exhibit the talents which Roland so admired and with which she hoped to contribute to the family reputation. At Mrs. Molineux's invitation, Blanche sat down at the piano and sang several selections from Gounod operas, then concluded with a favorite aria from Verdi's *Il Travatore* — "*Mira, d'acerbe lagrime.*" This tiny audience of three was certainly the most appreciative Blanche had ever sung for, and afterward there were emotional embraces all around, a marked departure from the usual Victorian decorum.

General Molineux even made a little speech. "Blanche, my child, I could feel in your songs the immense devotion of which you are capable. That one who bears the name Molineux is the object of your devotion is a blessing to us all. I would like now to present to you a token of our gratitude and also of our confidence that you will carry the Molineux name with all the dignity of those who have carried it in the past."

With this the general reached over to the sideboard, and grasping a large tissue-wrapped package, pressed it into Blanche's hands. As she tried to thank him, he bent to kiss her on the cheek, and in the nearness she could see the moisture in his eyes. Blanche removed the ribbon and tissue, then opened the box to find an ornate silver bowl with four delicate legs—a beautiful piece of a quality one might expect to find in some royal household. The sides of the vessel were encrusted with an intricate pastoral scene.

Blanche was moved beyond words as the general continued to speak. "This bowl was fashioned by Flemish artisans generations ago and was brought to England by my Huguenot forefathers. Dearest Blanche, it is now yours, given with the expectation that it will eventually be passed on to one of your children. You see, my dear, over the years my beloved wife and I have been blessed with many gifts, not the least of these being our three sons, Cecil, Leslie and Roland. If there is anything at all that Providence has denied us, it is a daughter of our own. Now, thanks to Roland's discriminating choice, and your acquiescence, we have been blessed once more, this time with a daughter incomparable."

Not to be outdone by his father, Roland now stood to make his own impassioned speech. "Father . . . and Mother, and Blanche, my dear, I have a surprise for you all. In recent years, the happiest hours for me have been those during which I have listened to the great opera performances at the Metropolitan. In fact, it was sharing this pleasure with Blanche that kindled our friendship and eventually my love. In the past, I was burdened by a dissatisfaction with life, which evidenced itself in ways that brought pain to you, dear parents, and more recently to you, my darling Blanche. And I too have suffered, even as you have. But during my voyage last summer, I had the opportunity to look deep within myself, and I perceived a man of profound sensitivity, a man whose musical talents have been stifled by the constraints of his profession and of society."

Roland's demeanor now changed from apology to triumph. "If a man does not act on his perceptions, he is no man at all, and therefore I have acted! For the past two months, I have been taking weekly lessons from one of the coaches at the Metropolitan, and he tells me that I have a remarkable baritone voice. Together he and I are working to perfect my delivery and control. It is my sincere hope that soon after we are married, Blanche and I will be in a position to sing together before our family, if not in public."

Blanche was amazed at this pronouncement. On one side, the intensity of his passion for music touched her deeply; on the other side, she found it somewhat presumptuous of him to imply that he possessed sufficient training, after just a few lessons, to sing a duet with her, a lifelong student of voice. She was left with a feeling of uneasiness, as though Roland had for the moment lost touch with reality.

NINE

Death of a Friend

As Blanche immersed herself in the preparations for the wedding—mainly the completion of her modest trousseau—Roland too had certain affairs to tend to before his marriage, mostly involving the future of his apartment in Newark. There was something about the situation there that did not fit with the wedded state he was about to enter.

Another matter that disturbed Roland the more he contemplated it was the disposition of his private laboratory, particularly the chemicals that were stored there. He was increasingly distrustful of the other Herrmann factory employees and suspected that some among them might occasionally have visited his quarters. He repeatedly examined the lock on the glass doors of his storage cabinet, and although he never found it other than locked, it often appeared to him that the bottles behind the doors were not as he had arranged them.

It was his intention to maintain the rooms above the factory as long as he had need for his experiments, possibly until the end of December. Then this chapter in his life, a chapter that had been fraught with unhappiness, would give way to the next, where sunlight and joy would reign. With the wedding little more than a month away, he also felt the pressure of find-

ing suitable quarters for Blanche and himself. He had engaged
a suite at the Waldorf for their honeymoon, but this was a luxury he could afford for little more than a month. One evening
as he sat is his apartment mulling over the alternatives, there
came a soft knock at the door. Roland froze, knowing that the
factory had closed hours earlier and that no one other than he
ought to be in the building, then warily made his way to the
door. He stood for a while listening for some sound on the other
side, until finally a familiar voice begged, "Roland, please, it is
Mamie. Please open the door."

Irritated that this problem he thought to have settled a year
ago had cropped up again, he unbolted and threw open the
door. Before him stood a woman of no more than twenty-four
years, yet her careworn, beleaguered appearance made her look
as if she were middle-aged. Here was a woman whom life had
treated very badly indeed. There was an air of melancholy about
her as she said, sadly, "I hear you are to be married, Roland—to
a very fine lady. Do you remember long ago that you promised
to marry me? Do you remember that . . . ?"

Infuriated, Roland lashed out, "You lie, Mamie! I never promised you anything! In fact, though I gave you many gifts, you
stole even more from me. I know that you were taking things
from my rooms for many months before I had you dismissed.
Don't think that I am a fool!"

And then, as though her mere presence had stripped him of
all self-control, he continued his bitter invective, "And what's
more, you . . . you trollop, it was you who brought disease into my life—disease that I am just now overcoming. Don't you
ever threaten me, for if you do, there is a great deal more I can
throw back on you. Now go, and don't ever let me see your face
again!"

Mamie did not move. In fact, she seemed to stand a little
taller than when Roland had first opened the door. In an even
tone, she said, "Roland, I need money very much. I have not
worked since Herrmann's let me go last year, and my family cannot carry me as their burden forever. I myself have not been well
for over a year. If you give me five hundred dollars right now,

I assure you that I will never bother you again in your life. If you do not . . . "

Enraged, Roland slammed the door in her face and barred it with his chair. For several minutes, he sat trembling with fury and listening at the keyhole. He could hear Mamie's uneven breathing, followed by faint sobs. At last, the scrape of her footsteps on the stairs brought an end to his vigil. He stood for a moment, trying to calm himself, then moved slowly toward his bed. Completely exhausted, he fell upon it.

Fortunately for Roland, he and Blanche had reached a tacit agreement that, with the exception of their Sunday afternoon meetings, they would not see each other before their November wedding. Thus he had several days to recover from the terrible scene with Mamie before they next met, and there was much to take his mind off of it. He was deeply involved in arranging a gala evening at the New York Athletic Club to honor one of its illustrious members. There were also his Saturday afternoon voice lessons, in addition to his duties at the Herrmann establishment, which would always occupy a major portion of his time.

In any case, Blanche was absorbed with purchasing her ensemble for that most important day. Isia had come down from Boston to help her select a gown from Isia's favorite dress shop. The dress was to be Isia's wedding gift to Blanche, and she insisted that the occasion called for one of Paris design. Blanche did not object, for she felt a bit cheated by Roland's desire for a quiet and simple ceremony. Alice's home took on a new liveliness, with the Chesebrough sisters flitting in and out, sometimes two or three times each day.

On the Sunday afternoon after his New York Athletic Club banquet, Roland called for Blanche, and enjoying the crisp November sunshine, the two walked down Sixth Avenue to a nearby cafe for afternoon tea. Blanche chatted enthusiastically about the wardrobe purchases made that week, and it was apparent that Roland took a great deal of pleasure in the delight of his intended. When it was Blanche's turn to inquire about

Roland's week, she pressed him for details of the New York
Club banquet. "Roland, tell me all about it . . . who was there,
what they had to say, and what kind of entertainment you provided? Unless, of course, it was not such as a lady would appreciate!"

Blanche laughed gaily at her little witticism, and Roland obliged with a recounting of the event. "Of course, General Watson was the guest of honor, and any entertainment suitable for
such a distinguished gentleman would be so for you also, my
dear. As a matter of fact," he went on, "the committee arranged
a Jim Crow review, with some of the more talented members
doing the vocals and dances themselves, all in black face."

"How delightful! Did you take part yourself, or did you sit
with the general," she inquired.

"No, on both counts," he answered. "I sat with Bartow Weeks
and his law partner, George Battle, whom I had never met before. He makes a good impression. You know, he is younger
than Bartow, yet he seems to be of another generation. I believe
that comes from being so successful at such an early age!"

Blanche's curiosity about Weeks, who always seemed so in-
credibly dull to her, prompted her next question. "How did the
two of them come to be partners? It always suprises me that Bartow has such good connections."

"Well, George Battle was an assistant in the District Attorney's office," Roland began, "and the best prosecutor they ever
had, according to my father. In fact, he was so successful that
he decided to try the other side—criminal defense. After he got
started, he found he had need of a partner, and remembered
Bartow from his days in the District Attorney's office. Bartow
has a reputation for thoroughness, though he never has had
much flair as a trial lawyer." This last was the only deprecating
thing Blanche had ever heard Roland say about Weeks.

"Good old Bartow," he continued. "He is indeed fortunate to
have made such a good connection. Sometimes I cannot understand him, though. Would you believe that after the terrible
beating he took from the Knickerbocker a year ago—those slanderous attacks by Cornish—he saw to it that several of the old

Knickerbocker crowd were invited to the dinner? Do you remember that fellow, Harpster, who used to be so close to Cornish?"

Blanche could only shake her head, for she knew nothing about Cornish, or Harpster, or the attacks on Bartow Weeks. She could only surmise that these men had to do with the "problems" at the Knickerbocker to which John Adams had alluded on the night she had gone there to see Henry Barnet.

"Both Alvin Harpster and Harry Cornish are insults to that club," said Roland, becoming more agitated. "I did my best to rid the Knickerbocker of such elements, but I failed."

For Blanche, the conversation was beginning to take a disturbing turn, and a sense of foreboding overcame her as she observed the intensity in Roland's eyes.

"You know, failure is like a disease, for it robs a man of his manhood," he continued. "But the time will come when I have the courage again to deal with the Knickerbocker affairs. In fact, one of the Knickerbocker fellows who agrees with me about Cornish was also at the dinner—his name is Rudy Heiles. He says that it is Harpster's influence that protects Cornish in his position, and he told me some things about Harpster that may be useful later. I want you to know, Blanche, that when I have set a goal for myself, I am not deterred by obstacles."

Blanche could not have been more in agreement with this assertion, but she wondered at Roland's obsession with the matter. However, Roland now spoke in a more relaxed manner. "I almost forgot to tell you that John Adams, Ballantine's secretary, was also present. He is certainly a gentleman, but unfortunately not powerful enough to control the vulgar elements at the Knickerbocker." Then, almost as an afterthought, he added, "By the way, my dear, he must have a special place for you in his heart, for he inquired of your health and made it a point to send his greetings to you."

Blanche flushed, more out of fear that Adams might have revealed her earlier visit to the Knickerbocker than out of embarrassment over his interest in her. Sensing her discomfort, Roland patted her indulgently on the cheek. "Blanche, dear, I was only teasing. I have no fear of competition from Adams. Anyhow, they say he is more interested in his 'nephew' than in any of the charming ladies he meets."

Blanche responded to Roland's grin and knowing wink with a smile, relaxing in the confidence that John Adams had made no reference to their Knickerbocker encounter. But her relief was short-lived, for Roland's next words, delivered almost without feeling, left her stunned. "Adams also reported a piece of bad news which may be of passing interest to you. Henry Barnet was among those Knickerbocker members invited to the dinner; however, according to Adams, he is confined to his bed, suffering from severe diphtheria. Two doctors and a nurse are in constant attendance, but as of Friday night there was no sign of improvement."

Blanche paled, and then instinctively tried to hide her distress as she could discern Roland's intense interest in her reaction to this news. In her confusion, she responded impulsively, "Oh poor, dear Barney . . . I mean Roland . . . perhaps we could send him flowers, sort of for old times sake?"

For an interminable moment there was silence; then Roland spoke. "A splendid idea. You take care of it in the morning."

For the next quarter hour, Blanche could barely concentrate on the conversation, though she herself contributed to it. The bloom of the afternoon tea had long since faded, and mercifully Roland suggested an early end to the meeting, particularly as darkness would bring a strong November chill.

Silently they walked back to West End and Alice's lighted doorway. Roland came only as far as the outer door and there kissed Blanche good night—a kind of obligatory kiss that Blanche perceived to be what occurs between a husband and wife. As she opened the door, Roland left to hail a cab for his ride to the Jersey ferry.

Blanche could hardly get inside quickly enough. The tears she had been holding back welled in her eyes, and she called aloud to Alice and Isia, who were sitting congenially together in the kitchen. "Alice, Isia, Roland had just told me that Barney is seriously ill! I fear that he may die . . . I must go to him, or at least call him. I'll ring up the Knickerbocker right now."

Alice knew enough of Blanche's temperament to realize that, if allowed to continue, she could very easily become hysterical. "Blanche, dear, stop right now. You cannot call Barney to-night," she cautioned. "First of all, it is too late, and secondly, if he cannot come to the phone, you will find yourself leaving a name, and this you cannot afford."

Although she conceded the wisdom of Alice's words, Blanche was still very upset. "But I am so worried about him . . . he is so very ill!"

"Wait until tomorrow, Blanche," said Isia. "Nothing can change that much between now and then, and in the morning you will be more rational." Both Alice and Isia helped her to her room and stayed with her until she was calm enough to sleep.

Roland had his own reasons for cutting short the afternoon tea. The whole Knickerbocker affair, which had so disoriented him in the previous year, had in recent months become blurred in his conscious thinking. He had been preoccupied with Bar-net's intrusion into his personal life, then his summer of recu-peration in Europe, and now his renewed courtship of Blan-che — at least until the recent dinner for General Watson. But somehow seeing Harpster there and his conversation with Heiles had stirred up past memories to a level that was again driving him to distraction. On the ferry back to Newark, he made a mental checklist of the Knickerbocker members, principally those whose position in society was akin to his own. His atten-tion fell upon William Scheffler, a good friend to Ballantine and a man of impeccable credentials in the community. Will and his wife, Sadie, had been friends of Roland's for a long time. He recalled afternoon teas at their home and Sadie's con-cern that he should find an agreeable wife for himself. She would certainly approve of Blanche, he thought, but that intro-duction would have to wait until the damn Knickerbocker affair was settled. Yes, the Schefflers were good friends, and Will in particular might be of assistance in this festering Cornish matter.

That night Roland began his letter to Will. The gist of it was that Cornish was a rogue, an employee of a gentlemen's club who was seeking to place his stamp of boorishness on the reputation of the club itself. Roland outlined the troubles he had had with the man when he was chairman of the house committee—Cornish's refusal to take orders, his taking on of airs, his slanderous remarks against Roland, and the insulting letter directed at the New York Athletic Club and its president Bartow Weeks. He also listed the various actions he had taken to rid the club of this unsavory element—his conversations with Adams, with Ballantine, and finally with the Knickerbocker Board of Directors, all without success. He reminded Scheffler of his own desperate action—that of resignation from the club to which he had devoted so much goodwill and energy. He concluded the letter with a paraphrase of Cornish's last words to him: "Cornish is in, and I am out."

The letter was phrased in such a way that Scheffler could go to Herbert Ballantine himself with it. Surely, if Ballantine would but listen to the facts as Roland had outlined them, he would act in a reasonable manner and get rid of Harry Cornish. Otherwise, Roland felt he would have to take matters into his own hands.

He did not sleep well that Sunday night. Nor did Blanche. As Alice predicted, she did take a more reasoned approach to Barney's illness on Monday morning. Very early, she made herself ready and left the house for Thorley's florists. As London had its stationers and florists to the Queen, so New York had it stationers and florists to the upper classes, namely, Tiffany's and Thorley's. Blanche had it in her mind that, for Barney, only Thorley's would do, and she made her way by trolley directly to the shop. She was foresighted enough to bring along her own stationery, on which to pen a note that could be enclosed. From among the beautiful selections, all fresh this early Monday morning, she selected shaggy chrysanthemums—a huge box full. She would charge them to Roland of course, as he was a

Thorley's patron and she was in fact acting with his approval. As the clerk was boxing and tying the bouquet, Blanche sat down at the little desk furnished for customers like herself. She drew out her paper, picked up the pen and dipped it in the inkwell. She pondered a moment and then began to write:

My dear Barney,
I am distressed to learn of your illness. I arrived home Saturday, and am exceedingly sorry to know that you are indisposed. Won't you let me know when you are able to be about? I want so much to see you. Is it that you do not believe me? If you would but let me prove to you my sincerity! Do not be cross any more — and accept, I pray you, my very best wishes.
    Blanche

Blanche read over her words and acknowledged to herself that it had been a while since she had been away, but the little fiction did add a certain drama to the note, and the slight inaccuracy was of no harm to anyone, least of all Barney. Her eyes became moist as she thought of Barney so ill. At least the flowers would give him encouragement, and perhaps he would even be strong enough to go down to the lobby and phone her. She hurried back home that she might be at the telephone before Thorley's messenger delivered the flowers to the Knickerbocker.

Monday went by with no response, no phone call, no message from Barney. On Tuesday morning, Isia left for Boston, unhappy at her sister's distress and also at her own unraveling marriage. That afternoon Blanche called the Knickerbocker and received no satisfactory explanation as to Barney's condition. On Wednesday morning, she phoned once more, leaving her name in the hope that Barney, or at least his brother Edmond, who the clerk had said was in attendance, would return the call. No word came.

By Friday afternoon, Blanche had decided that she must give up her vigil at the telephone. Roland had been after her to learn the duet from Verdi's *Il Travatore* so that they might perform together for friends and family. Blanche considered this aspiration of Roland's to become a concert baritone preposterous, yet she was about to become his wife, and she felt she ought to abide by his wishes. So she bundled up against a miserable drizzle and took the trolley down to Schirmer's music store at Union Square. At Schirmer's she made her little purchase, then looked around at the new editions, all to postpone for a while the long, cold ride back uptown.

When Blanche finally boarded the trolley for the ride back, she decided to take a little detour. She would disembark at Thirty-third Street, walk over to Fifth Avenue, and stroll through the Waldorf-Astoria. To think that in just three weeks she and Roland would be living there in the new Astoria section! It was more than she had ever dared dream of and enough to distract her from thoughts of Barney ill in his bed. The walk across to the avenue was a wet one indeed, but Blanche gracefully balanced her package and pocketbook while holding high the umbrella. Her mother had often reminded her that a real lady could maintain her composure, even in the most awkward situation. Surely getting about on such a wet November day without a carriage was a test for any lady. Blanche could thank her past struggles for the training that had prepared her so well.

Inside the hotel entrance, Blanche closed the umbrella and rearranged her hat and suit. One never knew whom one might meet under such circumstances. She had not progressed very far when she heard a now familiar voice: "Miss Chesebrough, Miss Chesebrough!"

Coming across the broad lobby was John Adams. His face was serious, though his greeting was warm. He spoke intensely to Blanche: "Have you heard the news? Did you know that Henry Barnet died yesterday?" Blanche was dumbstruck. *It cannot be true*, she thought. She grabbed Adams's arm, and he quickly steadied her. Together they went over to a large divan and sat down. Always the kind and compassionate gentleman, Adams did his best to comfort her. "I know Barney was your friend as well as Roland's. We all loved him . . . he was a man with no enemies . . . a splendid fellow . . . " Blanche barely heard him, as slowly a kind of sick feeling engulfed her, a feeling she could only identify as guilt.

Unknown to Blanche until much later was the peculiar nature of Barnet's fatal illness. It seems that in early October, coincidentally the very same weekend that Roland and Blanche were spending up at Fort Greene Place, Barnet received in the mail at his office a bottle of Kutnow Powders. Though he had not ordered any medicine, he retained the bottle of this well-known stomach remedy, taking it back to his room at the Knickerbocker and depositing it in his drawer. There it lay for several weeks, until the evening of November 1, when he experienced a mild case of indigestion and took some of the powder without much thought. Immediately he was seized with violent stomach pains, causing him to take to his bed. His condition worsened so rapidly that he rang the desk, and Paul, the young protege of John Adams, was sent up to attend him. Realizing forthwith that Barnet was severely ill, Paul summoned Adams, who quickly called in the Knickerbocker house physician, Dr. Wendell Phillips. Dr. Phillips sat with Barnet through the night, tending to him as best he could during his repeated, lengthy spasms of retching. The next morning, Barnet was still quite conscious and asked that his brother, Edmond, and his private physician, Dr. Henry Douglass, be summoned.

Dr. Douglass took over Barnet's care and ordered a nurse to assist him. He noted the persistent mucus around his patient's mouth and also the blood that Barnet was vomiting. The combination was unusual, he admitted, but he diagnosed the illness as diphtheria, not uncommon in those days. Barnet overheard the diagnosis and turned his head toward the ledge on which he had placed the Kutnow Powders bottle. Weakly he whispered to his brother, "Not diphtheria . . . it was those damned powders . . . they have done this to me."

For ten days the poor man struggled, ever more weakened as he could tolerate neither food nor drink. Day by day his condition deteriorated, while his physician and brother looked on helplessly. By Wednesday evening, Barnet had fallen into a coma, and on Thursday morning, November 10, he was dead.

Dr. Douglass filled out the death certificate—"cardiac asthenia, caused by diphtheria." He nevertheless picked up the Kutnow Powders bottle as he left the dead man's room. It would be interesting to have a chemist examine it.

Edmond Barnet began to pack his brother's belongings and to dispose of the floral bouquets, which had withered along with the patient. As he did so, he wondered who "Blanche" might be. There had been so many women in Henry's life, none of them serious as far as he knew; yet Blanche's note indicated something deeper. Perhaps he should look her up. At least he would save her note for the time being.

On Saturday, Alice Bellinger and Blanche Chesebrough joined a few friends and colleagues of Henry Barnet at a church on lower Fifth Avenue. Blanche sat silently behind her veiled hat, her eyes too full even to see the vicar who presided. Afterward she left the pew quickly in the hope of speaking with Barney's brother before he entered the carriage for the trip to Greenwood Cemetery.

She wanted to ask Edmond Barnet a question, rather to make a request. Something besides grief was troubling Blanche, and she dared not reveal it even to Alice. If she could only get to Mr. Barnet and inquire about a note that had been sent with flowers from Thorley's. Did he know the whereabouts of the note? Would it be possible to return it to the sender? Blanche found herself pushing between the other mourners to reach him, but when she reached the door of the church, he had already entered the carriage and the curtains were drawn. Silently she prayed: "Dear God, may the errors of my ways never return to haunt me."

That evening as she contemplated her rendezvous with Roland on the following afternoon, Blanche came to a decision. For fear that she might weep at the mention of his name, she would remain silent regarding the news of Barney's death.

On Sunday, Roland surprised her by attending church in the morning and waiting for her as she descended from the choir loft. He escorted her to a favorite cafe for luncheon, but their conversation lacked vitality, as if each of the participants was preoccupied with his and her own private reflections. Henry Barnet was uppermost in Blanche's thoughts and perhaps in Roland's also; but discretion prevailed on both sides.

Since the day was without sunshine, Blanched found herself huddling close to Roland as they walked back up Sixth Avenue to West End. Minnie met them at the door, and Alice came out of the kitchen to hug Blanche and offer them both a cup of hot chocolate.

The front parlor, which had once been the scene of Roland's rejection, now became his welcoming home. The glowing fire added a warmth that begged the visitor to remain. Roland, no less than Barney, warmed to Alice's unique combination of wit and wisdom. Throughout the afternoon, the three of them sat and talked of the wedding and of Roland's and Blanche's plans for the future. When Roland mentioned that he still had not found a suitable apartment, Alice insisted that she would be more than happy to accommodate the newlyweds in her home. In fact, she offered to move into Blanche's room so that they might have her own spacious quarters. By mutual agreement all around, the informal arrangement was accepted. The increased payment for room and board would mean that Alice could employ a cook in addition to Minnie. She also promised a fresh coat of paint and new damask window coverings, all in Blanche's favorite rose color. That night, Blanche slept in peace. Even Barney's recent death could not diminish the feeling of security that was enveloping her.

Roland's thoughts, however, were not as serene as Blanche's. The issue of living quarters had been settled very agreeably with Alice Bellinger's proposal, and any problems that might have arisen with regard to Barnet's illness and death also seemed to have been avoided. No doubt Blanche had heard the news, for everyone at both the Knickerbocker and the New York Athletic Club was talking about it. Fortunately she had not brought up the subject, and the affair was closed as far as Roland was concerned.

What bothered Roland was that he had expected to hear

something from Will Scheffler in response to his letter about Cornish. Instead he had received a note from Sadie, inviting him to tea. It was clear to Roland that Will had been too cowardly to act; rather he had discussed the matter with his wife and they had come upon this idea of an informal meeting. Roland perceived Sadie's invitation as an insult thrown by her husband, and he would of course decline, but in a manner that would not offend her. Sadie had always shown a sincere interest in Roland's well-being and had always wished him the best in his romantic pursuits. The proximity of the proposed tea date to his wedding date provided the perfect excuse. Thus he wrote:

> My dear Sadie,
> I am to be married on Tuesday next. Think of that! So you will excuse me from tea next Sunday, will you not? It is all very sudden a romance, in fact, and I am very happy. We go to the Astoria to live until our new home is ready, and the announcement cards will be sent out from there. Excuse great haste. I know you join me in my happiness.
>   Always most cordially yours,
>   Roland

So Will Scheffler too had disappointed him. As had happened before in his life, Roland concluded once again that he alone had the will to do what must be done.

TEN

A Curious Honeymoon

Tuesday, the twenty-ninth of November, dawned sunny and cold. New York had been blanketed with fourteen inches of snow over the weekend, and as so often happens after a snowstorm, temperatures had fallen sharply. Even with every horse and every wagon on Manhattan pressed into service for snow removal, two-thirds of the island's streets remained blocked. Roland's parents, communicating by telephone from Brooklyn on Sunday, had suggested that the wedding be postponed for a few days, but Roland had objected to any change in the date. From West End it was but a short drive to the church, he insisted, and beyond that only another short distance to the Waldorf-Astoria.

This, then, despite the inclement weather, was to be Blanche's wedding day. With the winter sun streaming in through the windows, she stood radiantly before the mirror in Alice's spacious room, unmindful of the out-of-doors. Rather she was admiring two sterling silver perfume vials, each containing a delicate French fragrance, which stood on the dresser nearby. Alice had left these with her card earlier that morning. The matching bottles were decorated with expansively engraved flowers in the style of *art nouveau*, and hidden within each design was Blanche's monogram—"BCC." Who but Alice would have selected a wedding gift with such flair.

Minnie was removing Alice's belongings from the wardrobe and carrying them across the hall to the little room Blanche had occupied for almost a year. The gowns that would accompany Blanche on her honeymoon were carefully laid out on the bed, and two large bags lay open across makeshift luggage stands, already partially filled. The scene was mildly chaotic, but a cheerfulness pervaded the entire household.

Blanche's gaze fell upon her wedding dress—the lovely Paris creation Isia had presented to her—and she decided it was time to begin dressing. Calling to Minnie for assistance, she slipped into the lace and satin finery, then turned to examine herself in the mirror. As Minnie began fastening the tiny cloth-covered hooks and eyes, the lines of the gown molded to Blanche's figure, and she was quite pleased with the effect.

The entrance bell sounded from below, and presently the new cook, a robust German woman from the Upper East Side, bustled into the room carrying a large florist's box. Blanche immediately recognized it as from Thorley's, and a shudder swept over her as a picture of chrysanthemums flashed through her mind. She quickly pushed the thought aside, refusing to dwell on the past this day.

"Meine Dame, huebsch, huebsch," blurted the coarse woman as she handed the box to Blanche, the harshness of the German words sounding more like commands for a horse. Blanche did not bother to ascertain what the woman meant. It amazed her that Alice had chosen to hire a cook who could not speak English, whatever her culinary abilities might be. But Alice prided herself on having studied German as a young woman and having learned it well enough to communicate competently. Blanche could not fathom why Alice had chosen this language over French—the language of culture.

Blanche took the box and dismissed the woman before opening it. Whatever the faults of the colored servants, at least they could speak and understand English well enough to communicate with their mistresses. She carefully untied the wide satin ribbon, a Thorley's trademark, and opened the box to find Roland's light blue stationery, beneath which rested a lovely corsage of violets and orchids. The message was as touching as it was simple: "This day I thee wed. Roland"

Blanche held the fragrant gift to her dress, and Minnie stopped her chores, wiped her hands and came to assist. Together they found a suitable anchoring, and Minnie affixed the long pin that had been provided with the corsage.

Roland's was not the first floral offering to have arrived that morning. As a matter of fact the room was filled with flowers— roses from Alice, a mixed bouquet from Blanche's choir colleagues, and another lovely arrangement from Roland's employer. By chance, Mr. Herrmann was to be married himself the following weekend, and Blanche made a mental note that she and Roland should send flowers to his bride, perhaps directly from their honeymoon suite at the Waldorf.

Surrounded as she was by a garden of flowers and a surfeit of lovely gowns, Blanche for a moment imagined herself to be a great diva on the opening night of some historic production. Lost in her fantasy, she returned to her mirror to put the finishing touches to her face and hair, paying little attention to Minnie, who continued to go about her duties in the room behind her. She smoothed on her long white gloves, then picked up the ivory kid-bound prayer book from which her marriage vows would be read. Like the *Mizpah* ring and the diamond butterfly, this too was from Tiffany's, a wedding gift from Roland.

As she glanced in the mirror for one last look, Blanche noticed Minnie's reflection beside her own, staring at her from behind. As their eyes met, Minnie dared to speak. "Ma'am, yous marry de wrong gentleman. Why you not marry gentleman caller, Mr. Barnet?"

Blanche dropped the prayer book and wheeled around to face Minnie angrily. "Silence," she cried. "Get out . . . and don't let me see your face again!"

As the terrified black girl dashed from the room in tears, Blanche immediately regretted her words, knowing they had been too harsh. She would have to make it up to her later, she thought, after she returned from her honeymoon. What Blanche could not know was that she would never speak to Minnie Betts again. She would only view her from afar more than a year later at Roland's trial as she testified for the prosecution.

Suddenly Alice was in the doorway urging Blanche to hurry. General Molineux's carriage had arrived, which meant that Roland and his parents awaited them at the Church of the Heavenly Rest. Blanche grabbed her handbag and her new fur jacket, also a gift from Roland, and quickly followed Alice down the stairs. Minnie would finish the packing, and a wagon would call for her luggage later in the day. Blanche found this aspect of her bridal role irresistible; at least for one day in her life, all responsibilities were taken care of by others.

The carriage stood elegantly at the street, the driver waiting obsequiously with his hand on the open door to help the two ladies into their seats. Blanche felt almost majestic as they made their way down the partially cleared road, snow banked high on either side. But as the carriage turned the corner to cross over to Fifth Avenue, she suddenly realized she did not have the prayer book with her. "Driver, halt!" she cried, and the whole company—horses, driver, Blanche and Alice—lurched forward. As they recovered from the sudden stop, Blanche changed her mind, recalling that it was bad luck ever to go back for that which was forgotton. But Alice disagreed. "Nonsense, of course we will turn back," she insisted. "You cannot begin a marriage by disappointing your husband at the altar."

At the appointed hour, Blanche and Roland stood before the altar, with Alice and the general at their sides as witnesses. The Right Reverend Parker Morgan, the ivory prayer book between his hands, faced them as he pronounced the timeless words of the nuptial ceremony. "Dearly Beloved, we are gathered together here in the sight of God to join this man and woman in holy matrimony . . . Wilt thou have this woman? . . . Wilt thou have this man? . . . "I take thee Blanche" . . . "I take thee Roland" . . . "With this ring I thee wed" . . . "In the name of the Father, and of the Son, and of the Holy Ghost."

Blanche lifted her face to Roland's and he kissed her tenderly. As Roland stepped down from the altar to kiss his mother, who had risen from the pew below, Blanche turned toward the general. Gently he lifted her left hand, on which the *Mizpah* ring now encircled her wedding finger, and eyes brimming, he pressed it to his lips. Then releasing her to Alice's embrace, he walked toward his wife and son, and clasped Roland's hand for a long moment. Emotions were overflowing as each one silently harbored hopeful thoughts for this marriage, which had come by such a circuitous route.

It was the Reverend Morgan who spoke first. "General Molineux, your driver awaits us at the back of the church." Recovering his dignity, the general ordered the small entourage out of the church and into the carriage. A wedding dinner was prepared for them in the Emperor's Alcove of the Waldorf-Astoria; they should not allow it to grow cold.

The banquet at the Waldorf was everything Blanche could have desired. Roland and his father had made all the arrangements and had outdone themselves to make the occasion as festive as possible. The lavish feast, the exquisite wines, and the admiring words spoken with every toast were enough to turn the head of any woman. It seemed to Blanche that nothing could diminish her joy on this wonderful day.

Yet as the evening wore on, it became clear that Roland wished to extend the banquet as long as possible. When the wine ran out, or rather when the general declared that they had all had enough, Roland began to tell anecdotes of his earlier athletic competitions, and when those ran out, of his schoolboy pranks. His mother hung on every word, but the general became increasingly restless. At last he rose to leave, persuading his wife to join him and promising to deliver Alice safely at home on the way to Brooklyn. The bridal pair was finally alone.

They retired to their rooms, one of the Waldorf's renowned bridal suites, and there Blanche found all of the bouquets which had stood in her room that morning. Her luggage also had been unpacked. Each gown hung neatly in the wardrobe and her personal items lay folded in the drawers of the armoire. She could see the hand of dear Alice in all of this.

Her first hours alone with her new husband were not at all what Blanche had imagined they would be. Where she had expected virility and forcefulness, there were none. Where she had expected Roland to take the lead, he did not. Instead, almost shyly, man and wife disrobed, their movements hesitant and uncertain. As they lay together in each other's arms, Roland did show an earnest tenderness toward her; she in turn was more than willing to submit to his caresses. Strange it was then that a man who had pursued her so doggedly and who now professed such devotion for her could be so inept on his wedding night.

On the first morning of her marriage, Blanche Chesebrough Molineux awakened well before her husband. In the soft light of dawn, her gaze wandered about the room in which she and Roland had begun their conjugal life together. She was surrounded by luxurious velvet upholstery, exquisite watered silk, and graceful damask draperies, a heavy elegance that was in no way unpleasant after years of privation. Ahead of her lay a life of relative ease and, she postulated, one not without the promise of adventure. She knew that she would not be content now to settle down to the boredom of family life, not when, for the first time, she had the means to travel to Europe and to develop her talent there. The thought of this exciting possibility thrilled her, and she hugged herself with pleasure.

If there was any cloud on the horizon, it had to do with the man who lay sleeping quietly beside her. Though innocent of Roland's past romantic encounters, Blanche nevertheless puzzled over the inadequacy of her wedding night. How different the consummation of her marriage was from the earlier intimate encounters with Barney; the comparison left her somewhat bewildered. Yes, the marriage had been consummated, but just barely. At a loss for where to place the blame and assuming that she must be somehow at fault, Blanche resolved that today would be different. She rose to bathe and rearrange her hair so that she might be attired in her lovely negligee by the time her husband awoke.

Some time later there was a knock at the door of the suite, and Blanche opened it to be greeted by a colored porter with a breakfast cart before him. The clatter of the little cart laden with china and silver aroused Roland from his deep sleep, and he did his best to pull himself together, scrambling from the bed and quickly donning his robe. Blanche bade him a cheerful good morning, then helped the porter arrange the chairs on either side of the little table. By this time Roland was sufficiently recovered to tip the man and dismiss him.

As the two shared their first honeymoon meal, Blanche was crestfallen, realizing that her careful preparations had been in vain. Roland regarded her with eyes that were barely half open, and their conversation was forced and punctuated with awkward silences. But she did not despair, thinking perhaps his condition might be due to the amount of wine he had consumed at the banquet. She could expect better for the midday when they would stroll through the lobbies of the hotel and out onto Fifth Avenue. The beautiful sealskin jacket and matching muff Roland had given her would make a fashionable combination for a winter promenade on the avenue.

Beginning with this first evening, there were to be activities and entertainments to last the entire honeymoon. Morris Herrmann had invited Roland and Blanche to dinner with him and his fiancée at Delmonico's; Bartow Weeks had arranged an evening at the New York Athletic Club for later in the week, with a number of friends invited; there was also the Molineux family party to be held at the home of Roland's two aunts, near the general's home in Brooklyn; and even the Opera Club was planning a special holiday party to honor them. In between they would attend several theater and opera performances. This was to be a honeymoon calendar that Blanche would always remember.

Though Blanche had absolutely nothing in common with Roland's employer Morris Herrmann, or with his fiancée, the evening with them contained a very positive note. Almost as an aside, Herrmann announced that Roland would have new responsibilities in the future—more in the line of sales—and that these responsibilities would require him to have his office on Manhattan, near Herrmann's own office. This was a relief for Blanche, for although she had never visited the Herrmann factory in Newark, her instincts suggested that it was not a happy place. The new position would begin in January, as soon as Herrmann and his bride returned from Hot Springs, Virginia, where they would spend their honeymoon.

The evening at the home of Roland's aunts held both good and bad omens. Blanche was totally captivated by the charm of these two well-bred English ladies—sisters of her father-in-law. Aunt Anne was a spinster, and Aunt Emma, who had married a Burnham, had been widowed for many years. The two lived together in a home reminiscent of a setting for some great English novel. For this dinner honoring Blanche and Roland, the festive table was decorated with beautiful old English silver flowers. At the close of the evening, Aunt Anne presented them to Blanche as a wedding gift. This gesture put Blanche on the verge of tears—tears of joy at being part of such a generous and thoughtful family.

Something happened that evening, though, that was to be a portent of later events. Roland had carried with him to the dinner party the score of *Il Travatore*, and although he and Blanche had not practiced together, he insisted that they perform the duet of Leonora and the Count. Blanche would have been delighted to sing the aria alone, but she cautioned Roland against trying the duet as she knew it required skills he did not yet possess. However, Roland was adamant, and dutifully she assented, providing the piano accompaniment and the soprano voice while Roland sang the baritone. It was indeed a painful experience.

Later that night, as they rode through the cold Brooklyn streets and back to Manhattan, Blanche was discomfited by a strange brooding silence in her husband. Thinking that he was perhaps angry at her reluctance to perform the duet, she asked,

"Roland, why are you so quiet . . . have I somehow failed in your expectations of me?"

"No, no, of course not," he reassured her. "There are matters pressing upon me that sometimes distract me even when I would have it otherwise. Perhaps tomorrow I can take care of some of these problems so that these precious days of ours will no longer be disturbed. I know I sang badly tonight, my dear, but I hope you will have faith in my potential . . . I feel sure that I have the makings of a great operatic singer, and I have such great expectations for our marriage and our careers."

So it was that the next morning Roland eschewed the honeymoon breakfast in their suite and left before Blanche was even out of bed. Boarding a trolley, he rode downtown to the establishment of Joseph Koch at 1620 Broadway. Known as the Commercial Company, the shop was in fact a letter box agency, similar to that of Nicholas Heckmann on Forty-second Street. However, Koch was also the proprietor of the Studio Publishing Company, an advertising and printing firm with which Roland had had occasion to conduct business a year earlier, in the interest of Morris Herrmann product advertising. Thus the name of Roland Molineux was known to Koch.

Roland entered the shop and was greeted by Koch himself, who recognized his customer from the encounter months earlier. Not expecting this instant recognition, Roland became a bit diffident, explaining to Koch that he was merely inquiring about letter box leases for a friend. After bidding Koch a cordial "Good day," he left.

Blanche occupied herself through the midday with shopping for a few Christmas trinkets. Since she and Roland would be spending the night before Christmas alone at the Waldorf, she wished to have some little gifts to mark the holiday. On Christmas Day, they planned to join the Molineuxs in Brooklyn, and later in the afternoon they would stop at Alice's. Alice would be alone that day as both Minnie and the cook were to be excused to be with their own families.

For the first time in many years, Blanche noted, she too was to spend Christmas within a family. It was a comforting thought, particularly in light of the incompleteness of her relationship with Roland. Lately she had found herself pondering this problem again and again, as something deep within her seemed to be asking, "Is this all there is?"

Blanche recalled that at one time she and Barney had discussed this very matter—what happens to lovers when they finally marry. It was the reason he was opposed to marriage, he had said. She could not help wondering whether it would have been the same with Barney. In one way, at least, it would have been different. It was rumored that Barney, who had speculated heavily on the Wall Street Exchange, had died penniless. His brother had even had to pay the funeral bill himself. Blanche's practical side told her that fate had been on her side, but her heart spoke otherwise.

Roland arrived back at the Waldorf in early evening. Blanche was already dressed for dinner and was somewhat chagrined that Roland had tarried so long. As on the evening before, he was downcast and uncommunicative, enough so that Blanche suppressed her own distress at his tardiness. He quickly changed to the formal dress required for the Palm Room, though, and with one look at her impeccably attired husband, Blanche's annoyance vanished. She had arranged with the *maitre d'* for a table in front of the Fifth Avenue windows, the very table at which Roland had proposed three months earlier. Her plan was well-conceived, for as they reminisced about that happy afternoon, the strain that had existed between them eased somewhat. The evening was at least companionable, if not intimate.

Their days at the Waldorf began to take on a certain monotony. Mornings found Roland rising early, ostensibly to take care of his business correspondence at the desk in the sitting room. Blanche was perturbed that Morris Herrmann, who had made such a point of telling Roland to forget business for these weeks, still expected him to attend to such matters from his honeymoon suite. At least, so it seemed.

After preparing his letters, Roland would leave for a few hours, during which Blanche would dress and breakfast in the room. Sometimes Roland would return for lunch, but most of the time she would be left to her own devices until they were reunited again for whatever evening engagement they had.

The night of the Opera Club party marked the first open breach in their tenuous relationship. Roland was again determined to take the Verdi score with him over Blanche's objection that the little performance at the Molineuxs had not been particularly successful. Roland disagreed vehemently, and in fact intimated that perhaps Blanche's reluctance to perform with him lay in the fear that she might be upstaged by him. Such words nearly brought Blanche to tears; she was learning that Roland had certain fixed notions with which she should never take issue. For the moment, the notion seemed to be that he possessed a great baritone voice.

Several of their fellow Opera Club members had magnanimously arranged a delightful holiday banquet, complete with vocal entertainment, to honor the bridal couple. It was gratifying to Blanche to realize that she had been accepted unequivocally by this group of cultured people who sincerely appreciated her musical talents. Her joy quickly turned to embarrassment, however, as at the close of the entertainment, Roland came forward and announced that he and Blanche would perform a duet from Verdi's *Il Travatore*. There was a murmur in the crowd, surprise at this vocal talent that had so long remained hidden, and Blanche knew that those present would form a most critical audience. Quietly she sat down at the piano and opened the music. She began with a little improvisation and a sort of silent prayer that disaster might somehow be avoided. Then she launched into the introduction and commenced with Leonora's aria. Roland stood proudly beside the piano with his hand across his diaphragm and listened for his cue to begin. Blanche reduced the volume of her own voice as she led into the duet, but as Roland began to sing, she knew that despite all her care, her worst fears were to be realized. Their voices were neither together in time nor on the same pitch. Mercifully the duet was not a long one. The friendly audience applauded politely, but no comments were forthcoming. Blanche begged to leave, pleading fatigue and the lateness of the hour, but Roland was visibly distraught at the lack of appreciation shown by the audience and turned to her for support.

"You sang wonderfully, Roland, don't worry about it. I think the others were just jealous. You know, there are some in that crowd who are professional singers and they do not like to be shown up by an amateur."

Blanche wondered if being a wife would always mean living such lies. It was all such a new experience for her, and Roland was so complicated, more so than she had ever imagined. Perhaps when the honeymoon was over and they could settle down at Alice's, with Roland working right on Manhattan, these disturbing elements would disappear.

As Christmas approached, Roland continued to spend time away. Although he did not disclose the purpose of his errands, seemingly they were related to his business responsibilities. He even found it necessary to visit the factory in Newark, much to Blanche's consternation. She began to chide Roland about his Jewish employer, who so thoughtlessly drove his loyal employee with no consideration for the Christmas holiday. Roland was quick to caution her not to accuse Morris Herrmann: "The matters which have so distracted me these days have nothing to do with my employment. Rather they go back to Knickerbocker Club times. I never told you, my dear, about the shameful things that went on there. When I resigned a year ago, I left some unfinished business, but I believe I have settled everything during the past few days. From now on, I will be yours alone."

The twenty-fourth of December brought a blanket of fresh snow, and as he had promised, Roland spent the entire day with Blanche in their suite. In fact he seemed to be more like his old self again. During breakfast, Blanche talked of the refurbishment that was being completed at Alice's. She had sneaked a visit during one of Roland's absences, and they would view the newly decorated rooms together for the first time on the morrow. Blanche also broached the subject of the European voyage,

Roland Molineux, in
athletic togs

Blanche Molineux before
her marriage

The Knickerbocker Athletic Club

A TUG OF WAR.
WAITING THE SIGNAL.

BOAT HOUSE.
HARLEM RIVER.

CLUB HOUSE.

The New York Athletic Club

The Claremont Hotel

The Metropolitan Opera House

Lobby of the Knickerbocker Athletic Club

Henry Barnet

The antique silver Flemish bowl

General Edward Molineux

The Atlantic Yacht Club

OFFICIALS WATCH THE RAISING OF THE COFFIN.

Henry Barnet's body exhumed from
Greenwood Cemetery

"IT WAS A DAMNABLE LIE!"

MOLINEUX'S PARTING SHOTS.

"I am absolutely and entirely innocent!"

"These hands never put pen to paper to address that poison package!"

"I denounce and despise the action of the District-Attorney in attempting to vilify and attack the character of the pure and lovely woman who bears my name!"

"It was the act of a blackguard!"

"It was a damnable lie!"

"I am not afraid, because I am not guilty!"

Roland attacks the prosecutor

Mamie Melando

Katherine Adams

Handwriting facsimiles

James Osborne, the
prosecuting attorney

Recorder Goff, the
presiding judge

The Murray Hill Hotel

General Molineux bids farewell
at Sing Sing

Blanche listens to
testimony at the trial

and Roland seized upon this to expound on his previous trip abroad and the sights that he wished to revisit with her.

That night they sat before a warm fire in the sitting room, which Blanche had decorated with lighted candles and pine branches from the florist, and they told each other stories of their childhood Christmases. Roland had prepared small packages wrapped in tissue and ribbon, each containing a small gift for Blanche. As she opened them one by one, she was reminded of her childhood, when her father too had prepared many packages, each with a trinket of little value. For this one evening Blanche and Roland were children again and they were happy together.

Christmas Day out in Brooklyn was almost like Christmas Day in the country. The Molineux clan was present in full force, including Cecil and Leslie, who had come over from Metuchen, New Jersey, with his wife and their five children. After the midday dinner, General Molineux ordered that a horse be hitched up to the family cutter for races up and down Fort Greene Place. It was as if all of the inhabitants of that stately neighborhood had shed their dignified exteriors, for out on the street were sleighs of all sizes, each finer than the other. The Molineux grandchildren climbed into the cutter and soon joined in the merriment, squealing in delight as they met and passed the heavier sleighs.

As the afternoon wore on, Blanche became impatient to get to Alice's. As much as she had enjoyed the day in Brooklyn, it was not the same as when she and Roland visited there alone. With grandchildren running about, General Molineux had little time for his new daughter-in-law, and even Roland was more intent on visiting with his brothers than with his bride. Left to converse with a mother-in-law and sister-in-law whose entire lives were bound up with domestic matters, Blanche found very little of common interest. She hoped that even if she lived to be eighty, her horizons would never become so narrow.

At twilight the cutter delivered Roland and Blanche to the foot of Brooklyn Hill. From there they boarded a trolley for the ride across the bridge and eventually made their way up to West

End. Alice had prepared a magnificent supper, both as her Christmas celebration and as her welcoming gesture to the bridal pair. Afterward she and Blanche vied with each other to show Roland the new wall and window coverings that had transformed Alice's former room into a lovely apartment for two. Roland was favorably impressed; for Blanche, it was good to be home again.

"Oh Roland, couldn't we move right in tonight and then return to the hotel in the morning to pick up our belongings? Please, please!" Blanche was acting like a spoiled child, but Roland was in an expansive mood. Besides, leaving the hotel a week early would do no harm to his pocketbook. He smiled and nodded in agreement, then graciously accepted an impulsive hug and kiss from his bride.

That night the two of them lay between Alice's best linens. Roland cradled Blanche's head in his arm and talked softly to her. "I have the feeling tonight that we both have been purified—that the demons who sought to destroy us have been overcome forever. Sleep well, my sweet, as will I; the future is ours." Blanche would have liked to protest that no demon had been after her, but sleep overcame her just then.

ELEVEN

Death of a Stranger

Late in the day on the twenty-first of December, no doubt while Blanche was strolling alone on Fifth Avenue, an unidentified man called on Joseph Koch in his letter box establishment. To this day no one has ever publicly identified this man, and if Joseph Koch knew his identity, he took it with him to the grave.

All that is known is that the unidentified man rented a letter box in the name of H. Cornish. On that same afternoon in New York City two letters were mailed, and although addressed to different destinations, they were not entirely dissimilar. Each was written on distinctive stationery, powder blue with three entwined silver crescents in the upper center. Furthermore, both letters were handwritten and signed "H. Cornish."

One of the letters was addressed to the Kutnow Brothers' firm, requesting a sample of Kutnow Powders—shades of *deja vous*. The return address, the place to which the powders should be sent, was 1620 Broadway, the letter box of H. Cornish. The other letter was a request by H. Cornish for a reference. It was sent to Frederick Stearns and Company of Detroit and it inquired as to the reputation of one Alvin Harpster. Harpster, a close friend of Harry Cornish and an employee of Herbert Ballantine, had formerly been employed by the Stearns firm and,

119

according to Roland's friend, Rudy Heiles, had been dismissed
for serious cause. The return address on the letter was 1620
Broadway, New York.

On that same afternoon, an unidentified man purchased a silver
toothpick holder at Hartdegen's jewelry store in Newark. The
purchaser carefully measured the diameter of the holder before
completing his purchase. Emma Miller, the clerk who sold the
holder, later said that her customer wore a full red beard that
could have been false. Like the renter of Koch's letter box, this
man was never identified.

The day before Christmas was the day that Roland and
Blanche spent together in their hotel room, arranging greens
and little packages for an intimate pre-Christmas evening. It
was also the day on which Harry Cornish over at the Knickerbocker Club received a surprise Christmas package in the mail.
Ever since Roland had succeeded in eliminating his private office and sleeping room, Cornish's desk stood out on the gymnasium floor. In such circumstances his private business never
stayed private very long, and so it was with the Christmas package. In the presence of several club members who happened to
be in the gymnasium, Cornish opened the package, removed a
small blue Tiffany box, then opened the box to find a lovely
silver holder packed carefully in tissue with a bottle of Bromo-
Seltzer powder. The bottle slipped easily into the holder — a
perfect fit. There was no card, just an empty envelope.

Cornish's baffled expression drew some good-natured ribbing
from the onlookers — so Harry Cornish, divorced and through
with women, had one out there somewhere. Cornish feigned
annoyance, but then such a reaction was in keeping with his
well-known blustery manner. Any friend of his would know
that he was in no need of a hangover remedy, even during the
holiday season. This must be a practical joke. But what friend
of his, male or female, would go to the trouble of purchasing
a silver holder for the bottle? Cornish admitted to those
gathered around that this was indeed a mystery. He tossed the
paper wrapper into the wastebasket, then as an afterthought

Death of a Stranger

reached in, cut off the handwritten address, and put it in his desk drawer. "I'll figure this one out later," he declared.

It was not until two days after Christmas that Cornish got around to taking his mysterious gift home, which at that time was the apartment of his aunt, Mrs. Katherine Adams, and her daughter, Florence Rodgers. Cornish's former wife and his young daughter lived in Boston; his parents lived in Hartford, Connecticut. He kept in close touch with his daughter, and she spent part of each summer with him in New York. But most of the time, at holiday time in particular, Aunt Kate and Cousin Florence were family to Harry Cornish. Thus he not only showed them the silver holder, but offered it to Florence as a token of his affection. She was delighted, particularly as she noticed that the pattern on the holder was a perfect match to the pieces of her dresser set. The leftover Bromo-Seltzer bottle Cornish slipped into his own dresser drawer.

The next morning, December 28, Aunt Kate awoke with a headache. It was severe enough that she mentioned it at the breakfast table, and Florence was quick to suggest Cousin Harry's Bromo-Seltzer. Cornish fetched the bottle, and Florence filled a glass with water, mixed in a teaspoonful of the powder, and handed the remedy to her mother. Mrs. Adams took a good swallow of the mixture, then complained of its bitter taste. At this, Cornish took a sniff of it and tasted it himself, but noticed nothing unusual. However, he was not in the habit of taking the remedy and had nothing with which to compare it.

Mrs. Adams left the kitchen and Cornish turned to his newspaper. Within a minute, however, Mrs. Adams raced to the bathroom, her body seized with a violent retching. Florence followed, and as her mother collapsed, she screamed for Harry. Cornish arrived to find Aunt Kate lying on the floor, clutching at her throat and gasping for breath. He tried to raise her but was himself seized by retching and a weakness in his limbs. He grabbed his coat and raced across the street to a pharmacist, bottle in hand, to ascertain an antidote, while another boarder aided Florence in an attempt to revive her mother. A young boy

121

ran for the doctor, but by the time he arrived, it was too late—Mrs. Adams was dead. In the next few hours, the apartment was a hive of activity as the police, the undertaker, and the coroner all came and went, along with various inhabitants of the building who milled about while the doctor, Edwin Hitchcock, fed Cornish mustard water to induce vomiting.

With the situation in the hands of others and he himself in no condition to assist, Cornish made his way to the office of his club friend, John Yochum. Yochum observed Cornish's condition and urged him to proceed immediately to the Knickerbocker and to go to bed in Yochum's own room. This was easier said than done, as the violence of Cornish's illness made even the trolley ride hazardous. When he did arrive at the club, he went promptly to bed. Good old John Adams, always at hand to help a man in need, summoned the house physician, Dr. Phillips, who had ministered to Henry Barnet in his last illness. It was Dr. Phillips who first made a connection between the symptoms of the two illnesses. He therefore proceeded to pump his patient's stomach, something he had failed to do for poor Barnet. Yochum himself stayed up throughout the night to assist Cornish in his numerous trips to the bathroom. After two days, the symptoms subsided and Cornish was well enough to be visited by police detectives.

Captain George McClusky, Chief of Detectives in New York City, had initiated an immediate investigation of Mrs. Adams's death. The handwritten address from Cornish's package, still available in his desk drawer, became the master clue, and a murderer was being sought. An autopsy on the body of Mrs. Adams indicated that she had died of poisoning by hydrocyanic acid. An analysis of the contents that remained in the Bromo-Seltzer bottle (in fact, it was not a Bromo-Seltzer bottle, but a chemist's bottle to which a Bromo-Seltzer label had been attached) revealed that it contained cyanide of mercury. The search for the poisoner proceeded with the evidence at hand: the bottle, the silver container, and the handwritten wrapper.

On the morning of December 29, the news of Katherine Adams's death was broadly covered in the New York press—by the staid *New York Times* as well as by the sensation-oriented *New York Journal*, the *World*, and the *Tribune*. However, as additional clues surfaced along with bits of gossip surrounding Cornish and others associated with the Knickerbocker Athletic Club, the political differences among the major newspapers soon became clear.

William Randolph Hearst was the owner of the *Journal*, which had grown and prospered while fueling the events leading to the United States war with Spain, the independence of Cuba and annexation of the Philippine Islands. In December of 1898 there was a dearth of material for the kind of journalism on which the *Journal* thrived. It must have been that the editors of the *Journal* recognized the beginnings of a good story before their competitors did. At least from the first day after Kate Adams's death, the *Journal* was suggesting that her death was somehow connected with affairs at the Knickerbocker Athletic Club.

Joseph Pulitzer's *New York World* was not slow in following the *Journal's* lead, intimating that there were dynamics in the Knickerbocker Club politics that could have led to a vendetta against the athletic director, Harry Cornish, and ultimately to the death of his innocent aunt, Kate Adams. In fact between the *World* and the *Journal*, both of whom were interviewing anyone with some connection to any of the club members, and even some who had no connection, a rather plausible case was building against John Adams.

There were several reasons to cast suspicion on Adams—a one-time divinity student, literary scholar, former editor of *Harper's Weekly* and secretary to Herbert Ballantine, the principal stockholder in the Knickerbocker Club. Although he professed concern over social issues, the newspapers pointed out that he nevertheless had befriended a young man and had taken responsibility for his education instead of marrying and having a family of his own. In fact Adams and his protege Paul Gloar lived together in a men's boarding house that was reputed to be home to several known homosexuals. According to the *World*, Adams's living room was furnished in the style of Oscar Wilde, even including a Japanese butler. Certainly John Adams, whose lifestyle was so inimical to the accepted standards of society, was a man to be investigated. The publicity surrounding John Adams's private life was enough to cause the owner of his boarding house to sell the building and disassociate himself entirely from its inhabitants. Even Herbert Ballantine, a close friend and confidante from his student days at Cornell, announced to the newspapers that although he had known Adams for many years, he really wasn't that close to him. Adams was simply in his employ and he had no reason to distrust him.

The *New York Times* was a bit more careful. Its coverage of Kate Adams's murder was front page on the first day, but then became more subdued. It was the policy of the *Times* to depend on the New York Police for its information, and the New York Police were being closemouthed indeed.

A political problem of utmost severity appeared to be developing. Captain McClusky had visited Harry Cornish at the Knickerbocker as soon as he was well enough to talk. Cornish was quick to suggest that he did have an enemy and that this enemy was Roland Molineux. He even recalled that there was an example of Molineux's handwriting in the files of the Knickerbocker, namely his letter of resignation written a year earlier. He suggested further that John Adams could probably locate it. Captain McClusky found John Adams in his office, taking care of Ballantine's affairs as usual. Adams was pleased to be helpful but put forth no accusations, even as his own character and reputation were being attacked and cut down by the eager press. He helped McClusky go through the files and together they came up with Roland Molineux's letter, which McClusky took with him back to headquarters.

The surfacing of this particular suspect was not a happy event in the office of the District Attorney. At that time the District Attorney of New York was Colonel Asa Bird Gardiner, a battle-field comrade of General Molineux in the Great War. But the friendship between the two men ended there. Colonel Gardiner was a product of the Tammany Hall faction within the Democratic Party. There were rumors abroad that the Republican

Party, of which General Molineux was one of the most influential leaders, would momentarily reveal the systematic corruption of Tammany Hall, which had infected the District Attorney's office as well as all segments of city government. The revelations were highly feared by Colonel Gardiner. It was his hope that the old wartime friendship with the general might insulate his office from the anticipated attack. To be in the position of even accusing, let alone prosecuting, the son of the general was something to be avoided if at all possible. This fear on the part of Gardiner was reflected in the care with which the police department, in particular Detective McClusky, conducted its investigation.

Between the *Journal* and the *World*, a mighty list of suspects was being accumulated. It seemed that, with the exception of Roland Molineux, no one connected with the Knickerbocker was immune. In addition to John Adams, Harry Cornish himself was suspect, along with Alvin Harpster and others, each having some obscure motive for malice against either Kate Adams or Cornish.

The silence on the part of the New York Police in those last days of December was conspicuous. If the *Times* was privy to McClusky's information, which suggested Roland Molineux as the prime suspect, its editors did not relish placing in public the name of General Molineux's son. They chose instead to follow the leadership of the official investigation.

On New Year's Day, 1899, Colonel Gardiner broke his silence with a long report on the status of the murder investigation. Preliminary conclusions were that Harry Cornish was the intended victim of the poison package and that there was very probably a connection between this case and the death of Henry Barnet in November. The evidence pointed to an as yet unidentified woman as the perpetrator of these two crimes. Gardiner's statement read in part:

> History shows that it is essentially a woman's method of action. Women acted thus in ancient times and following down through the ages we find the same traits of character,

the same outcropping of human nature. It is easy to surmise the reason for this trait. Woman's nature is essentially subtle. From deeds of blood and violence she naturally shrinks. What then follows? Her scheming brain begins to work. She turns to poison as the easiest and surest method, because if handled deftly and cleverly it insures less suspicion and less possibility of detection. In the Adams case there may be a man involved, but I think, as I have said before, that a woman is at the bottom of it and the prime mover, despite the many suppositions and rumors that Mr. Cornish has an enemy in his own sex.

With this first clear statement of Colonel Gardiner, the *Times* finally had something to report.

On the morning that Colonel Gardiner's statement was published, Blanche and Roland were preparing to attend the annual afternoon New Year's Day concert at the Metropolitan Opera House. As in previous years, it would feature a massed chorus, but unlike previous years, Blanche would be in the audience rather than on the stage. Lilli Lehman would be the soloist, and Blanche expected that there would be many in the audience whom she could greet for the first time in her new role as Mrs. Roland Molineux. She had not been following the newspapers, so she attended the performance innocent of any scandal brewing on the horizon. In fact she was counting on seeing some of the old Knickerbocker faces, possibly even John Adams; but in this she was disappointed. Furthermore, since Roland for the first time exhibited no interest in promenading during the intermission, the couple sat quietly in their seats, much to Blanche's consternation. For them, the entire day had been somewhat subdued as New York City once again lay covered with five inches of fresh snow. By the time the concert was over, the temperature had dropped to seven degrees Fahrenheit. With such weather, it was no evening for Delmonico's, where Blanche could have been assured of renewing old acquaintances. Rather, after the concert Blanche and Roland made a hasty run to the nearest cab and headed home to Alice's warm rooms and hot chocolate.

During winter, dawn always comes late in New York, long after much of the city is in motion. On the second day of the New Year, while darkness still engulfed the city, Blanche and Roland were awakened by a knock on their door. Roland jumped from the bed and opened the door to find Alice's cook standing before him and speaking excitedly as well as somewhat incoherently. Blanche could catch but a word or two, enough to know that two men were downstairs waiting to see Roland. He returned to the bed, kissed his wife gently, then donned his robe and slippers. As he left the room, he carefully closed the door behind him.

Blanche roused herself and lighted the night lamp next to the bed. She looked at the clock—6:00 A.M. She lay in her bed looking at the shadows on the ceiling, expecting that Roland would return quickly; but the minutes ticked on. As his absence continued, she threw back the covers, wrapped herself in a robe and slipped into her satin sandals. She opened the door, leaving it ajar, and sat down on the side of the bed to listen.

She could hear several men below, talking rapidly and with a kind of urgency. Blanche recognized one of the voices—that of her father-in-law. Why would the general be out at such an early hour? It must be that Roland's mother was either ill or that she was dead. This would explain not only the visit, but also the worried look on Roland's face when he kissed her. As she began to accept this plausible explanation, she also felt twinges of guilt at her own impatience with her mother-in-law. How bored she had been when Mrs. Molineux complained unendingly about her poor health and the stupidity of the physicians who attended her. Blanche chided herself about not being more sympathetic with this woman who was so adored by her son and her husband. As Blanche began silently to make amends for her own failings, she was interrupted by Roland's hasty tread on the stairs.

127

Blanche jumped to her feet as he entered the room. "Tell me, has something happened? Is it your mother?"

Roland took her in his arms and looked at her intensely. "Yes, something *has* happened, but it has nothing to do with my mother. Look at me, dear one, and tell me . . . are you brave?"

Roland touched Blanche's lips with his fingers as if to prevent a cry and his voice betrayed both hardness and anxiety as he spoke. "Look . . . you believe in me, don't you? They are attempting to implicate me in a crime. A woman is dead from poisoning . . . they have published my name in this morning's *Journal* . . . Blanche, are you paying attention to me?"

Blanche nodded defensively for she had not taken her eyes from Roland's face. Now she noticed beads of sweat protruding on his forehead. How could he be perspiring while she was so cold and trembling in the barely heated room? "My father and a reporter from the *World* are downstairs waiting for me," Roland continued. "I am going to dress and we will go immediately to see McClusky."

Of course Blanche did not know who McClusky was. She fell back onto the bed, as if in shock, her mind focused on this unknown name that Roland presumed would have significance for her. Her wide eyes followed Roland about the room as he hurriedly dressed. With a wave of his hand, as if tossing a kiss, he made for the door, then looked back at the bed for a moment: "I'll send Alice in to stay with you. Promise me you won't be anxious. It will all work out, I know. These are just lies from my father's enemies."

Blanche heard every word, particularly the last ones which seemed to mitigate the accusations. But her logical mind rejected that premise. With seeming clairvoyance she perceived that some dreadful disaster was at hand, one in which she would ultimately be involved. This thought was more than she could bear. She began to sob and the sobbing increased until it finally overcame her, causing her entire body to heave convulsively.

Alice entered the room and sat down on the edge of the bed. She touched her friend on the shoulder but otherwise waited helplessly for it all to subside. Unaware of what had instigated this early morning drama, Alice vaguely feared that it might be connected with the newspaper stories she had been reading in the previous days—stories indicating that poor Henry Barnet had been poisoned and that the poisoner was possibly a woman. She had no doubt that Henry Barnet had been a ladies' man, but it seemed to her beyond the realm of possibility that one of them would have wished to kill him. She had made no judgment, but she had at least tried to keep the news from Blanche, and in this she had been successful.

It seemed to Alice an eternity that she sat on the edge of Blanche's bed, faithful to her charge. Blanche now lay quietly, as if in a faint, and the clock ticked on while daylight finally forced its way through the windows. When it was light outside, Alice stood up quietly, tiptoed out into the hall and closed the door behind her.

TWELVE

Retreat to Brooklyn

The occurrence that had brought General Molineux to the door and roused Roland from his sleep was the appearance on the street of the morning issue of the *Journal*:

POLICE WANT ROLAND BURNHAM MOLINEUX IN POISONING CASE . . . CHIEF McCLUSKY AND CORNISH HUNTED THE CITY FOR HIM ALL OF YESTERDAY . . . HE MAY BE ABLE TO SOLVE THE MYSTERY . . .

A reporter from the *World* saw the newspaper in the wee hours of the morning and took it upon himself to engineer his own scoop. He hired a cab and drove over to Brooklyn, waking General Molineux from his night's rest at 4:00 A.M. Upon seeing the headline, the general immediately dressed and accompanied the reporter in the cab, driving through the bitter cold back to Manhattan and up to West End. The general had no trouble prevailing upon his son to join him in a visit to Captain McClusky, who lived only a short distance away. It was just 7:00 A.M. when they arrived at McClusky's home, but he was already dressed, knowing that a day of high drama lay ahead. He welcomed the three men and remained cordial, even when General

Molineux, angry and distraught, almost pushed the newspaper into his face: "If Roland Molineux is the man you want, here he is."

Captain McClusky tried to calm the general. "Sir, we do not want your son. At this point there is no evidence to link him to the poison affair. This article is a piece of scurrilous journalism; in no way does it represent the results of our investigation."

With this reassurance the general calmed down. Roland, who had stood by relaxed but sober, now smiled and addressed the detective cordially: "Captain, let me write down my address on Manhattan in case you have any reason to want me."

As Roland reached into his pocket for a slip of paper, his father turned to the reporter and impetuously grabbed both his notepad and pencil. The general tore off a small piece of paper and began to write against the wall. In his slow deliberate hand he set on paper Roland's Manhattan address, Roland's business address in Newark, his own address in Brooklyn, and finally the name of Bartow S. Weeks, Attorney at Law. With a contemptuous gesture he handed the slip to McClusky and marched haughtily out the door. Roland stopped to shake McClusky's hand and wish him a formal "Good morning." Then he raised his arm, inviting the reporter to go ahead, and followed the two men out of the house. It seemed that he, the hunted, was much less disturbed by the events than those around him.

The reporter begged to excuse himself, for he now had his story in hand. He offered the waiting cab to father and son and disappeared down the street on foot. Once in the cab Roland had to make a decision—whether to get in touch with Bartow Weeks or return directly to Blanche. He wished to do the latter for he imagined quite rightly that she was in dire need of him. But his father prevailed; it was necessary to get legal advice immediately and they should proceed to Weeks's home, where they could expect to find him at this early hour.

Bartow Weeks, whatever his personal feelings about the matter, welcomed his visitors most amiably. He had been following the news of Kate Adams's murder and the involvement of Harry Cornish from his own special point of view. He was well aware

131

of Cornish's failings, having at one time been a victim of his crude sarcasm. He was also well acquainted with Roland's smoldering resentment against Cornish and had noted the uncomfortable connection between Henry Barnet's earlier death and the Adams death. But Weeks was one of the most professional, as well as thorough, lawyers in the city. He listened to General Molineux patiently and sympathetically, read the entire article in the *Journal* carefully and instructed his clients quietly: "General, go home immediately. Roland, you do the same. Later this afternoon I shall call on you there and we can proceed together out to Brooklyn, possibly with George. Under no circumstances should any of you speak with anyone about this matter, neither with personal friends nor with servants."

When the general interrupted to insist on a lawsuit against the *Journal*, Weeks silenced him: "Let me make those decisions, General. This is a serious affair, one that calls for the talents of a lawyer, not those of a battlefield general."

General Molineux, then and there, relinquished his command. A terrible realization had sunk in—at this critical moment neither his reputation nor his political power could halt the moving avalanche. Only the power of legal counsel could protect his family and himself. He shook hands with Weeks, thanked him for taking over the matter, then took the arm of Roland and walked out to the waiting cab. Roland helped his father up to the seat and the two men rode together in silence. Roland alighted at his home and his father continued on alone. It was not yet nine o'clock in the morning, but in the five hours since his awakening, this proud and powerful gentleman had become an old man.

The *World* reporter must have been very swift in his work, for Roland was greeted outside of Alice's by a half dozen strangers, who barely allowed him to push through into the house. "Mr. Molineux, Mr. Molineux, have you a statement? Have you read the newspapers this morning? Do you know the poisoner of Mrs. Adams . . . or of Henry Barnet?"

Roland reached the door and huddled against it until it was mercifully unlocked and opened from the inside. The drapes had been drawn downstairs, and Alice, who stood behind the open door, had a worried look about her. "They started knocking about an hour ago and I can't get rid of them. In fact I am even frightened to leave the house myself and I must get to my shop to warn the girls. Roland, I have heard the news and Blanche must have heard it too. She is asleep now, but I don't know what to do if she awakes. You will stay with her, won't you?"

Roland assured Alice that he would be responsible for his wife. In fact he expressed his annoyance with Alice for making such a commotion about a fabricated story in a newspaper known for irresponsible journalism. He left the matter at that and went to be with Blanche. Alice returned to the kitchen, where she had been helping the cook, and soon came knocking on the door of the newlyweds to deliver a tray of strong hot coffee and croissants. Roland opened the door partway, thanked her for the tray, then closed the door again. It was clear that she was not welcome at the moment.

Inside the room Roland was explaining very calmly to Blanche the happenings of the last two hours. He repeated Captain McClusky's assurances and explained that his father had already ordered the attorneys to initiate a lawsuit against the *Journal*. There was little to worry about, but Blanche should expect to stay indoors for the next day or two, until the true story was told. Roland was careful to omit any reference to a connection between Mrs. Adams's death and either Harry Cornish or Henry Barnet. He guessed correctly that Blanche had not read any of the recent news accounts.

Blanche had recovered somewhat from the early morning trauma and she was reasonably alert and calm when Bartow Weeks stopped by later in the day. He brought with him a copy of the *Times*, in which the headlines referred to the inauguration of Teddy Roosevelt as Governor of New York that morning, an occasion for rejoicing. He could point to a lesser article, also on the front page, in which Captain McClusky of the New York police reported that although progress had been made in the investigation of Mrs. Adams's death, there were no suspects as yet. The news was mildly reassuring, but Bartow Weeks's advice to Blanche and Roland was not.

Weeks explained that unpleasant publicity was enveloping Roland and that the entire family, including Blanche, would no doubt be drawn into it. They would be vulnerable in many ways and would be exposed to many annoyances, such as the crowd that already was milling about the front door below. Blanche flinched at this bit of news; her intuition of that morning must have been not far off. Weeks went on to suggest that Blanche and Roland move from New York City out to the home of General Molineux in Brooklyn. Such a move would offer privacy and protection, as the Brooklyn police, unlike those of Manhattan, could be trusted in all matters. The move should take place within the next few days, as soon as Blanche was able to pack her trunks, including those that should go into storage.

This was a devastating message for Blanche. Roland, however, seemed nonchalant about the whole matter, merely promising to be helpful in the packing. With a cheerful farewell to Blanche, he and Weeks left her to proceed together to his father's house.

Once alone, Blanche finally got herself dressed so that she could appear downstairs. The hall and parlor were dim. She went to a front window and pulled back one of the drapes, expecting to greet the afternoon winter twilight. What she saw was a motley group of men gathered outside. As quickly as she put her face to the window, two ugly faces on the outside pressed against the pane. They were vultures, she thought as she dropped the drapes and fled to the kitchen. There the cook was sitting before a newspaper—not the *Times*, but the *World*. On seeing Blanche, she tried to hide the paper, as she had been instructed earlier by Alice. But she was not quick enough. "Nein, nein!" she cried, and held the paper behind her back; but Blanche reached around and snatched it from her hands, then ran back upstairs to her room.

Behind her locked door Blanche read the whole story—the poison package mailed to Harry Cornish, athletic director at the Knickerbocker, the suspicions directed against John Adams,

also of the Knickerbocker, and most terrible, the headline story
about the last days of Henry Barnet, her Barney:

HENRY C. BARNET DID RECEIVE POISON BY MAIL AND DID TAKE IT, AS *WORLD* TOLD

As if this knowledge were not devastating enough, Blanche
found buried in the article the worst news of all—Miss Adda
Bates, the nurse who had taken care of Barnet in his last two
days, told reporters that the morning before he died he had received flowers and a written message from a woman. Miss Bates
did not have the letter, however she remembered that Barnet
gazed at the flowers from his bed and remarked, "I wonder how
she knew I was ill."

When Roland returned several hours later, he found the bedroom door locked. He summoned Alice, who had also just returned, having fought her way through the unruly crowd, and
the two of them forced the door. Blanche lay stretched across
her bed, her clothes and hair in wild disarray. She had a wild
look in her eyes, spoke incoherently, and would allow neither
Roland nor Alice to come near her. Roland tried in vain to calm
his wife but was interrupted by Alice: "This is a case of pure hys-
teria; I shall call for the doctor immediately." Humbled by his
inability to control Blanche, Roland chose to leave the room. In
his absence Blanche relaxed.

That night and the next night and the night after that,
Blanche slept peacefully, for each evening the doctor came and
gave her an injection of morphine. It was Roland who packed
the trunks and Alice who helped. By the end of the week
Blanche and Roland were ensconced in temporary quarters at
the Molineux home—Roland in his childhood bedroom and
Blanche in the small guest room down the hall.

Fort Greene Place was a quiet residential street, and the
houses that faced it, erected a decade earlier, were massive and
uncompromising. The Molineux home itself was impressive,
with high stoops reaching up to the doors, long windows of
plate glass, and little balconies of intricate iron grillwork surrounding the major window groupings. Even the little plots of

grass in front of the house, now covered with snow, were bordered by iron fences.

Blanche had been delivered there late one night, alone in the Molineux carriage. It had been arranged that she travel separately from Roland in an effort to avoid detection by the press or the public. Of course the effort was in vain, for the next morning her change of residence was duly noted in two newspapers.

It had been made clear to Blanche that her residence there would be for an indefinite period; neither her father-in-law nor Bartow Weeks would promise how long. It seems that Roland had the least to do with managing her, or his, affairs. He behaved as if he were merely an onlooker in the rather momentous events that were taking place.

At first, the new environment had a beneficial effect on Blanche. She might grieve deeply over the circumstances of poor Barney's death, yet avoid making connections between him and herself or Roland. She came to believe that the slight mention in the news of a floral bouquet and note was an aberration that would not surface again. Even under the miserable circumstances in which she now found herself, she could not help but see some positive aspects of the move. After a few days she began to take comfort from the luxury that this massive home offered—the high ceilings, the polished walnut woodwork, the onyx fireplace mantels, the deep-piled carpets, all strong evidence of a prosperity of which Blanche had always dreamed.

However, it was not long before the terrible severity of the matter began to sink in. First, General Molineux made it clear to Blanche that she should at no time leave the house. The entire family was in seclusion, but Roland and he would have numerous errands on the outside in connection with the defense of their reputation. On the general's orders no newspapers were allowed in the house. Any information regarding events on the outside came from him or from Roland. Roland seemed to take an optimistic but rather disinterested view, as if secure in the knowledge that the truth would come out soon. His father, on the contrary, seemed to be always on the edge of anger, and Blanche was reluctant to press him. Rather she looked for ways to amuse herself in the house, where every matter was discussed in whispers, as if servants or strangers might be listening. The inside shutters on the high windows were permanently closed against the curious, adding a dreariness to the downstairs rooms. One winter morning as the sun tried its best to seep through the slits in the shutters, Blanche sat down at the piano to try a piece or two from her repertoire. It was not long before Roland's mother came storming into the parlor, her eyes blazing: "How dare you make music when the entire house is in mourning; how can you behave so frivolously when our family is being crucified? Have you no heart, no conscience?"

Blanche had always had a certain fear of her mother-in-law, though previously no cross word had ever passed between them—in fact they had exchanged very few words since Blanche had been entombed in the big house. Normally Roland's mother crept through the house in her black dress to be alone in the family sitting room with her mending or stitching. The sudden shock that she had aroused such violent anger in the woman sent Blanche running through the hall and up to her little room, where she dissolved in tears, aware perhaps for the first time of her utter isolation.

If Blanche was unaware of the events on the outside, her sister and brother were not. Speculation as to the relationship between Mrs. Roland Molineux and the deceased Henry Barnet finally found its way into both the *Journal* and the *World*, as well as other daily newspapers. It was first reported that Mrs. Molineux was not known in New York society and probably was an orphan; there was even difficulty in ascertaining her maiden name. As the days wore on, the Chesebrough name also appeared in print, along with a drawing of a photo taken when Blanche sang with the Rubenstein Society. The *World* even printed a short personality sketch:

"It has been said Mrs. Molineux wears a glass eye so perfect it hardly can be detected. This is a mistake, her friends say. According to them there is merely a cast in her eyes with which she was born. It is most discernible when she is excited. Mrs. Molineux, as has been said, is twenty-four years old. She is slightly over the medium height and possesses a graceful figure and carriage. Her friends declare she never has worn stays. Her eyes and hair are dark, her teeth perfect, and her complexion clear. Her nose is aquiline. Her manner is vivacious, but is at all times unassuming. Her friends agree that there are some things inscrutable about her; that they never are able to penetrate beneath the surface; that she stands mentally apart from them all. She is not only highly educated in music, but in other ways. Her diction is perfect and her accent fascinating. During the last year she has dropped out of musical circles. She has evinced all the signs of prosperity and her friends have understood some of her kin were aiding her financially."

Frank Chesebrough, Blanche's brother, felt obligated to come to New York from his home in Rhode Island. Upon his arrival he announced to the newspapers that he alone would speak for the Chesebrough family. He of course made his way to Brooklyn. With General Molineux's permission and in his presence, Blanche and Frank were permitted to spend an hour together in the Molineux parlor.

Not more than a day or two later, reports of Blanche's yachting trip to Maine with her sister, Mrs. Waldo Stearns of Boston, and of the meeting with A. J. Morgan and Roland Molineux on the *Viator* steam yacht appeared in print also. There were printed rumors that as part of the entertainment on board, "mock marriages" had been performed and the couples had then retreated to the various staterooms. There were further rumors that two of the male guests had died mysteriously in the year following the yachting adventure and that A. J. Morgan himself had been mysteriously ill following the cruise. One newspaper even reported that Mrs. Roland Molineux had been engaged to be married to A. J. Morgan. Morgan threatened to sue for libel.

With such stories appearing in the news, it was not surprising that Isia herself promptly came to New York. Certainly she felt responsibility for her younger sister, who was in such a dangerous position. In addition, however, the revelations—only partly true—had effectively destroyed the last tenuous bonds of her marriage. Isia established herself at the Majestic Hotel, while back in Boston her husband Waldo sued for divorce on grounds of adultery. This was bitter medicine for Isia. Her entire adult life had been molded through the reputation and the largess of the Stearns lumbering family. Her friends, her children's education, her style of living and the homes themselves derived from Waldo's means and his connections. It all was unraveling before the eyes of the entire world, yet Isia put her own troubles aside to go to the aid of her beleaguered sister.

Isia arrived in Brooklyn unannounced. It happened to be on one of the rare days when Roland was at home, sequestered in his room as was his custom. General Molineux arranged for the two sisters to meet in the parlor under his careful scrutiny and in addition sent the maid upstairs to alert Roland. He was not prepared for the emotional reunion of the sisters and was almost moved to tears himself. Isia found the situation most objectionable; under no circumstances would she conduct her filial visit under the eyes of the two Molineux men. She spoke frankly and persuasively to the general and prevailed upon him to allow Blanche to return with her to the Majestic Hotel for a few hours.

Roland joined the two women and his father in the parlor, and after exchanging pleasantries, announced that he had an errand in the city. He offered to accompany the charming ladies, as he himself phrased it, to the Majestic and then proceed in the Molineux carriage to his own destination.

The following day it was dutifully reported in the press that Mrs. Roland Molineux had left the house in the company of her husband and an unidentified middle-aged woman. The article went on to state that her husband had returned alone several hours later and to speculate on the state of the marriage.

Throughout the afternoon and evening the two sisters sat in Isia's hotel room commiserating with each other. Isia related to Blanche the story of the yachting cruise as she had read it in Boston—the lies as well as the facts. Then she went on to tell the several newspaper versions of Blanche's friendship with Henry Barnet, which had caused a rift between him and Roland. This information struck like a dagger at Blanche, perhaps because it was so close to the truth. It also offered an explanation for her father-in-law's growing detachment.

Finally Isia told Blanche of the case that was building against Roland, particularly through the efforts of the *Journal*. It was a complicated story, having to do with disguised handwriting and blue stationery and private letter boxes and patent medicines; and each day there was new evidence that pointed toward Roland as the poisoner. This was more than Blanche ever thought she could bear, but she did bear it that evening; with Isia, she at least could know the truth. In the Molineux home either nothing was told or it was cloaked and slanted so that the facts could not be recognized.

The two sisters wept together, and even this was more comfort to Blanche than weeping alone in her little upstairs room. At midnight she returned to her great stone prison—stronger than she had left it and relieved that she no longer shared a bed with Roland.

Roland's home away from home, the place where he spent a good many hours each day, was the private office of Bartow Weeks. Weeks was devoting all of his time to matters associated with Roland's interests, particularly as these related to the increasingly damaging newspaper stories that were appearing. During the early months of 1899, both Weeks and his partner were forced to abandon most of their other clients in favor of the son of General Molineux; for this sacrifice they were well compensated. The general had vowed publicly that he would spare no expense in defense of his son's name. When the affair was finally over, more than three years later, it was purported that he had indeed spent his entire fortune, most of it in attorneys' fees.

The law firm of Battle and Weeks, even in its first years, catered to the more privileged business interests in New York.

Each of the partners was active in the better clubs as well as the appropriate community activities. Both chose their social acquaintances with care.

One might believe therefore that their law offices reflected the opulence and extravagance of their society and their clients; however such was not the case. In those days, unlike today, the law profession generally downplayed its material success. The offices of even the greatest and most prosperous lawyers in the country were modest in size and furnishings, however extravagant the personal lives of the lawyers themselves might be. Perhaps the profession wished to display an image of restraint in material matters, which clients could interpret as reflecting on their fees.

So it was with the office of Battle and Weeks. To reach them, clients walked up two flights of stairs and entered through a windowed oak door. In the year 1899, a lone male secretary sat behind a single desk in a very large reception room. Along the outer walls were several wooden chairs and an unupholstered wooden settee, all in mission-style oak. Between this reception area and the secretary's desk was a simply designed wooden partition, no higher than the desk. To either side were wooden swinging gates, through which one walked to enter the office of Mr. Battle, on the left, or of Mr. Weeks, on the right. The only other furniture in this large area consisted of two wooden file cabinets, each with several file drawers. A visitor would certainly perceive the outer office of Messrs. Battle and Weeks as well-maintained, but spartan. The private offices of the two lawyers were slightly less austere. Mr. Battle's was somewhat larger than that of his partner, for he was the senior member of the firm. In all other respects the offices were identical — bookcases filled with law books lining the walls, large mahogany desks and chairs and a simple oak table.

Roland's daily routine usually began with an early visit to Bartow Weeks's office. There he and his counselor would sit — Roland at the table and Weeks at his desk — going over the morning *Journal* in an attempt to track down whatever malicious gossip had been printed that day. It was a strenuous and time-consuming task. For this reason Roland was spending very little time at his Brooklyn home and no time at all in the Herrmann factory or offices.

When the press reported that a man in a red beard had purchased the silver poison-bottle holder at Hartdegen's jewelry store in Newark, Roland and his counselor visited the store to assure the public that the clerk could not identify Roland as the purchaser. When Miss Emma Miller, the clerk, suggested that the beard might have been a false beard, Roland and his counselor visited several local wig stores to assure the public that Roland could not be identified by the proprietors as the purchaser of a red beard. When the press reported that a man had rented a private letter box at Joseph Koch's establishment under the name of H. Cornish, Roland and his counselor visited Koch's establishment to assure the public that Koch could not identify Roland as the man who had leased the box. It was a strange way for a defense attorney to spend his days, for it was the District Attorney, not the newspaper-reading public, who would present a case against his client if that were in the offing.

It was difficult for Weeks to know just what was in the offing. Somehow the fact that both Harry Cornish and his cousin Florence Rodgers were divorced lent a suspicious note to their common proximity in the apartment of Florence's mother, Kate Adams. The *World* suggested that they might have plotted against Mrs. Adams, though a motive had not really surfaced, and that Cornish's tasting of the poison was part of the ruse. Since no one could identify the lessee of Koch's letter box or the buyer of the silver bottle holder, it was no more difficult to accuse Cornish of engineering the whole letter box scenario in an effort to implicate Roland than it was the other way around. At least this was the gist of the *World's* story.

Both Roland and Cornish had been invited to the police department to give samples of their handwriting. This part of the investigation became more interesting and more complicated as various patent medicine firms around the country discovered letters in their files from "H. Cornish" or "H. C. Barnet" or "Roland Molineux." The eager press had indeed provided the police with a bonanza of "Barnet" and "Cornish" letters.

Harry Cornish was doing his utmost to cooperate with the District Attorney's office. He not only offered the most intimate details of his own life, but also passed on every bit of information and gossip about Roland that he could recall from his years at the Knickerbocker Athletic Club. This information included the incident two years earlier when Roland had received a desperate phone call in the gymnasium from Mamie Melando — Cornish even remembered her name — who had been incarcerated by the Newark police. He recalled how Roland had hurriedly dressed and left immediately for New Jersey. Cornish intimated that the Melando girl's arrest had something to do with a brothel and that Roland may have been involved with it also. The effect of this information in the hands of the District Attorney was not what Cornish might have expected. The entry of Mamie into the case would have far more impact on Roland's predicament than the mere character assassination in which Cornish was engaging.

Weeks and Roland also spent time with the Assistant District Attorney. In fact Roland invited him over to Newark to view his private apartment and laboratory, complete with his working chemicals. It was part of Weeks's strategy to provide all of the assistance requested, and more, in the hope of gaining insight into the direction that the case would take. Whom did the District Attorney consider to be the prime suspect — Cornish or Molineux? That was the question that even the best of the Tammany watchers could not answer.

Among the "Cornish" letters that came into the hands of the District Attorney were two written on a distinctive stationery — quality paper of robin's-egg blue with three silver entwined crescents in the upper center. The *World* one afternoon printed a facsimile of the crescents and drew a plausible connection between this stationery and Cornish's poison package. It probably occurred to Roland that Blanche had more than once received messages from him on such paper, but fortunately Blanche was well-insulated from the daily news.

On the morning following the appearance of the three crescents in the *World*, a damaging incident took place in the outer office of Bartow Weeks. He and Roland were sitting together in his private office going over the day's newspapers when they were interrupted by the secretary, who announced that a young woman in the outer office was inquiring after Attorney Weeks. When Weeks asked the name of the visitor, the secretary replied: "Mary Melando."

Roland leapt from his chair as if he were about to be assaulted and withdrew to the back of the room. "Get rid of her. That woman has no business in this building. I will under no circumstances see her; get rid of her now!"

Roland was so agitated and spoke so loudly that Weeks himself stood up and closed the door to his office. Then he turned to Roland and cautioned him to be more restrained, reminding him that the woman of whom he spoke had not asked to see him. It was Weeks whom she wished to see, and Weeks intended to find out what she wanted. Leaving Roland alone in his office, he went out with his secretary and closed the door once more. Beyond the front desk, in the reception area, sat the young woman, poorly dressed but with a certain smartness about her, probably due to the bright red scarf she wore and the matching feather in her hat. Weeks pushed through the little swinging gate and walked over to her; she stood up and offered her hand. Could she speak with him privately for a few minutes? Weeks suggested sitting down where they were as his office was occupied by others who could not be disturbed.

In a soft unaffected voice Mamie Melando introduced herself as an old friend of Roland's—a friend of almost ten years' standing. She went on to explain that she had worked for Roland while she was in his father's firm and also later at the Herrmann factory, where she became intimately acquainted with his apartment. Weeks was at first inclined sympathetically toward this woman whose status appeared well below his own; but as his awareness of her association with Roland heightened, he carefully drew away. Finally he interrupted to ask the reason for this visit. Mamie was quite candid: "Sir, I am in desperate need of money. My health is poor and I have not been able to find work for more than a year. You in your position cannot imagine how difficult life can be for someone like me. I have with me items that perhaps you would like to have; I could sell them to you, you see."

With that she reached into her ample bag and took out a flat package wrapped in ordinary brown paper. She opened the paper carefully and uncovered three envelopes and three sheets of stationery—robin's-egg blue paper with three silver crescents entwined in the upper center. No doubt Weeks was not pleased with what he saw. "Where did you get this paper?" he demanded.

"I took it from Mr. Molineux's drawer when I was alone in his rooms more than a year ago," Mamie replied. "I took this paper because Mr. Molineux sometimes let me take things that I needed. I took only a few sheets, which I doubt he even missed, for there were many other sheets there also."

Weeks may have wished to wrest the paper from the woman's hands, but he was an intelligent lawyer and he therefore knew that even without the paper in her possession, she could do Roland infinite harm. He would try a different approach: "Madam, you and Mr. Molineux were at one time friends. You must know that he is in great danger right now, falsely implicated in a murder due to malicious stories in certain of the newspapers. No doubt Mr. Molineux was kind to you at one time. You could do him a kindness in return by going home and forgetting about this paper. It would be best to destroy it as it can help no one, least of all Mr. Molineux."

Weeks then ended the conversation with a cold "Good morning," and rose from his chair to return to his office. Mamie was left alone with the secretary, who continued with his work as if no one were there. Finally Mamie stood up, wrapped her coat and scarf about her, and left the office. Once outside she reached into her bag, took out the paper and began shredding it with her ungloved hands as she walked, letting each piece be caught by the cold, wet wind.

THIRTEEN

The Inquest

By the laws of the State of New York, the District Attorney was required to call together a coroner's jury in the event of a suspected murder. The coroner of the borough—in this case the Borough of Manhattan—presided over the proceedings, out of which an indictment would presumably come forth.

Six weeks after the death of Katherine Adams, Colonel Asa Bird Gardiner, in his role as District Attorney, did indeed convene the coroner's jury; presumably his office had evidence that could lead to the indictment of at least one man or woman. Roland Molineux's name was most frequently mentioned in the major newspapers, but the names of Florence Rodgers, Harry Cornish and others connected with the Knickerbocker Athletic Club were also cited, particularly by those who believed strongly in the integrity of the younger Molineux. Because the District Attorney and the police had been so noncommittal as to the direction of their investigation, there was much room for speculation.

The coroner's jury was convened on Thursday morning, the ninth of February, at the Criminal Courts Building, and was presided over by Coroner Edward Hart. The day also marked the beginning of a winter snowstorm that would set records in terms of temperatures, winds, and snow.

On the same morning, in the midst of the snowstorm, a second noteworthy event took place, also initiated by Colonel Gardiner. He had earlier petitioned the court to exhume the body of Henry Barnet in Greenwood Cemetery, and the judicial order had just been issued. A small group gathered about the grave to witness the exhumation, including the appropriate city officials, Barnet's brother Edmond, a chemist, and members of the press. The coffin was taken to one of the cemetery buildings, where vital organs were removed. The chemist completed an analysis of the organs on the spot, confirming the presence of cyanide of mercury. Barnet's body was then returned to its grave, all within the matter of a few hours.

It was the inquest, however, that dominated the public's attention that day. Earlier it had been announced that entry would be by card only. Thus immense social and political pressures had been put on the District Attorney's office by those who wished to obtain one of these coveted items. On this opening morning those with cards were seated, but others continued to mill about noisily outside the courtroom. As it turned out, the first day's business was not all that interesting. The twelve jurors were sworn in, and Coroner Hart made a long speech admonishing them as to the seriousness of their deliberations, then explained to them the anticipated schedule for the inquest. Having taken care of these preliminaries, he turned the proceedings over to the District Attorney.

Prior to the inquest, Colonel Gardiner himself had been the principal spokesman for the District Attorney's office. However for reasons of his own, probably political, he decided to maintain a low profile at the inquest. Though present on this first and succeeding days, he relinquished control to his assistant, James Osborne.

For Osborne, this opportunity was to become the foundation on which he would build his reputation, first as a prosecuting attorney and later as an expert in criminal law. Osborne was just

40 years of age at the time, a handsome man with an aristocratic nose, born and bred in Charlotte, North Carolina. There he had obtained a bachelor's degree from Davidson College and then had come north to study law at Columbia Law School. In 1896, just at the time that Bartow Weeks left the District Attorney's office, Osborne joined the staff there. Colonel Gardiner recognized Osborne's excellent qualities very early and made him a direct assistant. Osborne was indeed a very hard worker, methodical and thorough. He had another side, also, which would distinguish him in the months that were to follow, and this was his bent toward the theatrical, almost to the point of ferocity. This latter quality, for which he was to be fondly remembered in later years, was precisely that which Blanche Molineux would neither forget nor forgive throughout her long life.

On the first day of the inquest, Osborne played his role quietly, merely explaining the framework within which he would call his witnesses and listing the names of each one, including Florence Rodgers, Harry Cornish, Roland Molineux and Blanche Molineux. These last two names caused a stir in the courtroom, for this was the first open acknowledgment that the District Attorney had made the connection between Roland Molineux and the deceased Kate Adams, a connection that had already been accepted by much of New York's reading public. This bit of information caused the representatives of the press to leave en masse; it would provide a tasty morsel for the late editions. By mid-afternoon the jury was excused and the remaining onlookers scattered into the cold streets. That night the temperature dropped to minus four degrees, the coldest in twenty-seven years.

By eight-thirty Friday morning, frigid as it was, the crowds at the door of the courtroom were so demanding that it was deemed prudent to allow them to enter and be seated. (For the remaining days of the inquest, entry was on a first-come basis—the cards that had been issued with such discretion ceased to have any value.) Long before Coroner Hart entered the courtroom the counsels' table below his bench was as bustling as a beehive. On one side sat Osborne and Gardiner, their papers spread before them, engrossed in conversation. The other side and the ends of the table were occupied by the attorneys representing certain of the witnesses, those perhaps who had the most to win or lose at the inquest.

Counsels for Florence Rodgers and Harry Cornish gravitated toward each other, as if their clients' interests were complementary. Roland Molineux's interests were also represented, by his friend Bartow Weeks and Weeks's partner, George Gordon Battle. These two men would appear daily together throughout the entire inquest.

The firm of Battle and Weeks, barely two years old, had already made a name for itself on Wall Street. The partnership was formed in 1897 after Bartow Weeks left the office of the District Attorney to enter private practice. George Battle's background was rather unlike that of his partner and remarkably similar to that of James Osborne. Battle too was a southerner—born in Edgecomb County, North Carolina, shortly after the Great War. His home was Cool Spring Plantation, one of the great antebellum mansions of the South. He studied at the universities of North Carolina and Virginia before coming north to study law at Columbia. Like Osborne, he had chosen to remain in the North, in fact had gone directly from Columbia law school to the position of Assistant District Attorney. One might have presumed that Battle and Osborne could form a compatible partnership out of their common heritage. Instead George Battle, the consummate southern gentleman, had joined with Bartow Weeks of the spirited athletic club set to form a partnership that would establish the reputations of both.

Roland Molineux sat with his father just behind his attorneys. The four chatted among themselves, and General Molineux made it a point to pass the time of day with Colonel Gardiner, his old comrade-in-arms. Roland avoided any glance in the direction of Cornish, and Cornish did likewise. Though the two men sat within a few feet of each other, they might as well have been on different planets.

When Coroner Hart finally took his place in the courtroom and brought down the gavel, James Osborne stepped forward, secure in the knowledge that he alone would orchestrate the entire drama that was to unfold there. He turned to Hart and announced his first witness—Harry Cornish. Cornish was a tall, well-built man who looked every bit the part of an athletic director. For this appearance he had attired himself as conservatively as possible, as if his dress might camouflage the hot temper that he frequently had difficulty in controlling. As James Osborne began his interrogation, it became clear that he did not intend to make it easy for Harry Cornish. In fact it almost appeared as though Osborne were trying to cause the witness to lose his composure, and perhaps his credibility. Osborne used a technique that would become his trademark throughout the inquest and later in the trial. He fired a series of questions at the witness, in rapid succession, introducing new subjects in the middle of the witness's testimony, interrupting the witness in his testimony, returning to previous questions, and thus confusing the witness to such a degree that even the most candid might be caught in contradictory statements.

Osborne kept Cornish on the stand for the entire day, questioning him not only about Knickerbocker Athletic Club politics and his long-standing disagreements with Roland Molineux, but also about his past professional life, his social contacts, his relationship with his former wife, with his deceased aunt, Kate Adams, with his cousin Florence Rodgers and with others in the house where Mrs. Adams had died. When it was apparent that Cornish was becoming exhausted and impatient, Osborne grew more strident, berating him for inconsistencies in his testimony and finally requesting that he return again on the following Monday to clear up certain mysteries that he had unwittingly introduced. James Osborne had done his utmost to uncover the worst in Cornish. An unbiased onlooker would surely have wondered to what end this would lead. Colonel Gardiner, who took voluminous notes throughout Cornish's testimony, made himself available to reporters afterward. He shook his head at the poor performance of the witness and was quoted as saying, "Cornish had better take care."

The weekend brought continued blizzard conditions to the

city, already short of coal from the previous storm. By Monday morning, when the inquest was reconvened, snow had fallen continuously for twenty-four hours. No trains were running and the city was isolated from the outside world. Governor Theodore Roosevelt, over the telegraph, had ordered the armories of the city and state to be opened to provide shelter and food for those who were without. One might have expected that the proceedings would be postponed, for the public transportation system had ceased to operate, but such was not the case. James Osborne was just reaching his stride, and he had no intention of allowing an interruption in his plan.

The storm notwithstanding, the courtroom was again filled by ten o'clock in the morning. All of the principals were there—Coroner Hart, the twelve jurors, Osborne, Gardiner, Cornish, Florence Rodgers, the Molineuxs, father and son, with their attorneys, and others who expected to be called as witnesses that day. Osborne finished his questioning of Cornish, reminding the bewildered witness that there would be more questions for him before the proceedings were completed and leaving the impression that Cornish might be holding back key evidence. Then he called his second witness, Roland Molineux.

Roland stepped up to the jury box and bowed formally to Coroner Hart before taking his place. His impeccable attire and gratuitous politeness set him apart from the witness who had preceded him and from most of those who would follow. His dignified manner seemed to have an effect on his interrogator, who began by treating him with great deference, even apologizing for asking the kinds of questions that this inquiry required. To some of the reporters it appeared that James Osborne was going out of his way to placate the man they believed to be the obvious suspect in the Adams murder. Those who perceived Osborne so would soon learn that they had greatly underestimated this formidable prosecutor.

James Osborne kept Roland on the stand most of Monday afternoon. He inquired into Roland's past—his education, his expertise in chemistry, and his various positions in the Raynolds and Herrmann paint firms. He asked about the yachting trip on

which Roland had met his bride and about Roland's friendship
with Henry Barnet, particularly as to any difficulties he might
have encountered during the courtship of his wife. Roland was
patient and cooperative, and always gracious. He indicated that
his life was an open book and that he was pleased to share perti-
nent details in the interest of clearing any suspicion that might
rest on him.

When Roland returned to the witness box on Tuesday, it became evident very quickly that the going would not be quite so
easy. Osborne began by directing his questions toward Roland's
athletic pursuits, which led directly into the affairs of the Knickerbocker and specifically to Roland's difficulties with the athletic director of the club. Roland patiently outlined the problems
he had encountered with Cornish—foul language in the pool,
insubordination at the time of the Amateur Circus, unautho-
rized use of the club stationery, and other attempts by Cornish
to enhance his status in the club beyond that of an employee.
Roland readily admitted his frustration in not obtaining Cornish's dismissal and he acknowledged his subsequent resignation. Osborne then led Roland into a summing up of his troubles with Cornish.

"How long were you trying to have Cornish removed from the
club?" he began.

Roland replied in a forthright manner, "Since the time of the
Amateur Circus."

Osborne inquired further: "What year was that?"

Roland remembered exactly: "1897—the twenty-ninth of
April."

Osborne led him further: "You felt that you wanted him removed?"

Roland's response took on a moral tone: "I felt that it was for
the good of the club. He could undo more good in a minute
than I could do for that club in a year."

"What do you mean by that?" Osborne interjected.

"I mean that I was entertaining there, spending money there
and putting new members in the club, whenever I could, and
trying to make a gentlemen's club of it, and Cornish was work-

ing against me." Roland's reply was memorable for its candidness.

What more could be said? So must Osborne have concluded, for he suddenly ceased to inquire about Cornish and rather turned his questions to the acknowledged friendship between Roland and Henry Barnet. In doing so he became a little contentious, introducing for the first time a touch of sarcasm.

"Did you know Henry Barnet?" Osborne began.

"Very well," replied Roland.

"Was he a warm personal friend of yours?"

"He was indeed," snapped Roland, somewhat petulantly.

Osborne's voice now took on a syrupy tone. "For how many years had he been a warm personal friend of yours?"

"He was a warm personal friend during the time I lived at the club," Roland responded.

"Lived at the Knickerbocker Athletic Club?" queried the prosecutor.

Roland clarified his statement. "He lived at the Knickerbocker Athletic Club and I met him there often, even when I no longer lived there."

Osborne continued to play his theme. "And he continued to be a warm personal friend of yours up to the time of his death?"

"He did."

"He did?"

"He did."

An expectant silence enveloped the courtroom. James Osborne's tone of voice and choice of words seemed to promise that he had something up his sleeve, so to speak. He paused as if to amplify the silence, then mounted his charge. "Do you know of any quarrel that Henry Barnet had with anybody in the Knickerbocker Athletic Club?"

Roland deftly turned the question: "I know he had a great deal of criticism to make about the affairs of the club, about the way the baths were run, and the bar and restaurant. We all made criticisms when we were on the house committee."

Osborne played along on Roland's digression for the moment by inquiring further, "Was he on the house committee?"

The answer was obvious: "He was, yes."

Osborne tried again. "Can you imagine any motive that anybody in that club would have to send poison to Mr. Barnet?"

"I can't," replied Roland. For the next hour the prosecutor sparred with his witness, but for all of the words very little information was forthcoming.

"Do you know, as a matter of fact, from closely connected evidence or hearsay, that he was poisoned?"

"I have read it in the newspapers."

"Did you never hear that Barnet was poisoned?"

"I did not."

"From anybody?"

"No, sir; I have never heard the statement made that he was poisoned."

"And the only information that you have that Barnet was poisoned was from the newspapers?"

"That is all I have."

"Did I understand you to say, with tears almost in your eyes, that Barnet was a warm personal friend of yours?"

"You didn't see any tears."

"I said almost. How many days was he sick?"

"I don't know."

"At that time were you a member of the Knickerbocker Athletic Club?"

"I was not."

"How long had you been out of it at that time?"

"I had been out nearly a year."

"How often did you see Barnet?"

"I saw him several times; I can't tell you the exact number; I never counted them."

"If he was a warm personal friend of yours, wasn't it quite likely you would see him frequently?"

"Not necessarily; it was in the summertime, when Mr. Barnet had gone to the Atlantic Yacht Club to live, and I had gone to Europe."

It was getting late in the day. Interest was waning, as if James Osborne had promised the crowd something that he had not de-

livered. A few of the onlookers left the courtroom, for the verbal
exchange between prosecutor and witness seemed to indicate
that the prosecutor was more bluff than substance. Indeed if
Osborne had been trying to draw out of Roland details of a
quarrel with Barnet, he had failed.

Osborne must have presumed that everybody, especially Roland, was weary of the endless and somewhat fruitless questioning. Osborne fell silent for close to a minute. He sipped his water, straightened his tie and stood a little taller, as if to empha-
size the fact that he was introducing a new dimension into the
testimony. Then he began by suggesting to Roland that a romantic triangle existed among "two warm personal friends" and
a woman, namely Blanche Chesebrough. It might have been
asked at the time, and certainly was asked later, what this had
to do with the death of Katherine Adams. If such a question occurred to James Osborne, it certainly did not deter him. He
flung his questions in rapid succession at Roland, and Roland
parried them as best he could in an effort to negate the prosecutor's assertions.

"Mr. Molineux, I want to know whether Barnet knew your
wife?"

"He did; he knew her before she was my wife."

"When did he meet her?"

"You mean, Mr. Osborne, when did I present him to her?"
(Roland would not be caught in a breach of etiquette, particularly not at the behest of James Osborne.)

"Yes. When did you present him to Miss Chesebrough?"

"I presented Barnet to Miss Chesebrough at the Metropolitan
Opera House; it was in the fall of 1897—I don't know the date."

"Do you know whether or not your wife was ever in love with
Mr. Barnet?"

"I think she admired him as a friend."

"Did she ever have any pronounced affection for him, to your
knowledge?"

"Not that I know of, sir."

"Were you in any way jealous of Barnet?"

"I was not."

"Did you ever express yourself as being hostile to Barnet at any time in your life?"

"Never."

"Did you ever speak to anyone about Barnet's attention to your wife?"

"I never did."

"To any human being?"

"Never."

"Did you ever complain of his attention to her?"

"Never, sir."

"Did you know whether he ever visited her at the house of Alice Bellinger before your marriage?"

"I know he did."

"Were you aware of that fact?"

"I was."

"And was it with your approval?"

"Yes, sir; he had a perfect right to call on her."

"Did you ever resent in any way his calling on her?"

"I never did."

"Were you at that time engaged to be married to your wife?"

"I was not."

"At that time were you paying her attention that looked to be anything of that sort?"

"I paid attention to her ever since I knew her."

It was a rapid exchange and Roland was flushed to the point of perspiring. Osborne himself was at fever pitch until he paused to wipe his face with his handkerchief. When he next spoke, his voice had cooled. "Mr. Molineux, I regret exceedingly that I feel compelled to ask you these questions."

Roland too relaxed in response. "It is in the interest of justice and I am perfectly willing and ready to do what you ask."

The respite was short, however, for Osborne continued by digging deeper. "Will you please state when you became engaged to be married to your wife?"

"In the latter part of September, last fall."

"And you were engaged to her for how long?"

"Two months."

156

"Did you tell Barnet you were engaged?"

"I did not; I did not tell anyone, except my family."

"When is the last time Barnet called on your wife, to your knowledge?"

"Either in the latter part of April or the first part of May, last year."

"Since that time?"

"Not to my knowledge."

"Just as far back as May of 1898?"

"That is correct; never to my knowledge were calls exchanged between them after May of 1898."

"Mr. Molineux, did you know whether there were any letters or anything of that kind passed between them?"

"Not to my personal knowledge."

"Have you heard of any?"

"I believe that they wrote to one another throughout the summer; I don't know how often, or what the letters were."

This shift by Roland, from the denial of any letters to the possibility of letters being exchanged, betrayed a growing suspicion on his part that Osborne was in possession of such letters. In any case, it did not go unnoticed by Osborne, and he concluded that the time had come to show his hand. He drew from his pocket a paper and passed it over to Roland, who recognized it immediately as Blanche's stationery.

"I show you a letter, Mr. Molineux, which is marked for identification. Is that in your wife's handwriting?"

Before responding, Roland read the entire note while Osborne waited patiently. When he had finished reading, he looked up at the prosecutor and replied: "Yes, to the best of my knowledge."

"In that case," Osborne continued, "would you care to read aloud from the letter, for the benefit of the jurors?"

Roland began to read aloud with great deliberation: "I am distressed to learn of your illness. I arrived here Saturday, and am so exceedingly sorry to know that you have been so indisposed. Won't you let me know when you are able to be about? I want very much to see you. Is it that you do not believe me?

157

If you would but let me prove to you my sincerity. Don't be cross any more, and accept, I pray you, my very best wishes. Yours, Blanche."

One must believe that Roland had never dreamed such a letter existed and that he was chagrined by the intimacy that it implied. Though his voice quavered not one bit while he read from it, the moment he had finished, he thrust the letter toward Osborne, as if to detach himself from it at the earliest possible moment. General Molineux had been leaning forward to catch every word concerning Henry Barnet, but the reading of the letter was more than he could handle with equanimity. The old man's head fell forward on his hands and it required a tap on the arm by George Battle to bring him into an upright position again.

Osborne found the scene to his liking and continued with the letter exposed in his hand. He asked of his witness, "Had you any reason to believe that Barnet was in love with Miss Chesebrough?"

Roland was still prepared to deny the obvious. "It is impossible to tell his state of mind; if he was, I don't blame him; no, I had no reason to think so."

The prosecutor was not convinced. "Then you had no reason that you can recollect to be jealous of Mr. Barnet?"

"Jealous of him?" queried Roland, as if to indicate that the question was ridiculous.

"Yes," replied Osborne, assuring Roland that there was nothing ridiculous at all in the question.

"No, sir," Roland answered emphatically, continuing his attempt to make light of the letter and its ramifications.

Osborne tried again, from a slightly different direction. "Did you ever complain to Miss Chesebrough about the attentions of Barnet?"

"Never," stated Roland flatly.

Osborne was undaunted. "Did you ever ask her to ask him to cease his attentions?"

Roland's entire body betrayed his annoyance at the direction of Osborne's questions. He looked the prosecutor in the eye and replied coldly, "I never did."

Osborne now became more specific: "Would this letter indicate to your mind a degree of intimacy between Barnet and Miss Chesebrough that you were not aware of?"

It was clear that Roland would eventually have to explain the letter away one way or another and so he gave it a try. "No, sir; we all called one another by the first name; Barnet called me 'Moli,' and I called him 'Barney,' and I think Miss Chesebrough did so too; we were all good friends. When Barnet called, I often was with him, and when I called, he often was with me. I might say, Mr. Osborne, that this is a characteristic letter of Miss Chesebrough; she writes in that informal style."

Roland's words were not all that convincing, apparently not even to himself, for he finished with an inflection that seemed to ask for the prosecutor's approval, something Osborne had no intention of giving. Rather he opened the letter and selected a group of words that he wished to amplify. " 'If you would but let me prove to you my sincerity'; do you know what Miss Chesebrough might have meant by these words?"

Roland was becoming very nervous, looking back and forth from his lawyers to his father, none of whom were in any position to respond. His voice, so firm and forthright a few minutes earlier, was now hardly audible: "No, sir, I may speculate on it, but I don't know what she meant at all."

Osborne seemed delighted with the response and tried to probe still deeper. In a voice filled with mock pique, he quoted again from the letter in his hand: " 'Don't be cross any more'; do you know of any difficulty between Mr. Barnet and Miss Chesebrough that could have prompted such words?"

Roland shook his head. "I don't know, sir," was all that he could say.

One can only surmise that Roland was contemplating for himself the meaning of the words, not only as they might affect the prejudices of the jurors, but also as they might influence the expected testimony of Blanche, which was already of some concern to his counsel as well as to himself.

Thereupon, James Osborne excused his prize witness and called another. Roland took his place next to his father and immediately conferred with the Messrs. Battle and Weeks, in loud whispers. As far as the lawyers were concerned, it had been a bad day for their client. It was agreed that Bartow Weeks should visit Blanche that evening and inform her of the events of the day. General Molineux's desire to shield his daughter-in-law from the trauma of the inquest was threatening to jeopardize Roland's interests. The Molineuxs were in this together, and as this day's testimony proved, Blanche would not be excluded.

FOURTEEN

Indictment

Of Roland's and of Cornish's testimony Blanche heard nothing. Instead she remained at Fort Greene Place, cloistered in the large house with her mother-in-law, while Roland and his father spent their days on Manhattan. Before and after the daily hearings at the inquest, they met with their attorneys to review and to anticipate the moves of James Osborne. In their absence Roland's mother, always dressed in full mourning attire, set the sombre mood in the household. Under these circumstances Blanche found it less oppressive to while away the time in the tiny room that she now called her own. There she read, wrote notes to Alice and her sister, and more often just contemplated. In such isolation, she was prone to exaggerate her unfortunate situation. As the days wore on, she became convinced that Roland's parents believed her to be the "woman poisoner." The general, totally preoccupied with the events at the inquest, completely ignored those around him at home, even as he shared the evening meal with them. Blanche misinterpreted this preoccupation, judging his distant behavior to be a confirmation of his belief in her guilt. Blanche's spirits sank so low that she truly wished herself dead rather than despised by the only living man for whom she felt any affection or respect.

The evening before Blanche's scheduled appearance at the inquest, Bartow Weeks paid a call. He informed Blanche matter-of-factly that her letter to Barnet, received as he lay dying, had been introduced and read into the court record. Blanche was almost disbelieving. So Barney's brother had delivered it into the hands of the authorities. What kind of brother would do that? Oh, if she had only wrested it from him at the funeral, she lamented. Weeks carefully reviewed for Blanche Roland's testimony as it related to this letter and to his friendship with Barnet and with Blanche. Implicit in Week's careful repetition of Roland's words was the obligation of Blanche to uphold his credibility. She listened intently but acknowledged nothing. Blanche never fully grasped just how it stood between her and Bartow Weeks.

Demoralized as she was over the publicity surrounding her letter, Blanche was besieged by greater fears that the prosecutor might know more than had been revealed so far — that some member of the Opera Club might have related the events of the late-night party on Washington Square, or that someone at the Knickerbocker, possibly John Adams himself, might have described her last visit to Barney, or even that knowledge of her many intimacies with Barney might have escaped the walls of Alice's home. These uncertainties were so onerous that a feeling of relief descended on Blanche when Weeks informed her that she should appear at the inquest the following morning, February 15.

Blanche had expected that she would attend the inquest alone, that is without her mother-in-law; but the older woman would have none of it. Thus the two women arrived together, each dressed in black and each on one arm of the general.

The news that Mrs. Roland Molineux was to be called as a witness that day had engendered renewed speculation among the reading public. Prior to the inquest the District Attorney's office had hinted broadly that a woman must have been involved in the poisonings, but the testimony so far had in no way pointed to the obvious woman candidate, Florence Rodgers. In anticipation of Blanche's arrival, there was an even larger crowd than usual, the majority of whom could not gain entrance to the courtroom. For many of them it was sufficient just to have a glimpse of the woman who seemed to fit so neatly into the scenario being constructed around a deadly romantic triangle.

James Osborne, for reasons of his own, chose to delay his questioning of Blanche and thus to let her be a spectator for a time. He preferred to fill the rest of the week with peripheral witnesses, who gave unenlightening answers to rather obvious questions. For instance, Dr. Hitchcock, who had tried in vain to revive Kate Adams and who had ministered to Cornish at the same time, was questioned in such detail that both jurors and onlookers became bored to the point of restlessness. The coroner who had arrived shortly after Mrs. Adams's death was further questioned about the same details. Florence Rodgers was also interrogated and in fact treated rather rudely by Osborne, but to any listener it was clear that she was able to shed no light on a motive for anyone wishing to poison either her mother or her cousin Harry. The inquest was beginning to drag and the newspapers were becoming increasingly critical of the lengthy proceedings.

All that changed when Blanche was finally called to the witness stand on February 22. That morning she was well aware that this must be the day, though she had not been forewarned. The crowd was particularly unruly, more like a mob, as General Molineux guided her and her mother-in-law through the corridors to the courtroom. Roland walked well ahead, flanked by Battle and Weeks. As Blanche entered the warm courtroom, she began to feel faint and to falter, no doubt from the stale air as much as from the excitement. The room had already been packed to the doors for several hours. George Battle looked back toward Blanche and immediately left Roland's side to assist her. He abandoned the southern courtesy for which he was well-known and aggressively pushed people aside to help the ladies through to their seats. Blanche found it odd that Roland and Bartow Weeks had not bothered to assist.

Once in her seat Blanche put herself somewhat in order. Each day that she had attended the proceedings she had made a great effort to dress elegantly within the constraints of the occasion and to comport herself appropriately. As a result the press had so far mentioned her name only with the most appreciative adjectives. She wished it to be so even on this day when her entire life would possibly be laid out before the heartless mob. On this morning she had fortuitously selected a plain black gown, over which she wore her black coat trimmed in Persian lamb. For a change she had modified an older black hat so that it looked like a turban, setting it forward on her head and decorating it with fresh silk violets, then tying about it a chiffon scarf. She carried the large sable muff which she had carried on previous days and which the newspapers had already described in detail, marveling at the sable tails which dangled from it.

Blanche sat quietly, ignoring the commotion about her, as if she could avoid James Osborne's questions by being as unobtrusive as possible. But that was not to be her lot this day, for Osborne promptly called her name — Mrs. Roland B. Molineux. Blanche rose and walked over to the witness stand, her terror masked by an unnatural haughtiness. Murmurs passed throughout the courtroom as all eyes followed the attractive young woman, who the onlookers hoped could furnish the missing link in the poison murders. Blanche entered the witness box near Coroner Hart and acknowledged his office by nodding to him after she sat down. Distracted by the noise in the room, he barely noticed this gesture of respect. Rather he picked up his gavel and pounded it so loudly that Blanche recoiled in her seat.

The action for which so many had waited was about to begin. Blanche was called to her feet, a Bible was held out before her and she was obliged to place one hand upon it while raising the other. Never having been in such a position before, she mistakenly interpreted this customary swearing in as a sign that she might be the accused. She was trembling visibly as she sat down.

Immediately thereafter, James Osborne walked nonchalantly over to her, placed his hand on the railing of the witness box, and cast a benign glance at her, as if to put the witness at ease. There was dead silence in the courtroom. He began innocuously enough by inquiring as to where Blanche had lived in New York since the time she met Roland. He wanted to know how she came to live at Alice Bellinger's home and who her family were, all questions to which Blanche could respond openly and courteously. It occurred to Blanche that Osborne might not be so bad after all, particularly if he filled the time with such silly questions as these. She began to relax and even to behave a little coyly with the good-looking moustachioed prosecutor, that is until he changed his tack.

He paused a moment and reached for a glass of water, from which he took a sip. He then pulled an envelope from his vest pocket and laid it on the table next to his glass. Taking a step closer to the witness box, he began to speak in a softer voice, one might say more intimately: "Mrs. Molineux, describe in your own way your relationship with Mr. Barnet."

Blanche drew back against her chair, thought a moment, and then replied cautiously: "Mr. Molineux presented Mr. Barnet to me in 1897. Being a friend of Mr. Molineux, he called several times, and at the suggestion of Mr. Molineux I attended the Amateur Circus at the Knickerbocker Athletic Club with Mr. Barnet. There was simply a friendship existing between us. I don't know what else to say, Mr. Osborne; that is all."

As if not quite believing this matter-of-fact explanation, Osborne continued with a touch of impatience: "State the occasions he called."

Blanche perceived a glint in the prosecutor's eyes and she took it to be a sign that he was all-knowing. She felt the urge to faint, to avoid the truth that she feared would come out now—the truth about her intimacies with Barney, a truth that had nothing to do with the poisoning of Mrs. what's-her-name and should have had little to do with Roland. As she looked past Osborne, her view encompassed the Molineuxs, father and son, and their lawyers—straining to hear her response. She would not faint, she resolved, as that would be an admission of guilt where she was not guilty. Blanche found she had more strength than she had believed possible. Her voice became stronger: "He called once with Mr. Molineux at number 251 West Seventy-fifth Street. He called at number 271 West End Avenue several times with Mr. Molineux and several times without Mr. Molineux."

Osborne continued: "Did Mr. Molineux know of these attentions paid to you by Mr. Barnet?"

Blanche replied, "Yes, he knew that we were friends."

Osborne stepped back as if to shift his attack. "When did Mr. Molineux first begin to pay his addresses to you?"

This time Blanche replied with her own questions. "How do you mean? I don't understand you. Do you mean when were we engaged?"

Osborne's tone was now blatantly sarcastic. "Oh, I think you ladies understand such a question as that. I mean when did he begin to pay you such attentions as to give you reason to believe that he was going to propose to you?"

Blanche's disdain for this cocky man before her peaked at these words. How could such an obviously well-educated man be so inhumane. She felt unequal to it all; her voice softened and her eyes filled with tears. "I don't know, I am sure. Mr. Molineux and I were always very good friends. I cannot answer you in any other way." Blanche wanted to add "and I think you are the most cruel man in the world," but she silenced herself. Osborne laid his hand on the witness box again and looked squarely into Blanche's wet eyes: "At the time was Mr. Barnet paying you such attentions as Mr. Molineux was?"

Blanche tried to relax so that her voice would not betray her distress: "We were all friendly with each other."

With his hand still on the stand, Osborne brought his face even closer to Blanche's: "But was Mr. Barnet paying you attentions with a view of proposing to you?"

At this point it occurred to Blanche that perhaps James Osborne knew nothing more than he had gleaned from Roland and the letter. If that were the case, she could play his game without compromising herself. She sat a little straighter and feigned surprise: "Why I never thought of a proposal from Mr. Barnet; he was a great friend of Mr. Molineux and we all saw each other frequently."

Osborne became more insistent: "Was Mr. Barnet paying you what might be called heavy attentions?"

Blanche hesitated, for fear that Osborne was about to spring a surprise; it was still possible that he knew more than he had let on so far. Cautiously she replied: "I don't know what you mean."

James Osborne appeared to have met his match. He paced back and forth before his witness, then faced her again: "Mrs. Molineux, you should realize that these questions embarrass me as much as they do you, but will you please tell me whether or not, in any sense of the word, Mr. Barnet or Mr. Molineux were rivals for your hand."

Blanche now regained some confidence and unconsciously raised her voice: "Never."

"Did they call as a rule on the same evening?"

"Sometimes they were together and sometimes they were not."

"Did you receive any presents from Mr. Barnet?"

"Flowers, on a number of occasions."

"Did you and Mr. Barnet ever have any quarrel?"

Blanche was now holding her own. "Never," she declared.

"Or any difficulty or trouble?"

"No," she reiterated, "we never had any trouble."

Now Osborne digressed a little. "How did you learn of the illness of Mr. Barnet?"

"Mr. Molineux told me."

"What did he say about it?"

Blanche had prepared herself for questions relating to Barney's death, and her voice took on its customary modulated quality. "He said Mr. Barnet was ill. He said he was awfully sorry and he thought it would be nice for me to send some flowers. I telephoned the Knickerbocker Athletic Club and found that Mr. Barnet was confined to his room. Then I carried out Mr. Molineux's instructions about sending him some flowers."

Osborne paused to take another sip of water. Returning the glass to the table, he picked up the envelope that lay alongside it and drew out the letter—written on Blanche's personal note paper—which was later to become known as the "Blanche" letter. He strode over to the jurors and began to read aloud, pausing to flaunt the letter in front of them. Blanche could not stand the sight and instead let her eyes rest on the blurred faces of the Molineuxs—the general and his wife looking like death, their son with that silly agreeable expression on his face. Did Roland never experience compassion or grief, she wondered, or even rage, such as she felt at this moment? Behind the Molineuxs were the staring faces of the sensation seekers, those who watched and waited for her to writhe under the dissecting knife of the prosecutor. Blanche would show them; she turned her eyes back toward Osborne.

When he had concluded his reading of the letter, Osborne returned to face Blanche once more. Silently thanking Bartow Weeks for providing her with the right words, she readily acknowledged her authorship of the letter in response to Osborne's query. Osborne then cleared his throat and continued: "Is it a fact that you were distressed to learn of Barnet's illness?"

"Most assuredly," replied Blanche with conviction.

"Did you want to learn when he would be about?"

"Indeed I did," she retorted.

"What did you mean by the words 'Is it that you don't believe me?' "

It was now Blanche who took on a patronizing air. "Why, I would call it a form of speech. 'Is it that you don't believe me when I say I would be glad to see you again' is what I meant."

Undaunted, Osborne continued. "What do you mean by the phrase 'If you would but let me prove to you my sincerity?' "

Blanche shrugged off any need for interpretation and continued as if trying to be patient with Osborne's foolish inquiries. "Oh that is only a phrase. I did not know whether he was piqued at anything. He had not answered my last letter."

"You also said in the letter, 'Do not be cross any more.' What did you mean by that?"

By now Blanche was perfectly at ease. "Well, it was an informal way of expressing myself. I simply thought he perhaps was piqued, because he hadn't answered my letter."

James Osborne had counted on this letter to show conclusively that Roland Molineux had an overpowering reason to wish Henry Barnet dead; Blanche was being difficult in his view, but he was determined to try again. "Had you ever before tried to *prove* your sincerity to Mr. Barnet?"

With a slight smile, she avoided the obvious. "No, I think that Mr. Barnet *always* regarded me as sincere."

Now it was the prosecutor's turn to be agitated. In fact it seemed to him that the witness was toying with him, and this he would not tolerate. He thus restated the previous question. " 'If you would but let me prove to you my sincerity?' Does not that seem to you to mean that you had not been permitted to show him your sincerity before?"

Blanche responded in a manner that was meant to communicate her increasing distaste for the questions and her contempt for Osborne himself. "I think not, Mr. Osborne. I had not seen him for such a long time and it was simply a manner of speech with me."

Osborne began now to show his own agitation in earnest: "So you mean to tell the jury that you had not before been trying to prove your sincerity to Mr. Barnet?"

Blanche remained firm: "That is simply a form of speech."

It occurred to Osborne that further reference to the letter could be counterproductive with a witness as unyielding as Blanche Molineux. Instead he asked her to expand upon other matters about which Roland had already testified — the yachting trip where they had met, the Amateur Circus, occasions when Blanche had visited Roland and Barnet in their rooms, whether others were present and whether liquor had been served, all matters that stirred little interest when compared to Blanche's previous testimony. In a little more than an hour it was all over. Blanche was excused.

George Battle rose from his seat to help Blanche back into the reserved section. As they walked together, he whispered, "You were magnificent!" Blanche had come away reasonably unscathed, certainly above suspicion as the perpetrator of a poison murder. She was no longer the mysterious woman of questionable reputation about whom the public could construct impossible scenarios. By her own admission, however, she was the object of attention from two men who had been the best of friends. Few would deny that such circumstances might easily have given rise to intense jealousy.

Blanche felt reasonably comfortable with her testimony. She had revealed nothing new about her relationship with Barney in spite of the attacks by Osborne, and she had left the stand on the arm of George Gordon Battle, one of the most distinguished attorneys in New York City. It might still be possible for her to find her place in society. However, her contempt for James Osborne was unbounded.

Osborne, having gleaned what he could from Blanche's testimony, proceeded to call his remaining witnesses and thereby succeeded in continuing the inquest for another entire week. He had saved the best for the last day, and in his opinion the best was Nicholas Heckmann, owner of the letter boxes at 257 West Forty-second Street.

Heckmann was a slight lean-built man, with sharp features accentuated by piercing eyes and a staccato voice. He had previously contacted several of the newpapers, indicating that he would identify the owner of Box 217, "Mr. Barnet," for a price. Not one of the papers appeared ready to pay his price, although monetary rewards for information had been promised earlier. Under subpoena now, Heckmann would be asked to make the identification for nothing. Osborne wasted few words with his witness, turning directly to the subject of Box 217. First he inquired as to how often the person who had rented the box had called. Heckmann guessed "fifteen or twenty times within one month." Osborne suggested that this was certainly frequently enough for Heckmann to make a good indentification of the man who leased the box. Then he pointed to Roland while continuing to address the witness: "Do you recongize Mr. Molineux over there as the man who hired the letter box?"

Heckmann's response was prompt and convincing: "Yes, I do."

That was all there was to it — the first and only positive identification of Roland Molineux in connection with either of the poison murders. Also for the first time, Roland's agreeable expression and pleasant manner disappeared. He stood up slowly and rested both hands on the table before him, as if to steady himself, then shouted: "It is a lie! I want to say I never saw him — I never saw him in Forty-second Street . . . I never rented a letter box from him, and what he says is a lie!"

Before Roland finished, Weeks was also on his feet. He too spoke in a shout: "I ask, Mr. Coroner, that this man who has offered to sell his identification be examined . . . "

The coroner interrupted and threatened to hold Weeks in contempt. Weeks finally sat down and motioned to Roland to do the same. Osborne excused Heckmann from the witness stand and called the handwriting expert, his final witness. When he had finished, he retired to the District Attorney's table and whispered a few words to Colonel Gardiner.

For three weeks, Gardiner had sat quietly while his assistant had orchestrated the entire inquest; only this last scene — the summing of the evidence — had he retained for himself. It was a moment for which he had waited patiently, and he now stepped forward to begin. Gardiner opened with a sort of confession. From the beginning neither the police department nor his office had suspected Harry Cornish of the Adams murder. All of the evidence pointed to him as the *bona fide* intended victim. However, since the prime suspect had already been judged guilty by a broad segment of the community, his office had tried a peculiar strategy — to play down the suspicion of this man in order to learn more about him. The strategy had induced the suspect to submit willingly to handwriting tests and to show off his chemical laboratory, which contained the poisonous ingredient ingested by Mrs. Adams. The strategy, though unusual, had been successful.

If Colonel Gardiner behaved a little smugly as he described his strategy, he abandoned all smugness when he came to name the suspect — Roland Burnham Molineux. He even became a little maudlin as he cited the wartime friendship between himself and the father of the accused. In a similar tone he regretted that duty demanded his office show Blanche Chesebrough as the woman for whom Molineux had murdered Henry Barnet. At Gardiner's use of the word "woman," Roland again jumped from his seat. His face was highly flushed and he pointed menacingly at the prosecutor: "Lady, if you please, Colonel Gardiner, lady." Weeks cautiously but firmly rose and took Roland by the shoulder. The two men sat down before the coroner found it necessary to intervene.

Gardiner concluded his summation by stressing the evidence that linked Roland with the death of Henry Barnet, even though the inquest had been called to investigate the death of Kate Adams. He posed a series of rhetorical questions, such as a query as to whether Blanche's letter at the time of Barnet's death was the sort of letter a woman about to be married to another man would normally write.

General Molineux, who had been visibly distraught that entire last day, moaned out loud and replied with a painful "Yes." In an unfortunate scene that surely must have distressed Gardiner in hindsight, he turned to the general and snapped, "No."

The general looked startled and in a commanding voice shouted back, "Yes! I say yes!"

Coroner Hart turned on the general and threatened to have him removed from the hearing room. The old man fell silent.

The District Attorney concluded his statement and the coroner charged the jury. The eleven men retired (one had been excused because of illness), and before the end of the long day they returned with their verdict: "We find that the said Katherine J. Adams came to her death on the twenty-eighth day of December, 1898, at number 61 West Eighty-sixth Street by poisoning by mercuric cyanide administered by Harry S. Cornish, to whom said poison had been sent in a bottle of Bromo-Seltzer in the mail by Roland B. Molineux."

On the basis of the verdict, Coroner Hart read his indictment of Roland Molineux and ordered his immediate arrest. It came as a surprise to no one.

Blanche and her mother-in-law were promptly evacuated from the Criminal Courts Building and herded into the waiting

Molineux carriage. Fortunately they were not present to see Roland led out of the courtroom and across the "Bridge of Sighs" to New York's famed old Tombs for incarceration.

FIFTEEN

Prelude to Prosecution

For all of the anguish and trauma associated with the inquest, it had at least provided a few, if infrequent, occasions for Blanche to venture into the light of day. With Roland's indictment and imprisonment, however, she once again found herself confined to the Molineux house in Brooklyn. Throughout the dreary days of late winter and early spring, all of the downstairs windows remained shuttered day and night, ostensibly to maintain the family's privacy. It seemed to Blanche that the intent was rather to create a pseudo prison for the wife and parents of the prisoner so that they might share in his sufferings.

Blanche and her mother-in-law led their separate, isolated lives during the day while the general was away, but during the evenings they joined him in the library before the fireplace. There he did his best to assure them that the situation was far from hopeless, even though his face betrayed a profound weariness and pessimism as he described the legal maneuverings that were just beginning.

While the *New York Times* concentrated on the complicated legal and judicial issues relating to Roland's predicament, other newspapers continued to investigate the circumstances surrounding the two murders, paying particular attention to a possible motive in the death of Henry Barnet. An exposé in March quoted a "witness" who had seen Blanche Chesebrough with Henry Barnet at a Jersey City hotel in May of 1897. General Molineux, in a rare departure from his own dictates, confronted Blanche with this news article, for if it were so, the entire testimony regarding Roland's friendship with Barnet, and her place in this friendship, would unravel. Blanche was devastated by this confrontation. Though she could honestly deny the report, it nevertheless spread the seeds of distrust between her and the Molineuxs, seeds that had been sown earlier by the testimony given at the inquest. Blanche retreated to her little room upstairs, taking her meals on a tray rather than dining with the family. There she composed a long letter to the press, in the hope of vindicating herself in the eyes of the public as well as in the general's heart. When she had completed the letter, she took it to the general and begged that he allow it to be published. The old man was moved sufficiently to agree to seek approval from Bartow Weeks. (This power that Weeks appeared to wield over the family was something under which Blanche constantly chafed.) After obtaining Weeks's endorsement, the general himself delivered the letter to the *New York Times* and it appeared on March 25 over the name of Mrs. Roland Molineux.

In part the letter read: "Since the terrible tragedy culminating in the death of Mrs. Adams and throughout the inexpressibly painful scenes that have followed, I have felt it to be my duty to bear in silence the cruel attacks that have been made upon me in the newspapers. . . ."

The letter went on to deny categorically the report that Blanche had been associated with Barnet prior to October of 1897, when they were introduced by Roland at the Metropolitan Opera House. It concluded with a final plea from Blanche: "In simple justice to myself, my family, and my friends, I ask the public press to refrain from printing such wicked accusations, which the slightest investigation would show to be unfounded."

Following the appearance of the letter in the *Times* there was evidence of increased public sympathy for the Molineux cause. The general must have sensed this subtle change of mood, for he became ever more solicitous of his daughter-in-law, insisting that she rejoin him and his wife for their evenings in the sitting room or the library, where he sought to bolster the family spirits. Blanche derived some comfort from the general's attempts at optimism, not because she believed in Roland's innocence—she had already come to the certain conclusion that he alone was responsible for the death of Henry Barnet and the death of Katherine Adams as well—but rather because his exoneration appeared to be her single chance to escape the Molineux prison.

Immediately following Roland's indictment in February, Bartow Weeks had placed before the court a motion for permission to inspect the minutes of the Grand Jury. An upstate justice, Pardon Williams, who presumably was immune to the various political pressures that existed in New York City (but possibly not immune to pressures from the upstate Republican Party) was sitting temporarily in New York City. Weeks submitted to Justice Williams a motion to have the indictment set aside due to a number of errors in the proceedings, as revealed in the minutes. The most serious error cited was that of admitting as evidence the handwriting of the "Barnet" letters. On April 12, Williams granted Weeks's motion and ordered the case resubmitted to the Grand Jury.

Since the time of the inquest, a new Grand Jury had been convened, under the jurisdiction of Justice McMahon. This was certainly no detriment to the Molineux cause for he was a member of the Loyal Legion, a patriotic organization of which General Molineux was a founder. It would also seem fortuitous that the foreman of this new Grand Jury was Colonel William Church, an old comrade-in-arms of the general. The new jury essentially disregarded all of the evidence collected by the District Attorney and instead called its own witnesses, completing its investigations on May 9. It failed to indict anyone in the death of Katherine Adams. Ordinarily this ought to have meant the release of the prisoner, but Roland was rearrested as he was about to leave the courtroom, this time on a charge of first-degree assault against Harry Cornish.

In due course, Roland was brought before a local justice, who set bail at $10,000. Insisting that this amount was excessively high in view of the lesser charge, Roland's counsel wrangled with the judge until the bail was reduced to $5000. The smaller amount was posted and Roland was released, but as before, he was immediately arrested again on a charge of murder. He then filed a writ of habeas corpus, but the petition was denied. Roland was to be held until the new Grand Jury convened in July.

In an effort to keep up appearances while these legal battles were being fought, the general from time to time prevailed upon Blanche to visit Roland. Thus she would join her mother-in-law to drive in the Molineux carriage, curtains drawn, across the Brooklyn Bridge to the Tombs. There they would meet with Roland in a special room set aside for such visits, a room in which the prisoner was separated from his visitors by a metal grille. The Roland whom Blanche observed there was almost like a stranger—the hard and bitter expression on his face belying the thin smile on his lips. She could not help making the comparison with the Roland she had first seen on Morgan's yacht—in spotless white flannels, smiling infectiously and exhuding self-assurance. There was now about him an air of patronizing tolerance, as though he were merely impatient to have done with the whole business so that he might resume normal living. Blanche's entire being recoiled at the thought; there was no way that she could return to normal living as the wife of Roland Molineux. This she had firmly resolved.

Shortly after Independence Day, the new Grand Jury began its deliberations. All testimony regarding the murder of Katherine Adams was taken in secrecy, with the District Attorney's office providing the witnesses and the evidence. In light of this, Bartow Weeks strongly advised his client that he should not appear before the Grand Jury, but Roland took exception to this. Without consulting his friend and counselor, he issued his own public statement from the Tombs: He regretted that his counsel would not permit him to appear before the Grand Jury and he further protested his innocence of any crime whatsoever. Bartow Weeks was now becoming painfully aware of Roland's enigmatic nature, something Blanche had observed more than a year earlier.

Ignoring Roland's personal protestations, Colonel Gardiner proceeded to present to the Grand Jury a parade of witnesses, most of whom had appeared at the February inquest. Although no startling new testimony or evidence was introduced, the result was the same. On the twentieth of July, Roland was indicted, and on the following day he was arraigned. Once again, Bartow Weeks moved that the judge allow examination of the minutes of the Grand Jury; this time the motion was denied. Roland was returned to the Tombs, where he would remain for almost four additional months before being brought to trial.

The weather continued to be hot and oppressive throughout July. At night Blanche often sat at the open window of her room, peering into the darkness as though it held the answers to her imponderable future. When the wind was in the right direction, she could detect the faint flavor of salty air as it drifted up from the bay. It filled her with a wistful longing to go away, to be where she could taste the out-of-doors, perhaps the sea. Her life was now utterly bereft of everything that had brought her joy in the past—her music, her summers at the seashore, even the small comfort of having someone with whom to share an afternoon's conversation.

It was at such times that Blanche felt an overwhelming need to confide in her sister, and she wrote of her loneliness and desolation in long, sad letters to Isia in Boston. Isia's growing concern over her sister's mental state, coupled with the news of Roland's second indictment, quickened her resolve to alleviate Blanche's pitiful condition, and she traveled to Brooklyn to present the general with a *fait accompli*. Arrangements had been made that Blanche should enjoy a holiday on Long Island. It would not be at *Craigsmere*, where her presence would surely be noted, nor at the summer home of her brother Frank. Rather

Isia had selected the home of a mutual friend, near the Meadowbrook Hunt Club, where Blanche could recover and yet remain out of sight. General Molineux reluctantly agreed to Isia's plan; even he recognized the limitations in his power to command.

For two weeks of that long, hot summer, Blanche basked in the warm sunshine of the Long Island coast, enjoying the special freedom of anonymity. Her identity was known only to her host and hostess, yet there were luncheons at the Meadowbrook Club, excursions on board a yacht, and even a harmless flirtation with a young equestrian who insisted on calling daily. In the late evening twilight, Blanche often walked along the beach with him, aware of his attraction to her and taking pleasure in the effect she had upon him, a reminder that she still possessed those charms that had so captivated Roland and Barney in happier times. This awareness gave her a renewed feeling of self-worth and lifted her spirits higher than they had been in many months.

As she knew it must, the interlude at the ocean came to an end, and Blanche returned to her cloistered life at the Molineux home in Brooklyn. For another three months, she spent her days and nights behind shutters or in the darkness before her open window, interrupted only by infrequent trips across to Manhattan to exchange amenities with a husband whom she viewed ever more distantly.

The trial of Roland Molineux for the murder of Katherine Adams began on the fourteenth of November, 1899, in the Court of General Sessions of the Peace of the City and County of New York. At that time New York County had two criminal courts, and cases involving capital offenses were normally brought before the Criminal Branch of the Supreme Court; however, since Roland's indictment had occurred while the Supreme Court was not in session, his arraignment, hence trial, by default fell under the jurisdiction of the Court of General Sessions.

This peculiar court, which had already become an anachronism and was phased out soon after Roland's trial, was presided over by a Recorder, one John Goff, the last of his line. Goff was a highly visible figure in New York, known for his fierce opposition to corruption in government as well as his lack of diplomacy when confronting it. He had come to New York from Ireland as a child and, essentially through his own resources, had trained for the law profession. At a time when the Tammany organization was dominated by New York's Irish element and was in control of most of the city's public institutions, Goff had made his way into the District Attorney's office without any Tammany connection whatsoever. When the so-called Lexow Committee was appointed to investigate corruption in the police department, Goff was designated special attorney in the investigation. It was in this role that he established his reputation as a relentless prosecutor and an unmerciful interrogator of witnesses. The facts that surfaced during this well-publicized inquiry swayed public opinion against the Tammany organization and drove from office many of its elected officials. These revelations also carried Goff into the elected office of Recorder of the Court of General Sessions of the Peace.

The anticorruption mood, however, did not prevent the election of Colonel Asa Bird Gardiner, a member of the Tammany organization, to the office of District Attorney. The enmity that existed between Gardiner and Goff was public knowledge, and in fact Goff's disdain for Gardiner was persistent and vocal to the point of paralyzing any official duties the two had in common. Colonel Gardiner would therefore have preferred to prosecute Roland Molineux before any other justice. With Goff presiding, he chose to step aside completely, leaving the entire prosecution to James Osborne. Fierce and unrelenting, Osborne was a totally effective trial lawyer and possessed precisely those qualities which Goff admired and in which he took obvious delight. The combination of Osborne's talents and Goff's prejudices could certainly work against the interests of Roland Molineux, a fact that was not lost on Bartow Weeks, who planned his defense accordingly.

The trial was set in the Criminal Courts Building, across the

street from New York City's famed Tombs prison and connected
to it by the Bridge of Sighs. This Baroque stone passageway over
which Roland would be escorted for each day's session was
named for its resemblance to the *Ponte Dei Sospiri* in Venice,
which spans the narrow canal between the Doges Palace and the
prisons beyond.

The *New York Times* reported that not within memory had
a trial generated such interest. On the opening morning, the
crowds were so large that almost all but visiting lawyers, the
press, and certain city officials were turned away. The visiting
attorneys included many who had come from the far corners of
the country, for the proceedings had already raised interesting
legal questions relating to the testimony of handwriting experts
and circumstantial evidence.

General Molineux was also present in the courtroom, having
arrived on the arm of George Battle. As he walked to the front
of the chamber, his spirits were high though his face had become noticeably more lined within the year. He acknowledged
the greetings of old friends along the way, assuring them that
he was relieved the time had finally arrived for his son to be vindicated. Sitting down next to Battle, he removed his hat and
replaced it with a black silk skull cap; it was already winter in
New York.

Just prior to the opening of the court, Bartow Weeks strode
in with the defendant at his side. Roland's face was pale, probably the consequence of nearly nine months of incarceration in
the Tombs, but he exhibited an air of confidence, smiling at
Battle from a distance and throwing a kiss to his father. Well-
dressed as usual, he wore a black double-breasted suit and a
starched white collar. On the little finger of his left hand were
two rings, one glistening with diamonds and rubies. This was
the *Mizpah* ring for which Blanche possessed an equally jeweled
counterpart.

At precisely 10:30 A.M., Recorder Goff entered the courtroom and all rose to acknowledge his presence. Taking his seat,
he peered down to assure himself that those required to be pres-

ent for such a proceeding were indeed present. Then he pounded his gavel, calling the court to order, and for a moment the room fell silent.

Bartow Weeks now began his defense by approaching the bench and moving to have the case dismissed. A murmur passed through the crowd, as the word spread from those in the front who could hear Weeks to those in the back who could not. Goff demanded silence in the room. He then turned his attention to Weeks, not only denying the motion but scolding counsel for wasting the court's time with such trivialities. This kind of exchange would occur continually throughout the proceedings— Weeks objecting and Goff overruling—and in fact would become one of the trademarks of the Molineux trial.

The first business at hand was the selection of a jury to hear the case. This process would last more than two weeks and altogether 504 prospective jurors would be interviewed to complete the panel of twelve men who would sit in judgment of Roland Molineux. Jurors were rejected either by mutual consent of Weeks and Osborne or by objection of either one, and in many cases jurors disqualified themselves. Some asked to be excused because they did not believe at all in the death penalty—in New York it was administered via the electric chair, a recent technological advance—or because they did not believe in the death penalty when a conviction was obtained based on circumstantial evidence alone. Others were excused because they did not understand the precise meaning of words that would become commonplace during the course of the proceedings—words such as accomplice, premeditation, and turpitude.

Among those interviewed was a man with a heavy German accent whose name was Sigmund Feust. Osborne requested that he be excused immediately as he would surely be unable to comprehend the vocabulary of the proceedings, even if he understood its other aspects. Weeks, however, was willing to give the man an opportunity to exhibit his command of English. Under questioning, Feust recounted that he had read most of the works of Herbert Spencer, Thomas Huxley, and John Stuart Mill, all in the English language. Osborne apologetically retracted his objection, and Sigmund Feust was seated as a member of the jury. It was the single instance throughout the long trial when the two legal adversaries exchanged a smile.

As tedious as the jury selection process was for the onlookers, no doubt Roland found it much more interesting than life in the Tombs. He kept his attention riveted on the prospective jurors as they answered the questions put to them, and he did not attempt to mask his pleasure as certain of them were seated. The general was always at his side, and the two would chat amiably from time to time during recesses in the proceedings.

As the process dragged on interminably, several newspapers began to print bits and pieces of gossip in their eagerness to get on with the case. One even reported that there was madness in the Molineux family and that Roland was expected to plead insanity as soon as the jury was complete. The following day in court, Weeks exploded at the outrageous slander. He confronted Recorder Goff and moved that the case against his client be dismissed on the grounds that he was no longer able to obtain a fair trial. Goff was not impressed and categorically denied the motion.

November 29, 1899, marked the beginning of the prosecution of Roland Molineux for murder. Ironically, it was also the first anniversary of his marriage to Blanche, and early that morning he issued a statement from the Tombs:

A year ago today was the happiest day of my life. It was my wedding day. I expect the anniversary to be a happy day also, for I hope again to see my wife and my mother.

Up until that day, neither his wife nor his mother had appeared at the trial, but Bartow Weeks had come upon the idea that a visit to the courtroom by Blanche on this anniversary might generate sympathy for Roland. Certainly the press would also make the most of it. Blanche considered the idea Machiavellian, but agreed to cooperate, knowing there was no way out. She steeled herself for the obligatory reunion and the strong show of affection that was expected.

Blanche and her mother-in-law arrived in the courtroom at

10:25 A.M., both dressed and veiled in black, followed by their entourage—General Molineux and the two attorneys. As the two ladies took their places, Roland entered with a deputy and walked briskly to his wife. She stood up, lifted back her veil, and threw her arms around him, kissing him twice. He gazed at her lovingly and patted her affectionately on the shoulder as they sat down together. Both were smiling through their tears. This bit of drama provided the newspapers with several paragraphs of prose the following morning.

SIXTEEN

The Trial

The trial of Roland Molineux would be remembered as a *tour de force* in the annals of criminal law. Beginning with the prolonged jury selection process, throughout the lengthy prosecution during which more than one hundred witnesses were called, and culminating in a summary by the prosecuting attorney that lasted two and a half days, the entire episode spanned four months. The story that unfolded during these months contained an abundance of facts intermingled with untruths and considerable innuendo.

James Osborne was faced with a situation in which there were no witnesses to the murder and apparently no accomplices. The successful prosecution of this case would require a deft hand to manipulate what was clearly circumstantial evidence. The most useful evidence he had at his disposal consisted of a number of letters, most of which were written to patent medicine firms around the country, some in the name of H. Cornish, some in the name of H. C. Barnet, and one in the name of Roland Molineux. Osborne made extensive use of handwriting experts from the United States Post Office and from banks across the country in an attempt to connect the handwriting on the poison package with that of Roland Molineux. The best he could do was to establish that there was a strong resemblance between the admitted handwriting of Roland Molineux and the handwriting on letters written to patent medicine firms in the name of H. C. Barnet. Unfortunately for the prosecution, Roland was on trial for the murder of Katherine Adams and the attempted murder of Harry Cornish. It was incumbent upon Osborne to convince the jury that the murder of Henry Barnet had any bearing on the case at all.

This connection could be forged in two ways. The first was to call out the obvious similarity between the writing paper on which Roland admittedly wrote a letter to a patent medicine firm and the paper on which two of the Cornish letters were written. The second was less clear and therefore required considerable testimony during the trial. James Osborne wished to show that Roland had a strong motive to kill Henry Barnet, namely jealousy over attentions paid by Barnet to his intended bride and fiancée. If this premise was reasonable, the corollary was that the successful poisoning of Henry Barnet gave Roland the courage to apply the same technique for disposing of another enemy, namely Harry Cornish. Osborne intended to show that the mind that had plotted Barnet's murder had also planned Cornish's murder, and that this mind could be none other than that of Roland Molineux.

To succeed, this strategy demanded extensive knowledge of the life and character of Roland Molineux. To draw out information useful in his plan, Osborne interviewed many members of the Knickerbocker Athletic Club. A common thread seemed to weave through all of their statements; Roland Molineux was not well understood, even by those who knew him well.

Osborne then set about to construct a romantic triangle of which Blanche Chesebrough was the apex, for this would undergird the premise that Roland had poisoned Henry Barnet. With Blanche, Osborne had difficulties not unlike those he encountered with Roland. His office had devoted considerable resources in its investigation of Blanche's recent past. Interviews were held with members of the choirs where she had sung and with her colleagues in the Rubenstein Society and the Damrosch

Chorale, but these yielded very little. Blanche was known to have been serious in her pursuit of music, at least until the time that she met Roland. Yet her colleagues, one after the other, admitted that she never shared her thoughts nor joined in their social activities. There was general agreement that Blanche, like Roland, was a loner.

Stymied by this lack of information, Osborne groped further, finally reaching out to Blanche's former places of residence. In testimony at the inquest, Blanche had freely given three addresses at which she had resided between the time she met Roland and her marriage—the Mystic Flats, where she had lived a short time with Isia, Mrs. Bell's boarding house, and finally the home of Alice Bellinger. Investigators from the District Attorney's office sought out the servants from each of these residences and came up with two who offered information. The first was Rachel Greene, the black girl at Mrs. Bell's whom Blanche found both impudent and undependable. The second was Minnie Betts, who had served Blanche cheerfully and faithfully during most of the months she had lived with Alice. One of the regrets that continued to burden Blanche was the memory of her last encounter with Minnie, when she had lashed out at the girl's disturbing words on her wedding day. Despite the calamities that had befallen her since that happy morning, Blanche still harbored the hope that she could one day make it up to Minnie. However, the events which were to take place in the courtroom would render this impossible.

Blanche's initial visit to the courtroom on the first anniversary of her marriage had created such a stir of sympathy in the press that Bartow Weeks arranged for her to be present almost every subsequent day of the trial. His decision was communicated to Blanche by her father-in-law that evening while the two sat together in the library. General Molineux was almost overcome by emotion as he discussed with Blanche the implications of her poignant reunion with Roland and the importance of her future presence in court. Blanche sat silently before him. As much as she wished to tell this honorable man of her changed feelings toward his son, her compassion for him dissipated her courage.

Dutifully she assented and left to prepare for the coming morning in court, wondering how long she could continue living the lie that her marriage had become.

At first, one day in the courtroom seemed like any other. Osborne called many seemingly unimportant witnesses to testify to various assertions he had made in his opening statement. Among them were members of the Knickerbocker Athletic Club — Alvin Harpster, Will Scheffler, and even John Adams — from each of whom he elicited statements to confirm that Roland was indeed a strange one. Although Roland was generally pleasant and reserved, it seemed he had a queer streak that surfaced occasionally during which he was condescending, petty and even quarrelsome. These descriptions caused Blanche to wince uncomfortably, for she had observed these same tendencies often during her short life with Roland. Still she felt a sense of redress, as she had previously placed the blame on herself.

Roland's demeanor throughout this testimony did very little to belie what was being said. He seemed totally at ease, almost detached, as though the witnesses were describing some stranger who possessed mildly amusing idiosyncrasies. At times, he would smile or chuckle when Osborne drew out some particularly disparaging reference to him. Roland's attitude made the testimony even more onerous for Blanche; worst of all was the knowledge that her presence next to her husband was a total fraud. She felt she had sacrificed her personal integrity by submitting to the will of Bartow Weeks and chided herself that she had not been forthright with General Molineux. Silently she vowed that, whatever the verdict, she would flee the Molineux fortress as soon as the dreadful trial was finished.

Having drawn from the testimony of many witnesses a less than flattering portrayal of the defendant, James Osborne now turned to the question of motive in the attempted poisoning of Harry Cornish, which had resulted in the death of Katherine Adams. He brought Cornish to the witness stand and also interrogated additional Knickerbocker Club members regarding the enmity that had festered between Roland and Cornish for almost two years. Each Knickerbocker witness was able to add some bit of gossip confirming Roland's deep dislike of the athletic director. But Osborne did not stop there. While denying that the murder of Henry Barnet had anything to do with the trial of Roland Molineux, he nevertheless moved on to the subject of Blanche Molineux and her relationships with Roland and Henry Barnet before her marriage. This direction in the testimony gave Blanche a heightened awareness of her own vulnerability in this court of law.

The first testimony involving Blanche was given by one of the club members who had joined her and Roland and Barnet in Roland's room after the Club Carnival. Although Blanche could not even recall the man's presence at the little party two years earlier, he seemed to remember every detail, including the fact that she had drunk at least two and probably three glasses of wine. Such a harmless party it had been, as Blanche remembered it; but when subjected to interpretation by James Osborne it began to resemble a Roman orgy. At least Blanche could derive some comfort from the fact that Roland too had been present and could tell his father later how it had been in truth. Blanche now perceived her father-in-law to be her only protection from some unknown abysmal fate; thus she weighed each word of testimony for its potential effect on his opinion of her.

The testimony regarding the party in Barnet's room was just the beginning. The following day, Blanche arrived in court to discover two black women among the witnesses. A feeling of trepidation came over her as she recognized them both— Rachel, the colored servant at Mrs. Bell's, and Minnie, the girl whom she had wronged in a thoughtless moment. The presence of two black women was unusual enough to introduce a certain element of mystery as the proceedings opened. James Osborne wasted no time, promptly calling Rachel Greene to the stand.

His first questions to Rachel merely established her identity and her address and confirmed that she had been employed as a maid by Mrs. Bell for several months some two years earlier.

Then Osborne began in earnest: "Rachel—I trust you are not offended by my using your Christian name—who was living at Mrs. Bell's during the month of November in 1897?"

The tone of Rachel's voice suggested an eagerness to share this bit of information as she replied: "Up in the second floor front room, right at the top of the stairs, lived Mister and Miz Chesebrough."

Blanche was aghast as Osborne, feigning surprise, queried: "Mr. and Mrs. Chesebrough? Could you identify them if they were in this courtroom?"

"Yas, sir." At this point, Rachel's dark eyes darted about the room until they lighted on Blanche. "Yas, sir—that is Miz Chesebrough," she said, with a nod in Blanche's direction. "I could not ever forget her face or her hair. She was very stylish and I even sometimes heard her singing. Yas, that is Miz Chesebrough."

Satisfied, Osborne thanked his witness, gestured to the defense attorneys that it was their turn, and sat down. Bartow Weeks now stepped forward and addressed the witness: "Miss Greene, you have stated that a Mr. and Mrs. Chesebrough were living in a room at Mrs. Bell's during the month of November two years ago. Tell me, how did you know the names of those two people who supposedly lived in that room at the top of the stairs?"

"Oh, that were easy, sir. Mister and Miz Chesebrough received lots of mail. I always read the names on the envelopes becuz Miz Bell had me deliver the letters to her guests."

"Are you sure that you can read that well, Miss Greene?" Weeks's tone suggested his distrust of her assertion.

At this, Rachel sat up straight and with a piercing look at her interrogator, replied insolently, "Mister . . . sir, I believe I can read as well as you."

Weeks reeled in surprise, then mumbled an apology for his *faux pas* and continued: "Miss Greene, you mentioned Mr. Chesebrough. Would you recognize Mr. Chesebrough if he were in this courtroom?"

This time Rachel hesitated, then affirmed: "Yas, sir." Her

eyes now moved left and right across the room and back to Weeks. "I don't believe Mister Chesebrough be here today."

Weeks smiled, thanked the witness, and returned to his seat. Osborne sat silently, perhaps pondering why Rachel's testimony had weakened rather than strengthened his contention that Roland and Blanche were engaged to be married that fall of 1897.

Blanche was dumbfounded at the testimony. How could anyone have construed her relationship with Roland at that time to be anything other than innocent courtship? She wanted to cry out, "Lies, lies," but she restrained herself. She could only wonder what amount of money James Osborne had paid this impudent girl to stand up and utter such falsehoods and slander. Little did Blanche know that Osborne was as baffled by the testimony as she was. Damage to Blanche's reputation was not his goal; his only interest was the connection with Roland Molineux which Rachel had failed to make.

Next Osborne called Minnie Betts to the stand. He counted on her to furnish the evidence that would complete the romantic triangle. His first question drew out the fact that Minnie had begun working for Alice Bellinger shortly after Blanche arrived there, that is, early in 1898. Further, Minnie testified that she left the Bellinger home for a Christmas holiday at the end of the year and did not return thereafter. As to why she did not return, there was no clear answer. "Missah Osborne, I were not happy there after Miz Chesebrough got married." She offered no further explanation.

"Minnie," Osborne asked, "Did Miss Chesebrough have many friends who called on her at West End Avenue?"

"No, sir," Minnie replied, offering no embellishments.

"Do you mean to say that no one ever called on Miss Chesebrough in the months that you were both at Mrs. Bellinger's?"

"No, sir, I not say that at all," Minnie retorted.

Osborne could now discern that despite their common color, Rachel Greene and Minnie Betts were not of the same substance. There seemed to be a reluctance, perhaps springing from a kind of loyalty, that inhibited the effectiveness of his witness.

"Minnie—I mean Miss Betts—look at the defendant who sits before you. Did you ever see that man at Mrs. Bellinger's home?"

"Yas, Missah Osborne, I saw him at Mrs. Bellinger's home."

Osborne continued the laborious task: "How often did you see the defendant at Mrs. Bellinger's home?"

"Oh, maybe three or four times, sir."

"When was the first time that you saw him at Mrs. Bellinger's home?"

Minnie fell silent as she ruminated: "I believe it was after Miz Chesebrough returned from the coast, after the summer."

"You mean you did not see him call at all in the winter or spring of 1898?"

"Yas, Missah Osborne, that is so."

"And you say that no one called on Miss Chesebrough before she went away for the summer?"

"No, I do not say that."

Osborne's voice took on an impatient tone as he sought to re-phrase his question. He had not expected this witness to be so recalcitrant. She was sounding more like a witness for the defense.

"Miss Betts, who called on Miss Chesebrough before the summer?"

"Sir, I do not remember his name now."

"Well, what was he like?"

"Missah Osborne, he was kind to me; he made jokes with me; he never ordered me about; he was the best white . . . " Minnie ceased what had begun as an avalanche of words and a look of fear spread over her face.

"Go on, go on, Miss Betts, did this caller come often?"

"I don't remember, Missah Osborne. That was such a long time ago."

"Did this caller, the man who was kind to you, did he call on Miss Chesebrough after she returned from her summer holiday?"

"No, sir, I never saw him again."

Osborne turned his witness over to the defense, but Weeks

signalled that he would not cross-examine and Osborne excused her. She left the stand slowly, her eyes glistening. To the spectators she appeared to be watching Blanche, but Blanche did not look up. With hands folded and eyes down, Blanche was fighting back her own tears—tears of sadness and of regret.

Days became weeks and suddenly weeks were months as December became January and January slipped into February. The trial progressed and it continued to go better for the prosecution. A very plausible scenario was emerging: Roland Molineux had met his future bride in the summer of 1897; they had courted, probably more intimately than was respectable, during the fall of that year; then Molineux had introduced his fiancée to his friend Henry Barnet; at the time Molineux was having problems with Cornish at the Knickerbocker; while he was distracted, his fiancée, Blanche Chesebrough, became involved with Barnet; by the time Molineux became aware of this state of affairs, it was too late; he therefore withdrew to his dreary attic rooms, with his potions and poisons, and plotted how to get rid of the impediment to his desired goal—marriage to Blanche Chesebrough.

Having established a reasonable motive for the poisoning of Henry Barnet, Osborne proceeded to bring forth evidence to link Roland with the poison package that Harry Cornish received in the mail. For this he used letters that he had obtained from several patent medicine firms around the country, even subpoenaing the proprietors of the firms to testify as to the authenticity of the letters. With one exception, all of the letters were written in the name of H. C. Barnet or H. Cornish. James Osborne hoped to prove, not only through the handwriting but also through the contents of the letters, that Roland Molineux was indeed the correspondent. With the contents, he had something more to offer the jurors—information on Roland's private life that would show him to be something quite apart from his public image. James Osborne hoped to expose Roland as a "degenerate," a Victorian label that covered a broad category of ills. To this end, he produced from his leather briefcase a diagnosis blank from the Marston Remedy Company at 19 Park Place in New York City. The blank had been filled out by "H. C. Barnet," Box 217, 257 West Forty-second Street, also in New York, and sent through the United States mail. A handwriting expert was called to the stand. He identified the handwriting as a disguised handwriting, probably written by Roland Molineux.

Osborne then began to read from the blank: " 'Patients desiring treatment for seminal weakness, impotency, loss of erectile power, gonorrhea, gleet, stricture, syphilis, neurasthenia, spermatorrhea, nervous debility, varicocele, urinary troubles, Bright's disease, gravel, etc., will please answer as carefully as possible the questions.' "

He paused, then continued: "Gentlemen of the jury, notice the writer's response to the first question on the diagnosis blank, that of age; 'Thirty-one years old' is the written entry. Now, how old was Henry Barnet at this time? He was thirty-three years old. And how old was the defendant? You know the answer as well as I do. He was thirty-one years old. The second question is that of occupation. The writer answers 'clerk.' We know from the testimony that Henry Barnet was no clerk; he was a broker, in stocks and in commodities. The defendant, on the other hand, is a clerk of sorts in the Morris Herrmann business. I go on to the third question: 'Are you contemplating marriage?' Here the answer is touching for its candidness—'Yes, if I may.' From all we have heard so far in the testimony, it is clear that the defendant was contemplating marriage at that time, and for some time previous. In fact he was married not more than five months after this diagnosis blank was completed."

Again James Osborne paused, this time to look at the jurors and the spectators, as if to assure himself that he had their complete attention; then he went on. "I regret that in the interest of justice I must read of matters that are not fit for the ears of gentlemen, and certainly not for the ears of the ladies in our midst, most particularly those in the family of the defendant . . . I shall pass over a number of questions about the general health of the writer, for the answers serve no purpose here.

Rather I shall begin with the thirtieth question—'Have you had gonorrhea?'—and with the writer's response—'Yes.' "

By now the courtroom was as quiet as it had been at any time during the trial. Osborne dropped his voice to a stage whisper: "If I thought there was another way, I would not read further. But I have a passionate interest in bringing to justice the murderer of one—nay, two—innocent human beings and therefore must go on to the next question: 'Are you impotent?' The writer replies, 'Not entirely.' 'Partially impotent?' . . . 'Yes.' " Here Osborne paused dramatically before continuing. "I cannot in good conscience soil this august chamber with the detailed description of the writer's unholy condition. It is described in minute detail on this paper in my hand, Exhibit S-2. I prefer to make available to the jury this piece of evidence, the Marston Remedy diagnosis blank."

Osborne now walked to the jurybox and handed the paper with its envelope to the foreman. "Each of you gentlemen can read on and draw your own conclusions as to the character of the man who would place such a burden on his worst enemy," he said, "let alone his friend, Henry Barnet."

At this point, Blanche noticed that Roland was writing something on a small tablet he held on his lap. Curious, she leaned toward him and discovered that he was marking out the circles and crosses for the game of tic-tac-toe. In disbelief she drew back to her previous position. If he did not care about that which had been read aloud, neither did she. Silently she reaffirmed her determination to wait out the trial, but never to return to her husband.

With the diagnosis blank fresh in the minds of the jurors, Osborne now summoned the rest of his army of handwriting experts. One after another they were brought to the stand—to identify exhibits, to identify Roland's admitted handwriting and then Cornish's, to compare one exhibit with another, and to draw conclusions. Hours and hours of testimony were required to establish a connection between Roland's admitted handwriting and the handwriting of letters that bore the name of H. C. Barnet, and then to relate the handwriting of these Barnet letters to letters that were signed H. Cornish, and finally, to make the most tenuous connection of all—the link to the poison package.

Bound up with the handwriting was the matter of the writing paper—the distinctive blue stationery with three entwined silver crescents—on which two of the Cornish letters were written. Roland had admitted that he possessed such stationery when questioned at the inquest, but the defense contended that since the writing paper was available at Tiffany's and at other quality shops in New York, there was nothing out of the ordinary in this. James Osborne, who of course intended to cross-examine Roland if he chose to testify in his own defense, ought to have expected that he would again admit to owning such writing paper. It was peculiar then that the District Attorney's office placed such high priority on obtaining the testimony of Mary Melando, more often known as Mamie, the erstwhile friend of Roland Molineux.

Osborne surely had something other than writing paper in mind when he called upon the resources of the New York police to seek out Mamie Melando, residing in New Jersey beyond the limits of a subpoena, and deliver her to the court as a witness for the prosecution.

Months earlier, Mamie had called on Bartow Weeks in his law office, expecting that he would want the sheets of blue stationery from Roland's room that were still in her possession and that he would be willing to pay for them. Mamie had approached him with all the assertiveness she could muster. However, as in all of her encounters with men, she was meant to be dominated rather than to prevail. She left Weeks's office as she had entered, penniless and still in possession of the sheets of writing paper. As she walked to the ferry that day, Mamie heeded the lawyer's admonition and divested herself of the paper by shredding it to bits. She returned to New Jersey with every intention of staying there until the Molineux affair blew over.

Mamie Melando's options in life were limited by the unenviable situation in which she lived and from which she could not seem to extricate herself. She might have aspired to nothing more than a dependable factory job had Roland Molineux not noticed her years earlier. The position at the Herrmann factory from which he had her dismissed in the fall of 1897 was that of forewoman, a position in which she and the members of her family took immense pride. Now, two years later, Mamie's condition was pitiable. She had become an habitué of Newark's disorderly houses, and although there was no evidence that Mamie was a prostitute, her notoriety in the local drinking establishments made it an easy task to find her. Thus the two plain clothes detectives who were sent to bring Mamie across the state line had little trouble locating her and even less trouble luring her to "a party on Manhattan." The following morning, Mamie found herself at the women's detention center in New York City, where she remained for a number of days until Osborne was ready for her testimony.

On the afternoon that Mamie Melando was sworn in as a witness, Roland Molineux lost his amiable smile and distant look. For the remaining days of the trial, his face bore an uncharacteristic grimness and his bearing could best be described as that of a beaten man. Blanche noted the change and interpreted it as a kind of poetic justice. Rachel Greene and Minnie Betts had demolished the last vestiges of her reputation. It was only fair that this pathetic young woman should do the same for Roland.

Mamie was dressed in a worn but decent dark coat which she had attempted to brighten with a colorful scarf, and there was a rather comical feather in her drab felt hat. Younger than Blanche, she appeared to be ten years older. As Osborne approached the witness stand in preparation for his interrogation, Mamie shied away in the manner of a cornered, frightened animal. Yet, under his questioning, she readily acknowledged her long friendship with Roland Molineux, and even implied that the nature of their relationship permitted her easy access to his private rooms and to his ordinary personal possessions. Osborne chose his questions carefully, intent on drawing out the fact that Mamie, a loyal Herrmann factory employee, had been summarily dismissed at Roland's whim. When he was finished, there was no doubt among the listeners that poor Mamie Melando was a wronged woman.

Bartow Weeks then took his turn with the witness. He rather cleverly led Mamie into statements that appeared to be contradictory. On the one side, she claimed to be such a good friend of Roland Molineux; yet it seemed she was poorly informed about all matters relating to him, even those that applied to the period when Mamie had acquired the writing paper. Mamie was beginning to sound like a spinner of tales at best, and a liar at worst.

Normally the defense attorney's cross-examination of the prosecution's witness would have concluded the testimony of that witness. However, in Mamie's case there was an unusual turn of events in the proceedings. Recorder Goff, whose role as presiding judge had been mostly that of a curmudgeon—scolding the spectators, the jurors, and the prosecuting attorney with equal frequency, and berating and threatening the defense attorney at every opportunity—now chose to question the witness himself. There was little precedent for such action, and Goff was later severely criticized for it.

Goff leaned over his bench to speak directly to the young woman in the witness box. It was clear he was trying to put her at ease as he inquired about her past: When she left school . . . "after the eighth grade, Mr. Goff" . . . why she left school at such a young age . . . "I needed to earn money, sir" . . . and who her father was . . . "he used to be a policeman, sir."

Then he became very specific: "Miss Melando, when did you leave the employ of Morris Herrmann and Company?"

"Well, two years ago, Mr. Goff."

"And what have you been working at since?"

Mamie looked to the floor in embarrassment: "Nothing, sir."

"You have not been engaged since then?"

"No, sir."

"You have not received wages from any person, nor from any source?" Goff began to lose his newfound mellowness.

"No, sir—no wages from anybody."

Goff must have felt that he had made a point, for he turned abruptly to the matter of the blue writing paper. "Miss Melando, these four sheets of note paper that the District Attorney has shown to you . . . you say that you saw them before, or that you saw paper similar to them?"

Mamie spoke somewhat timidly: "Yes, sir."

Then he asked Mamie to describe the paper in her own words—the color, the nature and color of the crescents, and the existence of the matching envelopes. From there he went on to the matter of Mamie's access to Roland's rooms.

"Were you in the habit of going to Mr. Molineux's rooms?"

"Yes, sir."

"You had the privilege of going into his room when he was not there?"

"Yes, sir, if Mr. Molineux was in the factory."

"Was he in the factory at the time that you went in and took the blue paper?"

Mamie hesitated: "I . . . I believe so, but I can't rightly say for sure."

Goff's questions were beginning to sound like reprimands to Mamie: "Why did you come to take away this paper, Miss Melando, when you knew it belonged to Mr. Molineux?"

"Well, I liked it; I liked the color; I thought it was the love-liest writing paper I had ever seen, especially with the silver moons."

"So you were attracted to it, eh; and did you also take some envelopes?"

"Yes, I took envelopes also, but just one for each sheet of paper."

The recorder shook his head and Mamie cowered beneath his judgmental glare. He continued: "Did you tell Mr. Molineux that you had taken the paper?"

"No, sir."

"Did he ever speak to you about it?"

"Oh . . . no, sir."

"Whom did you tell, if any person, that you had taken this paper?"

"I never told anybody, sir."

"Well then, how did Mr. Osborne know that you had this paper?"

Mamie relaxed a bit. "Oh, Mr. Osborne . . . I told him about it just last Friday when he came to see me in the place where they were keeping me. I didn't know that was what you meant."

Recorder Goff was not yet satisfied. He was clearly after some additional information from Mamie and he continued to press: "Miss Melando, did anyone ever speak to you about the paper before Mr. Osborne spoke to you?"

"Not that I remember of."

Goff sat back in his large chair, as if to gather some additional strength before pushing further. He picked up a nearby glass, poured himself some water, took a sip, and leaned forward to try again. He cleared his throat and began: "You know of course, Miss Melando, that you are expected to tell the truth here?"

"Yes, sir."

"And you are prepared to tell the truth to every question?"

"Yes, sir."

"You have been very friendly to Mr. Molineux?"

"Yes, sir."

"And he has always treated you very kindly, has he not?"

"Oh . . . yes, sir." Mamie's voice faltered and her body trembled.

"His kindness would not prevent you from telling the truth, would it?"

"No, sir."

The recorder was now speaking louder and in apparent anger. "Now tell me, just who was it that spoke to you about the paper?"

Mamie lowered her head.

"Just look at me, Miss Melando." Goff was now shouting.

Mamie looked up, her face flushed, and mustered a response: "I can't remember, Mr. Goff." Then she let her head drop and began to sob.

Goff lowered his voice. "Now, now, Miss Melando, you know it is only the truth that we want . . . only the truth. Look at it this way; did anyone ever talk to you about the writing paper?"

Mamie remained silent.

Goff reiterated his statement: "Did you ever discuss the writing paper with anyone?"

Mamie sat frozen, her head bowed. Goff's tone now changed. "Ah, someone did speak to you about the writing paper then."

Mamie broke her silence. "I can't remember, Mr. Goff."

In his kindest voice, Goff continued to remonstrate: "You are not afraid to tell the truth, are you? You are a good girl, are you not?"

Mamie raised her head and looked at her interrogator with red eyes. "I have always tried to be," she answered, and then the sobbing began again.

Goff continued in this gentler vein. "Well then, there is no reason why you should be afraid to speak the truth, is there? No one here wishes to hurt you at all. You should feel perfectly at home in this room. We will treat you always with kindness. All we want from you is the truth. You have nothing to secrete, have you?"

Mamie spoke: "Nothing at all; no, sir."

"Well, then there is no objection, no reason why you should not speak what you know. Now then, tell us who spoke with you about this paper?"

Mamie finally gave up the information that her interrogator sought: "Mr. Weeks spoke to me about it."

"Mr. Weeks?" Goff inquired.

"Yes, sir."

Goff probed further: "Where did Mr. Weeks speak to you about the paper?"

"In his office, sir."

"And when were you in his office, Miss Melando?"

"It was last January, just a year ago now."

Goff spoke hesitantly, as if he might lose the thread if he became careless. "How did Mr. Weeks know that you had sheets of Mr. Molineux's blue writing paper?"

Mamie's final reply was disarming in its simplicity. "I showed them to him, but he wouldn't take them."

With that, Mamie Melando was excused and her long association with Roland Molineux was thus concluded. In their extended duel, Mamie had reluctantly delivered the final thrust. Her testimony left little doubt regarding the ownership of the blue writing paper with the silver crescents. Moreover, the testimony had introduced ambiguities with respect to Bartow Weeks's role in the matter, ambiguities that were never resolved.

The threads connecting Roland Molineux to the poison package received by Harry Cornish were now pulled together even more tightly. The links from the letter boxes, through the writing paper, and to the patent medicine firms forged the connection to the poisoner himself. All that was missing was a personal identification of the renter of each letter box.

As its final witness, the prosecution called Joseph Koch, the owner of the "Cornish" letter box, and Nicholas Heckmann, owner of the "Barnet" box. Under oath Koch claimed he could not identify the lessee of his box. But Nicholas Heckmann affirmed that the defendant, Roland Molineux, was "H. C. Barnet," the lessee of Box 217. Of all the evidence presented in the long trial, this single identification was the most damaging to Roland.

SEVENTEEN

Conviction

James Osborne rested his case for the prosecution early in the afternoon of February 5. Bartow Weeks moved for an immediate adjournment so that he might consult with his partner, George Gordon Battle, who had been indisposed at home for several days. Recorder Goff granted the motion. This was a rare achievement for Weeks, who during the trial had raised several hundred objections, of which Goff had denied all but a handful.

Blanche and Roland bade one another their public farewells, and Blanche entered the Molineux carriage for the ride home. The dreariness of the early spring afternoon was accentuated by the expectation that Weeks would begin his defense on the following day, calling upon his host of witnesses to counter the claims of the prosecution. Blanche had been led to expect that she too would be asked to testify, though Weeks had barely spoken to her during the trial, let alone coached her.

That evening, Blanche suffered through the obligatory family meal with her mother-in-law, for the general had not yet returned. Too often of late this had been the case, and on this particular night it was an excruciating experience for Blanche.

She retreated to her little room upstairs as soon as courtesy allowed.

Some time later, just as Blanche was about to retire for the night, there was a knock on her door. She opened it to find her father-in-law in a somewhat agitated state. He quickly explained that he had just come from Battle's home, where the two defense attorneys had been discussing their latest strategy. Blanche invited the general to sit with her by the fire, offering him tea from the pot the maid had brought her earlier. He seemed eager to talk of what had transpired during the late afternoon and early evening: "My dear, Mr. Battle and Mr. Weeks have advised me that they will enter no defense."

Blanche gasped, for she was convinced that the evidence so far would convict Roland overwhelmingly. The general reassured her: "No, do not fret, for our counsels are wise men. They believe that the jury will convict Roland no matter what evidence they produce, and they conclude it would be poor tactics to present the favorable evidence at this time. This trial has been a travesty of justice, and Mr. Weeks plans to appeal the decision immediately. This grieves me beyond words, but we will prevail in the final judgment. I am in touch with justices of the Appeals Court, and Mr. Weeks assures me that the appeal will succeed — both Goff and Osborne have committed egregious errors."

Then he took Blanche's two hands in his own and spoke tenderly to her. "This means of course that you will not have to testify, nor will your friend, Mrs. Bellinger. Daughter, you should take heart this night, for Roland will be free and he will return to you by and by."

Blanche's eyes were moist as she gathered her courage to speak. "General Molineux, you have always been kind to me, like a father in many ways, and for this I thank you. What you tell me tonight does make good news. Today I thought it was the end for Roland. But, sir, I must tell you something else — I can never go back to Roland. I can no longer be his wife. After tomorrow, or the day after, or whenever this miserable trial is finished, I must leave New York. I am not sure where I shall go;

I only hope that my sister or my brother will have me for a while so that I might leave the public eye and withdraw into obscurity. I know it has been the worst for Roland, but you cannot believe how I have suffered through the entire experience. It is simply too much for me, and I must now go away forever. Please understand and give me your blessing."

General Molineux let go of her hands and clasped his own together. For some moments there was silence, as slowly he considered his reply. "No, that is not possible, Blanche. You must remain here longer; you cannot leave before the appeal is completed, and if there is another trial, as I expect there to be, you must be here for that. We cannot have it otherwise. I shall try to be understanding of your wishes—that is, that you now do not wish to continue the marriage. For the moment, it makes no difference, for with Roland incarcerated, there can be no marriage. If later you feel the same way as you do now, then it will be your privilege to go where you wish. But this is not possible now. For the sake of Roland—mind you, of Roland's life—you will stay in this house as you have up until now."

Blanche dropped her head in her hands and gave her body over to piteous sobbing. The general sat a little straighter but did not move from his chair. Not until Blanche raised her head and looked at him through tearstained eyes did he speak again. "Blanche, you will stay with us now; you will not abandon your husband in this most cruel moment of his life; you will not desert him at this time when evil persons dare call him a murderer.

"For the time being, all of your needs are supplied. You receive a stipend from Roland that should amply cover your personal needs. In addition I am providing for you this home—my home—so that you are relieved of all the ordinary burdens of a household. You should consider yourself very fortunate that you no longer must fend for yourself in a world that can be harsh indeed.

"One day Roland will be declared innocent; my boy will be free and he will come home. At that time you may choose to stay or to go. If you choose to go, I personally shall see that you never want for material goods. I promise this to you even as I order you to remain here now. You know that I am an honorable man. Do not believe that I am without understanding for your suffering; we all suffer, however, and my boy Roland suffers most of all."

General Molineux stood up and left the room, closing the door behind him. Blanche rose from her chair and prepared herself for bed. Through the night she alternately slept and sobbed.

On the morning of February 6 an atmosphere of excitement filled the Criminal Courts Building, for it was generally believed that the case for the defense in the trial of Roland Molineux was about to begin. The case for the prosecution had indeed had its high points, particularly those details relating to the death of Henry Barnet and the affair that preceded it, but there had been too many witnesses to sustain the interest of the crowd. As the prosecution wound up its case, the members of the press found much of the testimony tedious to the point of boredom. Still, the reading public demanded news of the trial and the reporters obliged.

It was expected that Roland Molineux would testify in his own defense, and his wife also, with the possibility of new revelations. Long before the doors to the courtroom were unlocked, there was a sizable crowd milling about in the corridors of the building. Even the faithful reporters, wrung out from weeks of testimony in the stuffy courtroom, appeared to have gotten their second wind as they leaned against the pillars and banisters, smoking their cigarettes and chatting amiably. At 10:00 A.M. the double doors swung open and the crowd pressed forward into the courtroom, filling all but the few reserved seats within minutes.

As on every previous day, General Molineux, his wife and his daughter-in-law arrived at 10:25 A.M., and a minute or two later the defendant strode in with his attorney at his side. George Battle slipped in at the last moment, with a heavy scarf draped about his neck and extending down both front and back. He had not been present for a number of days and was still recovering from the grippe. The last to enter before Recorder Goff and the jury was James Osborne, this time accompanied by the District Attorney himself. Distracted by other matters, namely revelations about his conduct in office, which continued to make front page news, Asa Bird Gardiner had been absent during most of the prosecution. However, since this day was to be the start of the defense (and there was no telling whether Weeks would make it a long or a short matter), Gardiner overcame his reluctance to appear in public.

The twelve members of the jury then filed in and took their places. One juror, Manheim Brown, had missed much of the defense testimony due to illness, but he was back in his place. Like Battle, he was bundled up against the cold, and he appeared to be very ill.

The last to enter was Recorder Goff. The entire assemblage rose as one and sat down again only after he had taken his own seat. As Goff pounded the gavel to begin, Bartow Weeks rose to be recognized. "Your Honor, the defendant Roland Molineux has been indicted on four separate counts of murder. I move that the court compel the People, as ably represented here by the Assistant District Attorney, Mr. Osborne, to elect on which count of the indictment they would go to the jury."

Goff slammed down his gavel: "Motion denied," he bellowed. This was the last time the now familiar words were heard at the trial. There were no regrets, as they had become a tiresome litany.

Weeks was now expected to do what virtually every defense attorney does at this point in the trial — move that the case against his client be dismissed for failure of proof. Instead he made a startling announcement: "We believe that the prosecution has failed to establish its charge and we rest the defense upon the People's case."

The chambers exploded in noisy exclamations as members of the press beat a hasty path to the doors. Osborne showed profound shock at the move and entered into frantic consultation with Gardiner. Roland smiled and reached for Blanche's hand, but she kept it well hidden in her large muff and he had to settle for a wrist. General Molineux also was smiling as George Battle leaned over to speak with him. Bartow Weeks stood smugly in his place while Recorder Goff pounded his gavel for attention.

Five minutes later, order finally prevailed. Goff addressed Weeks, who had been standing quietly during the confusion, and asked for the defense's summary. Weeks was ready and turned to the jury, addressing the twelve through their foreman. First of all, he made the customary compliments to those who had, at such personal sacrifice, performed their civic duty. He began summing up the case with a discussion of the motive in a crime, his contention being that no motive had been shown to exist in the death of Mrs. Adams. Then he turned to the character of the defendant and began to attack in earnest the gossip and hearsay that had been slipped into the record in the name of evidence. Weeks attacked particularly the wealth of testimony relating to the petty politics at the Knickerbocker Athletic Club—schoolboy antics, he termed it, in no way contributing to a motive for murder. He spoke soberly, with a touch of sadness, as he recalled the excessive amount of testimony and exhibits devoted to Roland's courtship of Blanche and to his friendship with Henry Barnet. In righteous indignation he condemned those who pried into the private lives of individuals—the dead who could no longer defend themselves, as well as the living. All this, supposedly in the name of justice, had nothing to do with justice, and certainly nothing to do with the death of Mrs. Adams. It was a sorry day, according to Weeks, when a conviction for murder was asked for based on evidence as far removed from the victim as that relating to the death of Mr. Barnet. Weeks lay blame for this misuse of the People's trust directly on the Assistant District Attorney. He warned the jurors that they must not succumb to the temptation set before them by the prosecutor: "The wrong you may do can never be repaired. Unless you are so well satisfied of such an abiding conviction in your hearts, hesitate long before you render a verdict that can never be repaired. . . .

"We know that this mass of matter that has been placed before you, you will examine well, and will winnow the chaff from the wheat, and after you have gotten rid of all these matters which are only to becloud and befog your vision, you will see clear as day the verdict that your conscience demands that you shall. render. . . .

"We rest the case with you, confident in your verdict, because we believe, and know, that you are men of conscience. We ask no maudlin sympathy; we ask no favors. We ask only as a man to his fellow man: 'Do unto others as you would they should do unto you,' and doing that, we are sure of the result."

Weeks wiped his brow and his nose and returned to his seat. His summation, which had lasted four hours, had been somewhat lacking in fervor and had only partially held the attention of the jurors. In fact a low hum had pervaded the room throughout much of his speech as the bored spectators whispered among themselves. Weeks himself did not consider this his greatest moment in the courtroom; he later blamed it upon a cold and a hoarseness that had limited the volume of his voice as well as the length of his presentation.

James Osborne now stepped forward and, like Weeks before him, faced the jurors: "May it please the court, and you, Mr. Foreman, and each of you gentlemen of the jury." Thus began his summing up of the case for the prosecution, or rather the People, as he frequently reminded his audience. The discourse was to last two and a half days and would consist of more than 88,000 words, much of it repetitive but none of it boring.

The fact that Weeks had entered no defense became the keynote of Osborne's speech. In fact Osborne directed his initial attack on the attorney: "I have noticed that whenever the District Attorney speaks a very particular truth in this courtroom, Mr. Weeks objects. And his whole defense in this case may be expressed as made by one great objection, 'I object.' To what? To the light, to the truth? . . .

"I tell you he is an Anglo-Saxon man. He has been advocating the truth all his life, while he was in the District Attorney's office, and, when he suddenly undertakes to pull down the blinds—guilt always pulls down blinds—innocence is willing to have them lifted as high as heaven — when he undertakes to pull down the blinds, he always gets caught. . . .

"And is not that the reason why Mr. Weeks did not dare to put in any defense in this case? . . . That he did not dare to put on the stand this defendant's wife? I say, and I mean it, that there is not enough force or power under the sun to keep a woman from going on the stand and giving the lie to the District Attorney — if it was a lie. I assert that she, in her person, represents a living, concrete form of the motive in the Barnet case. . . .

"You must remember that this defendant was married on November 29, 1898. You must remember that Barnet died on November 10, 1898. . . . You must remember that the defendant testified at the inquest that he had been trying to marry this woman from a time running back to January 1898. You must remember that he also testified at the inquest that this woman refused to marry him. That is his own testimony. . . . The plain, cold facts are that this defendant had been trying to marry this woman and that this woman had refused him until Barnet was cold in his grave. . . .

"This brings us to the bedside of Barnet, and I wish here to tell you, gentlemen, that you must not regard the Barnet case as a crime, that is, you must not allow the Barnet case to prejudice your mind against the defendant, as a criminal matter, but you must only regard it as a transaction, tending to prove the existence of the Adams case, if it does do that. It is not proved as a crime, but proved as a separate and similar transaction, tending to show that the defendant committed the Adams crime. It is introduced in evidence here, by the District Attorney, for the purpose of getting a description of the murderer; because every man of any common sense must know that the man who killed Barnet, or sent him that powder, is the same man that sent it to Cornish. . . .

"I say that Mr. Weeks has not been able to suggest any other person in the world that disliked Cornish, or any other man in the world that had any motive against Barnet.

"And you have already conceived here in your mind that the man who destroyed Barnet, and sent poison to Cornish, must have had some motive, strong or weak, adequate or inadequate, good or bad, sufficient or insufficient; must have had some motive, and that this defendant is the only human being in the world who had any motive.

"Now we come to the next proposition here, the next link in the chain. On the fourteenth of January in 1898 it appears in evidence here that Captain McClusky, having reasonable common sense, came to the conclusion that if he could find the man who did away with Barnet, he could find the man who sent the poison to Cornish. And so Captain McClusky sent a photographic copy of the address on the poison package to a little girl at Kutnow Brothers along with this request: 'Find that letter among the hundreds of thousands of letters that Kutnow Brothers have.'

"And the young woman, sitting down and carefully comparing the poison package address with the mass of letters, found this letter."

Osborne picked up the letter and waved it toward the jury, toward Goff and toward Weeks. Then he continued: "Captain McClusky called in his handwriting expert and Mr. Weeks called in his own expert and they both looked at that letter and agreed that the man who wrote that letter wrote the address on the poison package; both of them agreed on that. That is sworn evidence and not denied. Mr. Weeks's expert agreed that the man who wrote that blue letter also wrote the address on the poison package. His exact expression at the time was 'Find me the man that uses the blue-crested paper and you will have found the murderer.' Those were his exact words.

"Gentlemen of the jury, we will discover—if our theory is right—that the man who hated Barnet, the man who hated Cornish, the man who had the motive, and the man who used that paper must be the same man. . . .

"Great heavens, can it be so? . . . Does the name of any person suggest itself to the minds of the jury as the man who did use that blue paper? . . . Does the still, small voice of the conscience of the jury suggest the name of any human being as using that blue letter paper?

"Is there a name upon the lips of every human being within

the sound of my voice? . . . Does anybody's name suggest itself to you? A name suggest itself to me — the name of the defendant, Roland Molineux. And here is the letter."

Osborne laid down the letter and picked up another of the blue sheets. He pointed to the entwined crescents embossed upon the paper: "There is the fatal crest and there is the envelope. Now, I will read this letter to you. 'Dear Sir, Please find enclosed 25 cents, for which send remedy, and oblige, Very truly, Roland Molineux, number 6 Jersey Street, Newark, New Jersey.'

"What kind of a remedy is that? . . . For what disease was that remedy sent? . . . What did the man who sent that letter need the remedy for? . . . To what use was he going to put that remedy?

"We have evidence here that the remedy was used to cure impotence — impotence, a lack of virility — a lack of manhood — a lack of strength — a lack of power. I ask you, under your oath as jurymen, if that is not exactly the kind of man from whom you would expect this crime to come?

"Have you not already said, in your hearts, in your consciences, when you first heard of this cyanide of mercury being sent by the mails, sent on its deadly mission, like an arrow flying in the nighttime, to kill, not perhaps the man for whom it was intended, but some innocent child or some old woman, you knew that the man was *outré*, peculiar, abnormal, in some respects; that he lacked a man's strength and a man's virility? . . . And what do you find?

"You find that the man who hated Cornish, and the man who found Barnet to be an impediment, was the same man who used the fatal blue paper with the fatal crest on it; and it turns out that that man is found to be in need of a remedy for impotence.

"Doesn't that explain the whole thing? Is it necessary for the District Attorney to say another word in this case?

"I leave it to you, as men of honor, I leave it to you, as twelve ordinary businessmen, if that does not explain this whole crime. There is your man — abnormal; there is your man, who has something of him lacking in manhood. There is your man, from whom you would expect conduct like that. There is your man, who believes he needs a remedy for impotence.

"Mr. Weeks—the great Mr. Weeks, one of the most intelligent lawyers in America—Mr. Weeks undertook to explain to you all the evidence in this case, but that was one bit of evidence that Mr. Weeks did not refer to—one bit of evidence that he did not undertake to explain—the contents of that letter and the necessity that the man had for a remedy for impotence. He passed it over in silence and said nothing about it.

"But the prosecuting officer declares that letter to be the most eloquent thing in this whole case. The prosecuting officer claims that an honest jury, contemplating the contents of that letter, knows now the man who was of such a moral nature as to commit that crime.

"Only one human being has been suggested in this case as having a motive for hating Cornish, a motive in Barnet's case, and as using the blue paper with the fatal crest, and that one human being turns out to be exactly the kind of man from whom you could expect such deeds as these. . . .

"Mr. Weeks asked wonderful questions, but when he asked questions, it seemed to me I heard the voice of one crying in the wilderness. He asked why I did not show something about the moral character of this defendant. He inquired how I could expect a man from his social position, from his surroundings, to commit such a crime.

"You must remember that this defendant did not live at home—that he left the parental roof—that he went to clubs—that he had rooms in Newark, away off in that barn of a factory.

"Think of the nights of debauchery—think of the nights of sexual excesses—think of the nights of sexual depravity that must have brought a young man to such a pass, a man acrobatic, a man athletic, a man with the measurements of an athlete—thirty-seven inches in the chest and thirty-two inches in the waist—a man who was one of the best horizontal bar performers on the trapeze; think of the nights of self-indulgence in that lonely room in Newark, over the canal, that must have brought a man of that vigor to such a pass that he needed a remedy for impotence.

"And Mr. Weeks wants to know why I did not put in evidence of his moral nature. Why, he knows I cannot do it. He knows that the law does not allow the District Attorney to attack the moral character of the defendant. He knows that I cannot say one solitary word against the moral character of that prisoner at the bar, unless it comes out of the testimony which happens to be relevant to the case.

"But the thought will undoubtedly occur to you, gentlemen of the jury, that perhaps the existence of the little piece of blue paper, signed by the defendant and conceded to be written by him, is the reason why no witnesses have been called for the defense."

As Osborne concluded this emotional recounting of the testimony, weaving together the various threads to make his case against Roland, he became even more melodramatic: "There have been times in this case when I began to think of poor old Mrs. Adams, stricken down, stricken down without an opportunity to make her peace with her God, stricken down while she was in the performance of her family duty, leaving alone and unprotected her daughter and her son; stricken down in the most cruel and the most brutal manner. . . . Sometimes it seems to me in the nighttime that I can almost hear the voice of Mrs. Adams, calling to me. . . .

"And then Barnet, Barnet, in the vigor of his youth and manhood, stricken down in that same manner. . . . And will a jury of my countrymen quail before the honest and just verdict? I think not.

"I believe that you are made of that stalwart nature, that nature which has heretofore represented the northern races, the northern races which can say with pride, 'Poisoning is not our crime. Poisoning is not one of our faults, but is a comfit of Italy.'

"The question is: Do you want to make poisoning one of our sins? Do you want to make it one of our crimes? It has been the proud boast of our race that, when we struck an enemy, we struck him down in the light of the noonday sun.

"They have been guilty of atrocious, of brutal crimes, the northern races, but they have not been a race of sneaks and cowards and poisoners, and I do not believe that a jury of my countrymen is going to countenance any such crime.

"Gentlemen, in conclusion I say that this defendant has degraded the traditions of the race to which he belongs. I say that he is chargeable with the death of Mrs. Adams and the death of Barnet. I say that the evidence from every direction points to that conclusion. . . . I leave this case in your hands, knowing that you will find your verdict in the sight of God, in the sight of man, without fear and without favor."

There were many in the courtroom who would remember James Osborne's legendary summation with fondness and admiration, and among his peers in the legal profession it earned him high praise. But there was one who would remember it otherwise.

During Osborne's performance, Blanche had rarely taken her eyes from him. In vain she hoped that he might show some compassion, if not for Roland, at least for her. That he did not instilled in her a lifelong loathing for the man and his tactics. This animosity would have little effect on the life of James Osborne; within Blanche, it would grow and spread like a cancer and would remain with her until her dying day.

On that last morning of Osborne's speech, General Molineux conspicuously exchanged seats with his wife that he might be next to his daughter-in-law. He patted her and spoke softly to her as the prosecutor engaged in his final histrionics. When it was all over, Goff beckoned to a deputy to whom he whispered a command, after which the deputy went immediately to the Molineux family. He informed the general that the ladies were invited to await the verdict in Goff's private chambers; then he escorted the women through the private door behind the bench.

Goff now spoke privately with the jury foreman, who relayed an urgent message that Manheim Brown was on the verge of physical collapse and requested that the deliberations begin immediately so that he might return to his home and his bed as quickly as possible. Goff was not sympathetic. It was noon now, time for dinner, and he was of the opinion that all of the jurors, Brown included, would benefit from a hot meal. A coach was ordered and arrived shortly to carry the jurors across to the Astor House, where they could enjoy a comfortable meal in seclusion. Afterward they were returned to the juryroom, where the deliberations took place. Manheim Brown had to be supported on both arms and pleaded to be excused, but Goff and others impressed upon him the importance of his participation and the cost to the State if he should fail to complete the verdict. (No one bothered to calculate the cost to Manheim Brown, who within a few days would be dead from pneumonia.)

While the jury dined, the Molineux women sat silently alone in the judge's anteroom, without food or drink. When the deliberations began, George Battle and the general joined them to wait out the verdict. As the afternoon wore on, messengers came to announce that the jury had requested this exhibit or that and that the deliberations were swaying in Roland's favor or against. There was a rumor that three jurors were prepared to acquit; nay that two were leaning in Roland's favor; and finally that only one was holding out. The hours passed slowly. Lights were lit in the room and, later, outside. Through the windows the cries of newsboys could be heard; the rumors had found their way to the printed page sooner than they had reached the family's ears. When the clock struck six, Battle went out, returning a short time later with the news that there was no news, only false alarms and rumors. At last General Molineux announced that the ladies must be taken home; there was no telling how long the jury would deliberate. The Molineux carriage stood waiting at the side door of the building to receive the two ashen-faced women dressed in black and to speed them across to Brooklyn.

Of all the arrivals at Fort Greene Place in which Blanche participated, this was the most welcoming. In spite of the furs that enveloped her, she was chilled to the bone and in much need of a hot drink and some nourishment. This one evening above all others, the lighted brownstone residence and the warm greeting by the maids were most gratefully appreciated. Strong tea and little sandwiches awaited the two women in the library, and though it was not her usual custom, Blanche joined her mother-in-law before the blazing hearth.

They had only a short wait. From a distance they could hear the shouts of those who were following the carriage that bore the general and George Battle. The sounds were muffled, but they had the eerie quality of a death knell. Presently the general came in with the news: "They have found him guilty."

He need not have said the words.

EIGHTEEN

Sing Sing

Early in the morning on the day following Roland's conviction, the two Molineux women arrived at the Criminal Courts Building to make their way across the Bridge of Sighs and into the Tombs prison. Though Roland had walked this depressing path almost daily for three months, neither his mother nor his wife had visited him since the trial began. Roland had wished to spare them this ordeal. However, with his sentencing imminent, Mrs. Molineux was disconsolate, and not even the general could dissuade her from going to her son's side.

Through the gray stone corridors the women followed two police officers until they reached a pair of iron barred doors. These were unlocked by an officer on the other side, and as the two women entered, the massive doors swung closed behind them. They continued on through an enclosed space surrounded by stone and iron—a space that was neither a corridor nor a room. At the far end stood a few chairs, a bench and a table. This little grouping of furniture, arranged as if to resemble an informal parlor, was surrounded by an iron cage. Inside stood Roland, freshly groomed and looking quite as though he had just stepped from his quarters at the club, or so it seemed to Blanche as she approached. The officer opened the gate and the women entered, each in turn embracing the sole inhabitant of this cordoned space. The three sat down together while several officers stood outside, a respectable distance away but close enough to hear every word that was spoken.

There was little conversation to exchange. All three knew the expected outcome of the sentencing which still lay ahead, and although each chose to believe the general's prediction that Roland would eventually be freed, they were well aware that it would be months before his appeal would be heard and even longer before a new trial would begin.

A quarter hour later the gate to the cage was unlocked. The two women embraced the prisoner once more, then left the enclosure and followed the two police officers back through the long stone corridor, their echoing footsteps underscoring the bleakness of the surroundings. The general's carriage awaited them just outside the courthouse.

Six days after his conviction, Roland was brought before the bar to receive his sentence. Flanked by his attorneys, he stood at the counsel table, prepared to hear his fate. Recorder Goff, perhaps aware that this was to be his own final scene in the drama, addressed the convicted in a funereal tone: "Roland Molineux, have you any legal cause to show why judgment of death should not be pronounced upon you?"

Roland pulled from his pocket some scribbled notes and was about to speak when Weeks interrupted him to introduce a motion for a new trial. Goff impatiently denied the motion. Undaunted, Weeks put forth a second motion, which was also denied. Then he prepared the way for his client: "The defendant, your Honor, desires to speak in his own behalf."

Roland began in his well-bred, modulated voice, calmly asserting that he had been unjustly convicted of a crime of which he was wholly innocent and that he had been wrongly implicated in a second crime of which he was also wholly innocent. As he continued, his voice became more strident and his fingers nervously twisted the paper in his hands. He declared that he was stunned by the testimony that had been given in what was purported to be a court of justice. He denounced the "yellow journalism" practiced by the newspapers and vehemently denied ever using his hand to address the poison package.

Roland then turned away from Goff and looked directly at District Attorney Gardiner, seated next to James Osborne. His entire body was now trembling visibly and he began to shout: "Your Honor, all of this is nothing to what is in my heart at this moment. Above and beyond everything else, I denounce and despise the action of the District Attorney in attempting to vilify and attack the character of the pure and lovely woman who bears my name. It was the act of a blackguard. It was a damnable lie!" He paused for a few seconds, gripping the bar before him in an effort to compose himself, then quietly spoke his last words: "And now, your Honor, I am prepared to hear you sentence me. I am not afraid, because I am not guilty."

Recorder Goff solemnly passed sentence—death by the electric chair, to be effected sometime during the week of March 26, 1900. Later that afternoon, Roland was delivered to Sing Sing prison at Ossining, New York, to await his execution.

For several days thereafter, General Molineux did not leave his home. There was little he could do for his son while the attorneys prepared to mount their appeal, and he chose instead to remain close to his wife, who presided over the family sitting room in full mourning as she had done throughout the trial. But burdened as he was, the inactivity soon made him restless, and he left her side in favor of his books and mementos in the library. As a diversion, he took out the albums with the papers and letters from the war years in the hopes of immersing himself in those fond memories. One afternoon as he sat at the library table, Blanche appeared in the room, and the long-absent sparkle returned to his eyes at the welcome sight of her.

"My child, what a pleasant surprise," he said. "I have worried of you day and night, knowing that you leave your room so seldom. These are sad times for all of us, but they are saddest when we face them alone. No burden is intolerable when it can be shared with another."

Blanche's heartbeat quickened at these unexpected words of friendship. The general drew up a chair so that she might sit beside him, then spoke with an intimacy that reminded Blanche of their first meetings in this same room what now seemed like a lifetime earlier. "My dear, in my own sorrow I am not insensitive to yours. It is exceedingly difficult to suffer when one is young. We who are older and who have lived long have learned how to endure. With you it is different; the days must seem interminable and the suffering intolerable. Is it not so?"

He took hold of her arm with his firm hand and drew himself closer as Blanche answered in a choked voice, "Yes, sir, it is so."

"I know that you have changed your attitude toward Roland," he continued, "but you won't do anything rash, will you? Please don't try to leave now. I have worried about this, particularly in these last days, but I want you to remember that just because they have convicted him, that doesn't make him guilty. I know the awfulness of it all, my child, but . . . (here his voice broke) it has been twice awful for my boy!"

For the first and last time, Blanche saw the tears in his eyes and heard the weeping in his voice. Overwhelmed with compassion for this kind man whom she had come to respect immensely, Blanche patted his hand comfortingly and reassured him: "I will do whatever you ask of me."

At this the general cleared his throat and took his hand from Blanche's arm. His spirits buoyed, he stood up and began to pace the floor as if engaged in a debate over his son's innocence, speaking as he walked: "You know . . . you know he is innocent. . . . We cannot weaken now. . . . And so much depends on you."

Blanche slipped out of the library as quietly as she had entered. She returned to her room feeling better than she had in a long time. She had actually given comfort to another human being, one for whom she cared a great deal. There must be something of value within her, something on which she could eventually build a new life.

The future no longer seemed as unsure, and Blanche began to make plans. If Roland was to die in March, she would leave the house then. If his execution were stayed for the appeal and if there was a second trial in which he might be declared inno-

221

cent, it would take at least another year. But it had already taken more than that and she had managed to survive; yes, she could hold out for that long.

How much easier it would be, though, if she could go out a little—to the theater or the opera—to dine at Delmonico's once again, or to sit on Isia's veranda. But she reconciled herself to the reality of her situation—her soiled reputation and the possibility that she would never again experience such joys. A vision of James Osborne standing smugly in the courtroom and pointing his finger toward her obliterated all else; she threw herself on the bed and began to sob.

Day by day, activity in the Molineux household picked up as plans for the appeal began to take shape. Bartow Weeks was a frequent visitor and could often be found in the library discussing the matter with the general. He was more civil to Blanche than he had been at any time during the trial and even inquired as to whether she would like to make a public statement. It was evident that Weeks felt such a statement would be useful in contradicting any rumors of trouble in Roland's marriage. Blanche viewed it as an opportunity to salvage her good name, and she immediately went to work setting down on paper her rage against James Osborne. When she submitted the statement to the general, he expressed amazement that it encompassed so much beyond a declaration of a wife's loyalty to her husband. But both he and Weeks let it stand. It was a rare opportunity for Blanche to have her say, and certainly it could do no harm to Roland.

On the third of March the statement appeared in the *New York Times* over the signature of "Mrs. Roland B. Molineux." It began innocuously enough with a declaration by the wife of the convicted that she believed her husband to be innocent and that she had been happy during the first weeks of their marriage. She vouched for his character, knowing him to be "brave, strong, true."

Having stated what would be expected of any steadfast wife, Blanche launched her diatribe against Osborne.

"I cannot remain longer silent; I appeal to the women of the land—to the mothers, the wives, the daughters of the American nation. I ask you to feel for me—for one moment to put yourselves in my place—can you wonder that I break the silence so long enforced on me, that I cry aloud in my own behalf against the malicious, the cruel, the wanton lies? Shall a man because he is vested with the power of a public office—because he is the prosecuting official in a charge brought against the unfortunate husband of one American woman—shall he, I say, be permitted to make that hapless wife the target for his merciless invective, his unfounded and unproved accusations? Is she to be defamed and robbed of her fair name? Are her honor, her dignity, her character to be wantonly sullied? It is not for me to dwell upon the unprecedented attitude of the public prosecutor, who to bolster his case attacks the wife of the defendant. But was it not irrelevant? Was it not inconsequent? Besides, it was unfounded and untrue.

"I have remained dumb, with closed lips, while my name was being constantly associated and connected with that of my husband's friend Henry Barnet. The absurd rumors developed into infamous lies, and I know now at too late a date that credence was given to statements that had not a scintilla of truth for their foundations. . . . Every scrap of so-called evidence introduced at the late trial, every innuendo, every insinuation uttered by the District Attorney wherein he sought to connect my name with Mr. Barnet's and to show the existence of something more than an ordinary friendship, originated in his own very convenient and elastic imagination. He offered no proofs as to the veracity of his utterances regarding this phase of his case for one very simple reason. They did not exist; and the whole accusation brought against me regarding Mr. Barnet was one of huge fabrication, grossly and atrociously false.

"Why was so much that was virulent, so much that was slander introduced? Could it be possible that this same public prosecutor resorted to the introduction of such baseless, such utterly false and unsupported testimony as that given by a paid negro witness to strengthen his lamentably weak case? Did he fail to bring other witnesses to support the paid testimony of a negro serving maid because he knew such testimony could not be supported? I ask you, the mothers, wives, and daughters of our fair land, was it just? . . .

"In respect to it all, I have borne the absolutely unjustified and unwarranted reproach to myself, my womanhood, my dignity, my honor. I have suffered unspeakably, but that suffering has been naught compared to the anguish which has filled, and still continues to fill, my heart because of the atrocious injustice, the result of cowardly persecution, which one man, brave, calm, courageous, is enduring today, that man, my noble husband, in whom my faith, my trust, my confidence is absolute."

Early that morning George Battle delivered a copy of the *Times* to the Molineuxs in person. He burst into the house without waiting for the maid to announce him and called out to the inhabitants. General and Mrs. Molineux rushed from the back of the house, and a quick reading of the statement brought smiles to their faces. A maid was sent to fetch Blanche, and when she glided down the stairs, she was embraced in turn by her father-in-law, her mother-in-law and Battle.

"Splendid, splendid—a masterpiece of prose . . . so well-timed for our case." Battle was exhuberant as he spoke these and other words of praise, intermingling them with appropriate phrases read directly from the newspaper. He assured them all that the appearance of Blanche's statement was a good omen for their cause and informed them that Bartow Weeks was already on his way to Ossining to deliver a copy of the *Times* to Roland.

Within a few days, Battle and Weeks filed the appeal to set aside Roland's conviction and in so doing obtained an indefinite stay of execution. With this turn of events, the Molineuxs leased a house in Ossining so that it would be more convenient for Mrs. Molineux and Blanche to exercise their visiting privileges at Sing Sing.

Either because she had made a firm decision regarding her future or because she felt more at ease in upstate New York, away from the prying eyes of reporters, Blanche approached her visits to Roland with a new-found equanimity. She soon en-

deared herself sufficiently to the warden that visiting days
became for her luncheon occasions in the Death House. Sitting
at a little table especially prepared for her, she often ate her
meal while engaging in conversation with Roland through the
cell bars. Gradually her interest extended beyond her husband
to the other inmates of the House. She became less obsessed
with her own misfortune as her empathy increased for the
pathetic inmates, most of whom would only leave the Death
House by way of the "little door" at the end of the cellblock
which led to the electric chair.

Between her visits to the great prison, Blanche spent hours
walking along the bluffs of the Hudson River, enjoying a kind
of spiritual recovery. It was a time of waiting that held hope for
the future. No one in the family, least of all Roland, doubted
the outcome of the appeal nor held any fear as to the result of
a new trial. With renewed hope for Roland's future, Blanche
viewed her own with more optimism. Always in the back of her
mind was the assurance by her father-in-law that she would
never want for financial security.

There were interminable delays associated with the appeal,
for it was a time of political turmoil in the State of New York.
Governor Theodore Roosevelt, a Republican, had removed
Democrat Asa Bird Gardiner from his position as District Attorney of New York County on charges of incompetency. Soon
thereafter New York's Republican Party conspired to remove
Roosevelt as governor. In the summer of 1900, its leaders saw
to it that he was nominated for the vice presidency of the United
States as the running mate of William McKinley. In the election
of 1900, McKinley defeated William Jennings Bryan, taking
Roosevelt with him to Washington.

The New York Court of Appeals sat in Buffalo. Both the
defense and the prosecution found it convenient therefore to be
represented by counsel from upstate New York. In spite of the
unsettled affairs in the District Attorney's office, a highly
respected attorney was selected—David Hill, a former United
States Senator, a former governor of the state, and a leader in
the upstate Democratic Party. For the defense, Battle and

Weeks engaged John Milburn, a Buffalo attorney who had previously appeared before the Court of Appeals on a number of occasions. Milburn was an active Republican and a personal friend of General Molineux. His credentials were impeccable.

The hearing on the appeal did not take place until June of 1901. The arguments lasted just three days, with Milburn speaking for five hours. His argument was threefold. First he attacked the admissibility of any evidence relating to the death of Henry Barnet and to the leasing of a letter box in his name; he also attacked the inferences drawn from the separate handwriting exhibits; finally he assailed the conduct of Recorder Goff-as being prejudicial. Any one of these arguments, by itself, was sufficient grounds to set aside the conviction. Nevertheless the court, taking the arguments under advisement, waited another four months to issue its verdict.

During the summer months, the Molineuxs traveled back and forth between Ossining and Brooklyn. Roland used his time to write letters and take notes with the thought that this unique experience could be the vehicle for launching a literary career.

On September 6, President McKinley was shot while visiting Buffalo. John Milburn was one of the key Republicans in his entourage that day, and it was to Milburn's home that McKinley was carried. He died there eight days later, and Theodore Roosevelt became president of the United States.

The Court of Appeals handed down its verdict on the fifteenth of October. Three separate opinions were issued since the justices did not concur on what constituted inadmissible evidence. These minor disparities were of no consequence to Roland Molineux, however, since the seven justices unanimously reversed his conviction and ordered a new trial.

Roland was immediately returned to the Tombs prison in New York City, and the house at Ossining was vacated. The tone of the newspapers had plainly altered in the two years since his first trial. Even at the Tombs, where Roland would be forced to wait another twelve months, there was exhilaration over his return, as if this was but the first step to freedom.

The mood in the Molineux home also reflected the hopeful

prognosis. The newspapers had little to report, and public interest in the Adams murder and the fate of Roland Molineux waned. The wooden shutters were opened, and once again sunlight streamed into the downstairs rooms of the house. Blanche was given certain privileges, such as permission to visit the shops on Manhattan and occasionally to take luncheon there. General Molineux provided her with sufficient funds that she might acquire a new wardrobe for the summer and for the fall. The implication was that Blanche would be present at Roland's second trial as she had been at the first.

The taste of Manhattan life rekindled Blanche's interest in the theater and the society that revolved about it. She began to talk about her little excursions at mealtime with the Molineuxs. Her mother-in-law, still garbed in black, raised immediate opposition to the frivolities that sparked Blanche's enthusiasm. In late summer the mutual resentment that had smoldered quietly during Roland's long imprisonment broke into the open when Blanche asked for permission to attend an evening theater performance. General Molineux took the matter in his own hands and quietly arranged for Blanche to move to the Murray Hill Hotel on Manhattan. He provided an unheard of amount for Blanche to cover her additional expenses — $300 monthly. In return Blanche promised that there would be no theater nor opera performances until Roland was a free man.

The trial opened on October 13, 1902, just two days short of one year from the decision of the Court of Appeals. The proceedings were conducted before Justice John Lambert of the Criminal Branch of the Supreme Court. If it could be said that Recorder Goff was prejudiced against the defendant, the opposite could be said of Justice Lambert, who was brought to New York City from Buffalo to preside. George Battle and Bartow Weeks turned over the leadership of the defense to attorneys from upstate New York — former Governor Frank Black and his partner William Olcott. David Hill, who had represented the District Attorney in the appeal, refused to continue with the case. James Osborne, still Assistant District Attorney of New York, found himself chief prosecutor once again, but with a case substantially weakened under the constraints set down by the Court of Appeals.

Early on it became evident that Justice Lambert intended to make the trial a brief one. The pace was set during jury selection, with all twelve jurors agreed upon within twelve hours. Lambert continually prodded Osborne during the prosecution, and he sarcastically belittled the handwriting experts on whom Osborne's case rested heavily.

Roland took the stand in his own defense. With no difficulty he was able to account for his whereabouts at all times during the crucial days prior to Katherine Adams's death. The defense presented witnesses who confirmed Roland's whereabouts, including a professor from Columbia University who testified that Roland had been with him during the afternoon when the poison package was presumably mailed. The fact that Roland's testimony did not agree with his testimony at the inquest almost four years earlier was not seized upon by Osborne. This time it was he who faltered during the five-hour cross-examination of the defendant. When it was finished, Roland was as unruffled as he had been at the start. He had avoided any contradictions and he had made no damaging admissions. In his father's own words, he "bore himself under fire like a true Molineux."

Blanche was not present to savor the defeat of her archenemy James Osborne nor to share in the exaltation over Roland's expected victory. No longer a necessary ornament to the defense strategy, she had already been discarded by the Molineux family.

NINETEEN

The Last Chapter

With Roland Molineux's acquittal, the Molineux trials and the events that precipitated them faded from public consciousness and eventually from the memories of all but a few. The Knickerbocker Athletic Club, where the lives of Roland Molineux, Henry Barnet, Blanche Chesebrough and Harry Cornish had collided, fell on hard times and was disbanded. The building was sold and later demolished. The neighborhood surrounding Fort Greene Place in Brooklyn soon started a slow deterioration and eventually became the classic example of urban decay. The Waldorf-Astoria, where Blanche and Roland's aborted marriage was consummated, gave way to the Empire State Building. Alice Bellinger's home, the Murray Hill Hotel, Delmonico's, the old Metropolitan Opera House, and most other settings of the events that played into the drama also disappeared. Even the old Tombs prison was eventually replaced by a modern Tombs.

From time to time during this century the Molineux story has manifested itself in a variety of ways. In 1916, the great American novelist Theodore Dreiser sent his lawyer to the New York State Library to investigate the court records of the first trial, with the thought of fictionalizing the story. However, the project was abandoned in favor of *An American Tragedy*, his highly acclaimed novel based on another historic murder. In 1929, an entire volume, *The Molineux Case*, published in London, dealt with the legal issues raised in the trial, principally those relating to the use of handwriting as circumstantial evidence. Throughout the years there has been an occasional retelling of the story—at least those parts that had been published earlier—in one or another periodical. However, no new information ever came forth.

Shortly after Roland's release from the Tombs, a collection of his prison essays, *The Room with the Little Door*, appeared in print—dedicated to "My Father General Edward Leslie Molineux, with Reverence." Soon thereafter two more books dealing with prison life were published under his name—*Death Chamber Stories* and *Tales of the Tombs*.

With Blanche no longer in the picture, Roland devoted all of his energies to his blossoming literary career. Trying his hand at romantic fiction, he published a full-length historical novel, *The Vice Admiral of the Blue, a Biographical Romance*, which claimed to be the chronicle left by Lord Nelson's friend, Thomas Masterman Hardy. Following the success of this novel, he wrote a number of romantic short stories, several of which appeared in the Sunday supplements of the *New York Herald* and the *New York Tribune*. Then he turned to the theater and completed a one-act play entitled, "Was It a Dream?" This little drama attracted the attention of Broadway producer, David Belasco, who engaged Roland to write a full-blown stage play on the reformation of a criminal, "The Man Inside," which opened at the Criterion Theater in November of 1913.

Unfortunately, any satisfaction the Molineuxs might have gained from their son's literary and theatrical successes was dampened by the deterioration of his health. Roland, now forty-seven years of age, was frequently beset by nervous episodes and tantrums, not unlike those he had experienced in 1898 prior to Henry Barnet's death. Once again, General Molineux encouraged his son to consider matrimony, and a few days before the opening of "The Man Inside" Roland was married to Margaret Connell, a young woman of twenty-eight who had assisted him in completing his play. His ailing mother declared that she could now die in peace, as there was someone to take care of her youngest son. She passed away soon thereafter, in February of 1914.

Shortly after the opening of "The Man Inside," Belasco began complaining to Margaret Molineux that Roland had become very belligerent and disruptive at the rehearsals. Then one evening during a performance, he caused such a disturbance that he had to be forcibly removed from the theater. Unable to cope with the situation, the young woman sought the help of her father-in-law. The general issued a statement to the effect that Roland had suffered a nervous breakdown due to overwork connected with the opening of the play; he then quietly arranged for his son to be sent to a private sanitarium at Babylon, Long Island.

Roland's mental condition continued to deteriorate at the sanitarium, and in September of that year he escaped from the grounds in the early hours of the morning. He ran through the village of Babylon, wearing only his nightshirt and bathrobe, assaulting several people who tried to stop him. Finally, a local police officer recognized Roland and convinced him to return to the sanitarium in a taxi. Once inside the vehicle, however, Roland attacked the officer and was promptly escorted to the local jail. His father, now 82 years old, was summoned from Brooklyn. He engaged two physicians to evaluate Roland's condition, and they recommended that he be committed to a hospital for the insane. General Molineux acquiesced and arranged for Roland to be taken to the King's State Hospital for the Insane on Long Island.

About this time an odd incident took place in Rockaway, New Jersey, at the country home of Captain Hennessey, Director of the New York Fire Department Recruiting School. His wife had placed an advertisement in the newspaper for a housemaid, and a woman by the name of Mamie Molineux responded and was hired. The woman claimed to be related "by marriage" to Roland Molineux (still a household name in that area), but explained that years earlier her husband had abandoned her and her daughter. Without means of support, she had been forced to send the child to an orphanage. She begged Mrs. Hennessey's permission to bring her daughter, now in her teens, to live with her in the Hennessey home.

Gossip about Mamie Molineux traveled quickly through the surrounding villages, and she soon became known as the "mystery woman of Rockaway." One morning in February of 1915, she announced to her employer that she and her daughter would spend the weekend visiting friends in Brooklyn. When the two did not return, the Hennesseys investigated and discovered that they had taken not only their own belongings, but all of Mrs. Hennessey's jewelry as well. The news item was reported in the press and no doubt came to the attention of General Molineux. Roland, however, comprehended nothing, for his mind had completely disintegrated.

In June of 1915, the general died. At the time of his death he still controlled three major businesses—the F. W. Devoe Company, C. T. Raynolds, and Devoe and Raynolds of Chicago. Earlier it had been rumored that the general had spent his entire fortune on the legal defense of his son; however, the probate records show that he left an estate of more than a half million dollars, a tidy sum in those days.

Roland succumbed the following year to the ravages of "cerebral syphilis infection." In retrospect, he no doubt had been afflicted with the disease for at least two decades. Predictably, the symptoms had gone unrecognized for years—the rashes, the chronic impotence, the nervous episodes, the gradual changes in personality, including delusions of grandeur, violent rages, and impaired judgment. This most dreaded form of syphilis, known medically as "paresis," had reduced Roland to a raving maniac by the time of his death at age fifty-one. The hospital records put it simply: "General paralysis and progressive mental deterioration, leading to complete dementia."

And what of the legal adversaries? The partnership of Battle and Weeks was soon dissolved, as Bartow Weeks became Chief Justice of the New York State Supreme Court. His partner George Gordon Battle went on to become one of the best among the great Wall Street attorneys. In later years he wrote occasionally of the Adams case and of the superb strategy he and his partner had employed in the defense of Roland Molineux. James Osborne, the triumphant prosecutor in the first trial, was fondly remembered for his adept handling of the prosecution and his virtuoso performances in the courtroom. Later he ran unsuccessfully for the Office of District Attorney, then left government to become one of New York's most noted criminal lawyers.

Of the three attorneys, Osborne was the first to die, passing on suddenly at the age of sixty-one. His old adversary, Chief Justice Bartow Weeks, interrupted the proceedings of the New York Supreme Court to eulogize his distinguished colleague and friend and to request a moment of silence in his honor. A private funeral service was held in Osborne's New York apartment, with only family and friends present, among them George Battle.

Five years later Justice Weeks died at his home on Park Avenue. Among the honorary pallbearers at his funeral were his former law partner George Battle and retired Justice John Goff, who during Roland Molineux's first trial had overruled several hundred objections tendered by Weeks. Among the organizations represented at the funeral was the New York Athletic Club, of which Weeks had been a highly respected member twenty-five years earlier when his name was maligned by the athletic director of the Knickerbocker Club.

George Battle lived on until 1949. Known throughout his life as a southern gentleman, he died at his country home in Orange County, Virginia. Nevertheless he had been a respected community leader in New York for many decades, devoting most of his energies to his adopted city. Over the years he had served on countless committees to promote children's playgrounds and parks throughout the city, and he fought with particular passion the commercial development encroaching on Central Park. George Battle's other great crusade was against anti-Semitism, which he carried on through various organizations. Although he had no children of his own, he provided for the education of at least one promising young man, who later joined him in the practice of law. This man acknowledged his debt to his benefactor by naming a son after him—George Gordon Battle Liddy of Watergate fame.

With Battle's death, it was said that the last survivor of the Molineux affair had carried to the grave all that was not published earlier. That was not true, however, for Blanche still lived, and she had forgotten nothing.

When Blanche quietly boarded the train for Sioux Falls, South Dakota, the day after Roland's acquittal, she had a single goal in mind—to dissolve the marriage as quickly as possible. By adding to her private knowledge the public evidence, she had arrived at the certain conclusion that her husband was afflicted with a disease which was slowly destroying his brain. As far back as the yachting cruise he had exhibited occasional lapses in judgment and strange fantasies. She now recognized the ramifications of Roland's disappearance and reappearance during her affair with Barney and the implications of his veiled warnings to Barney in the year prior to Barney's death.

It was clear to Blanche that Roland had arranged for Barney's death to occur in July, while he was in Europe and she was at the seaside, but that he had not counted on Barney tossing away the remedy for impotence so casually. Blanche found a certain satisfaction, if not amusement, in Roland's misjudgment of Barney's virility. Although the September reconciliation with Blanche belied Roland's obsession with his perceived rival, there was no doubt in Blanche's mind that he gave it another try—this time with a remedy for indigestion for the connoisseur of good food and drink—and Barney was certainly that. The Adams death was but a logical progression for a brain already warped and beyond repair. If Roland was capable of taking the life of his good friend, certainly he was capable of doing the same to such a boor as Harry Cornish. Blanche did not bother herself with the details of *that* "transaction," as James Osborne had so quaintly termed it.

With all of the publicity and scandal now a matter of history, the truth seemed so matter-of-fact to Blanche that she was surprised at herself. She had not shared her knowledge or deductions with anyone; still she had a naive conviction that General Molineux also knew the truth and hence would support her resolve to leave Roland. If he did not understand before she left, he surely would after reading her farewell letter.

All of Blanche's material possessions were with her on the train west—her ample wardrobe, hurriedly packed into a trunk, and several bags, plus the old Dutch silver bowl presented to her by the general before her marriage. Everything else of value was left behind, for Blanche prided herself on being correct in these matters. Furthermore, she had the promise from her father-in-law that he would continue to provide for her. With this assurance, even the unknown future held promise.

William Olcott, one of Roland's defense attorneys, had made all of the arrangements to ensure Blanche's comfort and privacy enroute to South Dakota. She changed trains alone in Chicago, but at Sioux Falls she was met by Wallace Dutton Scott, the junior partner in the law firm of Kittridge and Scott, whom Judge Olcott had engaged to handle the divorce.

When the *New York Times* finally figured out that Blanche Molineux was in South Dakota and not reunited with her husband, there was a flurry of speculation that prompted George Battle to make a public statement on behalf of the family: "Neither General Edward Molineux, nor his son Roland Molineux, nor any member of his family will make any statement in regard to the report in the press that Mrs. Roland Molineux has gone to South Dakota with the purpose of instituting an action for divorce against her husband. They regard it as a private matter concerning which no public utterance should be made. General Molineux desires to say further that all the members of his family have at all times treated Mrs. Roland Molineux with the utmost kindness and consideration. This is the last word on the subject."

It appeared that the Molineux family wished to have nothing further to do with its erstwhile daughter-in-law.

Since Blanche believed that the general would be kept informed of her whereabouts, she fully expected that the monthly stipend he had provided her with in New York would simply be remitted to her in Sioux Falls. In this she was sorely mistaken; not one penny was ever forwarded to her.

Within a year, Blanche's divorce from Roland became final. The proceedings were handled so discreetly that to this day it is not known in which county the divorce was granted nor on what grounds. A short time later, Blanche made a brief trip to New York, hoping to prevail upon the Molineuxs to provide for her. Their only response was silence. Through ill-advised counsel, Blanche threatened a $100,000 lawsuit against them, claiming that she had been promised a monetary settlement for standing by Roland throughout the entire four-year ordeal while suffering unspeakable humiliation. The threat was quickly squelched. In the State of New York, the Molineux family was not to be trifled with.

Not long thereafter Blanche married Wallace Scott, the attorney who had represented her in her divorce suit. At first the couple resided in Sioux Falls, but Blanche found it to be an exceedingly provincial town. She soon prevailed upon her husband to provide her with the means to spend time in New York, with the thought of pursuing her musical career there. In 1905, she signed a contract with the Proctor Theater to perform on stage at the unheard of salary of $1000 per week. However the public announcement that she would be billed as Blanche Molineux Scott brought an immediate challenge from the Molineux family. Roland's threat to sue his former wife to restrain her from using his name was enough to cancel the contract and abort Blanche's stage career.

Blanche returned to her husband in Sioux Falls and in the following year gave birth to a son, whom she named Rogers but chose to call "Boy." Continually restless in what seemed to her a frontier environment, Blanche found reasons to return to New York, sometimes with her husband Wallace, but more often without. Though she adored her young son, she seemed emotionally unable to give him the sustained attention normally provided by a mother. Boy spent much of his childhood in his grandfather's home, then was sent east to boarding school. Among Blanche's effects at the time of her death were the poignant letters of this lonely child written to his mother.

Eventually, in 1921, Wallace Scott prevailed upon Blanche to give up her wanderings and settle down with him in Minneapolis, Minnesota. It was a risky move for Wallace as he attempted to establish his law practice in a city with which he was unfamiliar. With financial help from his father, he purchased a fine home on Minneapolis's Park Avenue and refurbished it to Blanche's tastes. Boy was taken out of school and reunited with his family in what was supposed to be his permanent home. But this was not to be, for Boy soon contracted rheumatic fever and died of complications resulting from the disease. Blanche Scott's grief over the loss of her son and her accompanying feelings of guilt constituted a debilitating burden that she would carry the rest of her long life.

Less than a year after Boy's death, Blanche and Wallace were divorced. It was the custom of the time that a divorced woman be addressed formally by her maiden and married names, in this case "Mrs. Chesebrough Scott." Blanche had other ideas, however, choosing to assume Wallace's middle name, and henceforth she was known as "Mrs. Dutton Scott." In the divorce settlement, she obtained sufficient funds to make the long-postponed trip to Paris, under the guise of enhancing her musical credentials. Then, at the age of fifty, she took up residence in New York and prepared her vocal repertoire; but as before, opportunities to perform professionally eluded her.

Somewhat humbled by her failures, Blanche returned to Minneapolis in 1926 and was reconciled with Wallace Scott, who still lived in the home on Park Avenue. In the speculative frenzy of the late 1920's, he invested heavily in agricultural property while pursuing his law business. The market collapse of 1929 and the ensuing economic depression dealt a harsh blow to him and to Blanche. In 1930, her troubles were compounded when Wallace was killed in an automobile accident that gave evidence of being a suicide.

Wallace left no assets of his own, only debts. Blanche discovered that most of the income on which they had lived came from a trust left by his father, who had died in 1925. The stipulation was that the trust should terminate upon Wallace's death, with the assets to be distributed among the Scott relatives. Blanche claimed the Minneapolis home as her own, but after lengthy litigation the court determined that this too belonged to the Scott heirs. When it was all over, she had no home and no funds.

Commenting on the outcome of the litigation, the editor of the *Sioux Falls Daily Argus-Leader* was moved to write: "Mrs. Scott's pleasing personality, devotion and refinement are said to have brought high respect from all her acquaintances, and her long series of episodes involving crime, hardships, unhappiness and sorrow have won for her a genuine sympathy by all who knew her. It may perhaps be said that Mrs. Scott has drained life's cup to the last bitter dreg."

Blanche Scott spent the rest of her days in Minneapolis, living in a succession of ever-smaller apartments and rooms as her meager resources and belongings dwindled. The silver bowl, Blanche's single remnant of the Molineux years, became her most valued possession. At regular intervals, when funds disappeared altogether, she pawned the piece—always for the sum of five dollars—retrieving it when she was able to. By 1938, when she joined a newspaper indexing project organized by the federal Works Project Administration, better known as the WPA, her appearance marked her as an eccentric. She was often noticed in the older parts of the city—a stooped old woman with hennaed hair, a painted face and outlandish garments; however her exterior belied a beautiful speaking voice and considerable inner charm. Those who ventured to speak to her discovered a proud woman who might graciously accept the gift of friendship while rejecting any gift of material value.

At the WPA project, Blanche Scott avoided her fellow workers, retreating from them with what appeared to be a mixture of distrust and contempt. However, one of the trained librarians on the project, Irene Hauser, perceived in this peculiar woman a human being of some depth and refused to be put off by her haughty ways. It was not long before Irene became her friend and confidante, and it was she who encouraged Blanche to write down her own story of the Molineux affair. Blanche seized upon this suggestion as an opportunity to dispel the untruths and half-truths that James Osborne had thrown at her in the courtroom, despite the fact that his words were long forgotten, as were the murders themselves. Nevertheless Blanche persisted and set down on paper most of what she remembered of her strange courtship and marriage, not omitting her own indiscretions along the way.

When the WPA project ceased at the start of World War II, Blanche relied on public assistance to sustain herself in a rented room in a house on Kenwood Parkway. In what had previously been a front parlor, not unlike the parlor in Alice Bellinger's home, she sat day in and day out, admitting no one past the sliding doors but the handful of friends who refused to abandon her.

There Blanche brooded on a failed life over which she had only regrets. She who loved life and particularly the men whom she perceived to be life's drivers, had married twice—both times without love. If she had ever loved at all, she had loved Henry Barnet; but Blanche was shrewd enough to know that Barney had never loved her. In turn, she blamed the newspapers, James Osborne, the Molineux family and the Scotts for her destitute condition; but in the end Blanche openly and courageously, and probably unfairly, took upon herself the entire responsibility for all that had happened to her.

In March of 1954, at the age of eighty, Blanche suffered a fatal heart attack. Irene Hauser called on her in the hospital the evening of the night she died. Blanche was more alert than she had been for several days. In her friend's presence she sat part way up in bed and called to her in a strong voice: "Irene, Irene, I have so much I want to say . . . I have something that I *must* tell you." The nurse, overhearing the conversation from the hall, rushed in and urged Irene to leave. It was late and the patient should rest; Irene should return in the morning. But in the morning, Blanche Chesebrough Molineux Scott was dead.

The Molineux Affair was inspired by the legacy that Blanche left to my mother, Irene Hauser—a chronicle of the painful events as she remembered them many years later. It is also influenced by my memories of Blanche, childhood memories of an old and painted woman who spoke with the voice of an elegant lady from an earlier time, her conversation laced with French expressions I could not understand—a woman who lived in a tattered room of an old house, with drapes drawn and rose-colored cloths covering the shades of lighted lamps.

From my study window today I look across Kenwood Parkway to that old house where Blanche once lived and to the win 'ow of her room. In the last decade the house has been home to a large family, and happy children run through the small front parlor with its comfortable fireplace and sliding doors that are never closed. They have not heard of Blanche Scott or the Molineux murder trials. But in the evenings when the drapes are drawn, it is not difficult for me to conjure up the ghost of Blanche sitting next to the fireplace and setting down on paper, sometimes wet with tears, her agonizing musings and memories.

For all my acknowledged debt to Blanche, *The Molineux Affair* is primarily the result of several years' research into the newspaper records, the court records and every other published source of information that is extant. Where even the most intense research failed to turn up desired information, I have occasionally made obvious interpolation between the published facts. And when Blanche's account differs from a published account, I have usually opted in favor of Blanche, for the newspapers and the prosecution erred in many ways. It is my hope that the reader will not judge Blanche harshly, at least not as harshly as she judged herself. Like the seed of the cottonwood, Blanche was carried hither and yon by events which she was unable to control.